ARCHAEOLOGY OF CAMB
VOL. 2: SOUTH EAST CAMBR
AND THE FEN EDG

CW00802110

Wandlebury hill fort from the air, photographed by Geoffrey Robinson.

Archaeology of Cambridgeshire

VOL 2: SOUTH EAST CAMBRIDGESHIRE AND THE FEN EDGE

Alison Taylor

Series Editor: Christopher Taylor

Cambridgeshire County Council

To the memory of Jack Ravensdale

Published in 1998 by Cambridgeshire County Council Resources Unit, 19 Gordon Avenue, March, Cambs., PE15 8AL. Printed by Burlington Press (Cambridge) Limited, 1 Station Road, Foxton, Cambridge CB2 6SW Tel. 01223 870266, Fax 01223 872113.

Layout and design by Pen to Print, 196 Lincoln Road, Peterborough PE1 2NQ Tel/Fax 01733 706675.

© Cambridgeshire County Council, 1998.

© Maps, Sarah Wroot, 1998

Except for brief quotation or reproduction of photographs in a review, no part of this book may be photocopied, recorded or otherwise reproduced, stored in a retrieval system or transmitted in any form or by any electronic or mechanical means without prior permission of the copyright holder and publisher.

ISBN 0-902436-50-3

Contents

Acknowledgements

Like the previous volume, *South West Cambridgeshire*, this book could not have been written without information being readily available from many sources. The principal published sources are the Royal Commission on Historical Monuments' *North-East Cambridgeshire* and volumes of the Victoria County History. The final volume of the VCH for Cambridgeshire has not yet been published, and I am deeply grateful to Dr. A P M Wright and Dr. C P Lewis for providing me with information about the villages that this will cover and allowing its use in advance of publication. This book has also benefited from the timely publication of David Hall's final volume of the English Heritage sponsored Fenland Project, which includes results of many seasons' fieldwork in fenland and fen-edge villages.

Cambridgeshire County Council's own historical and archaeological records have supplied much of the information used in this text. The Sites and Monuments Record holds huge amounts of archaeological data; the Conservation Section has a similar record of historic buildings; the County Record Office contains readily-available collections of maps and documents; and the Cambridgeshire Collection is an invaluable source for local publications, typescripts and cuttings of all dates. Works such as this publication would be impossible if these resources were not so expertly maintained.

Many other historians and archaeologists have been helpful in providing information and ideas. Sadly, Jack Ravensdale died before work on this book began, but I learnt much from him in his lifetime and have used his own books, especially *Liable to Flood*, extensively. The explosion of new archaeological data in the 1990s has largely been due to the work of newly-formed professional units and the more old-established voluntary groups. Cambridgeshire is exceptionally lucky to have the County Council's own Archaeological Field Unit, led by Tim Malim, and the University's Cambridge Archaeological Unit, led by Christopher Evans, both undertaking about a hundred excavations every year. The County has also benefited from outstanding voluntary work by the Haverhill and District Archaeological Group, especially their field surveys in the parishes of Castle Camps and West Wickham, and the long-term programmes of field-walking by the Cambridge Archaeology Field Group.

Other authorities that have helped enormously in this work include South Cambridgeshire District Council, whose officers have given me the latest information on historic buildings and on Planning matters; Cambridge University Museum of Archaeology and Anthropology, which has very kindly supplied superb photographs and also detailed information about its collections; the Cambridge University Committee for Aerial Photography, whose data is the backbone for studying prehistoric and Roman settlements and which has also provided photographs; Cambridge University Library, particularly its Map Room, which holds many maps that have been consulted and also Cambridge Antiquarian Society's collection of Relhan drawings; and the British Museum, who have given permission to reproduce the Cole drawings. These drawings and Cole's other documents can be used as microfiche in the County Record Office. I was also very fortunate in being given access to the aerial photograph collections of Geoffrey Robinson and Ben Robinson, with permission to reproduce some of their fascinating views. Cambridge Antiquarian Society itself, through the Proceedings it publishes and its collection of drawings, is a major resource for anyone studying the past in this County, and many illustrations in this book are drawn from its publications.

This book also owes an enormous amount to the map illustrator, Sarah Wroot, who has provided such clear representations of the development of the villages, and above all to the editor, Christopher Taylor, who has helped to illuminate several difficult sections and, as in the previous volume, has provided ideas and criticism throughout.

Cambridgeshire County Council gratefully acknowledges the financial support made towards this publication by South Cambridgeshire District Council

Foreword

It is a pleasure to welcome this second book in the County Council's series 'Archaeology of Cambridgeshire'. Together with the first volume, it provides a full and detailed study of the archaeology of our District. We are proud to have been able to support a publication which makes so significant a contribution to our understanding of our local heritage.

Alison Taylor, a leading local archaeologist, uses knowledge accumulated over twenty years of research to present information about all periods of our past. She shows how cropmarks and earthworks identify ancient sites and reveal much of the past, some of it hidden for over 3000 years, giving us a greater understanding of the importance to our region of water transport, the significance of the fertile Fen Edge and of the Fen itself for its own specific products. She tells us about the major Roman pottery industry once carried on here, about Anglo-Saxon settlement, and about the impact of the manorial system and later of the enclosure acts upon our villages. This generously-illustrated book, with its ground and aerial photographs, drawings and maps, gives us a dimension within which we can all take our place in the life and history of our surroundings.

In this publication, Alison has been greatly aided by the research and assistance of many notable local historians. One of them, the late Dr. Jack Ravensdale, who lived at Landbeach, both she and I are privileged to have counted a personal friend. As our countryside and townscapes change and adapt in the face of massive development in the Cambridge area, I can do no better than repeat Jack's words:

Particular care should be taken of our heritage. The whole area demands protection to ensure that what has come down to us can pass on to following generations and by no means find ourselves shamed by them when it is revealed that at the end of the 1990s, lack of vigilance and vision destroyed in a moment the inheritance of long centuries.

Councillor Alan W Wyatt

Chairman of South Cambridgeshire District Council

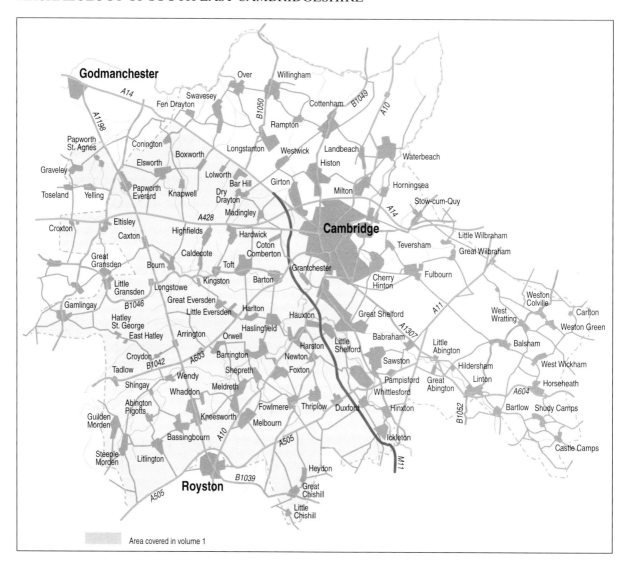

Area covered in volume 1

Introduction

From prehistoric times the lives of people living in this varied region have been affected by their natural environments. The economies of all the villages described in this volume were dependent on mixed agriculture from Neolithic times until the second half of the 20th century, but the presence of the fens meant that many inhabitants benefited from natural resources such as plentiful fish, wildfowl and rich summer pastures, and to some villages there were navigable rivers that brought international trade to their wharves. In other parishes there were vast sheepwalks on undisturbed downlands, and many villages grew where trade-routes from eastern to western England passed, or where there were stopping places on the drove roads that took cattle to fatten on fen pastures. Attempts to control the environment, such as draining the fens, digging canals to carry building stone and other goods to the hearts of fen-edge villages, and barring access along the Icknield Way with long ramparts and ditches, could affect the lives of villagers for centuries after they were first thought necessary, and these constructions have left many traces for us to see today.

Our villages range from minute and picturesque settlements such as Hildersham and Bartlow to virtual towns such as Cottenham and Linton, from the busy industrial and shopping areas of Sawston to the tranquillity of Fen Drayton, and from the densely built-up, regularly planned settlements of Willingham and Over to the scattered hamlets of Carlton and Castle Camps. Few fit the neat pattern of development around a church, manor house and green which is commonly found in the villages of south west Cambridgeshire, and instead have developed varied and interesting layouts reflecting different historical processes. Some have been moved about and kept small by powerful local lords, while in others there was a living for incoming labourers and younger sons and populations continued to expand well beyond the Middle Ages.

Natural Regions

The fens and the economies they supported are key factors in understanding the development of this region. In Mesolithic times, approximately 7000-3000BC, much of the area that later became fen was above sea level and could support hunter-gatherer societies in a forested landscape. Sea levels rose with the melting of ice-caps in warmer conditions during the Neolithic and Bronze Ages, roughly 3000-700BC, and this caused sea water to flood periodically into more and more areas. Repeated flooding, with sea water sometimes trapped between islands of higher ground, created saltmarsh conditions which killed the forests and left thick layers of marine clay. Marshy conditions impeded drainage and eventually prevented fresh water that had previously run down rivers to the sea from flowing freely, and so floodwaters deposited alluvium near the Cam and Ouse, especially at Willingham and Over. The combined effects of silted-up marshland and alluvium deposited by flooding meant that the land in the lower parts of the fens was becoming higher, causing sea water to recede. However, fresh water from uplands around the fens could now move very sluggishly and, apart from islands of higher ground, the whole area was now frequently flooded. The marshes this slow-moving water created led to steady growth of peat for more than 2000 years. Exceptions to this pattern were bays where water was trapped. These became meres, most notably, in our area, Willingham Mere, and were open water until the end of the medieval period or later.

A wealth of natural foods and other resources were abundant in this fenland landscape. Fish, eels, wildfowl and mammals such as beaver were widely available, turf and reeds were gathered for fuel and building material, and pastures that were flooded in winter provided exceptionally rich grazing for cattle and sheep in the summer months. In the 17th century there were even complaints about the unfortunate social effects on 'poore and meane people' of living 'an easy and idle life, by Fishing, Fowling and Feeding of Cattle'. The land was too wet to build settlements within the fens, except where islands of higher land still protruded above the marsh, but sites around its edge, with easy access to fenland riches but with dry ground for houses, growing crops and over-wintering stock, supported unusually high populations. As the area covered by fen expanded this desirable 'fen-edge' moved from Neolithic times until the 17th century

3. Occasionally the sea rose enough to flood the fens, depositing layers of marine clay before retreating again.

6. Small-scale drainage began in Roman times.

7. Peat deposition continued until intensive drainage began in the 17th century.

8. The peat wastes away as drainage lowers the water table.

2. As sea levels rose the fen basin flooded and the forests died.

4. Peat formed by rotting marsh vegetation and soil deposited by blocked rivers covered many settlements.

5. Shallow lakes or *meres* formed on the peat surface.

1. Early people hunted in forests of oak, yew and pine.

10,000 BC   **3,000 BC**   **AD 100**   **AD 1650**

Please note that the vertical scale is greatly exaggerated!

How the fens were formed.

ARCHAEOLOGY OF SOUTH EAST CAMBRIDGESHIRE

The Cam at Horningsea.

as the fens developed, and so the pattern of settlement shifted slowly southwards.

River valleys are other natural regions that attracted settlement. Here, light gravel and alluvial soils and good communications made farming easy, and at points where rivers could be forded permanent settlements arose, the origin of many villages in the Cam and Granta valleys. North of Cambridge the Cam and Ouse are navigable to the Wash, and villages near to them, such as Horningsea, Fen Ditton, Fen Drayton and Swavesey, often engaged in trade.

Areas in the east of Cambridgeshire, near to Suffolk and Essex, were largely on clay soils, where arable agriculture and communications were more difficult, though never impossible. Natural woodland in this region was a valuable resource, and there was always much economic activity and settlement, though large permanent

occupation sites were less common. Archaeological evidence makes it clear that by Roman times many areas had been cleared, and the forest-economy enabled the population to grow and wealthy villas to be established. These Roman clearances often show remarkable continuity into Anglo-Saxon and medieval times.

Areas of chalkland that were not close to springs or other supplies of water were never suitable for permanent settlement, but they served a vital function in providing dry open countryside across the county, giving well-used thoroughfares that linked Cambridgeshire to southern England and to Norfolk. Travellers and traders could therefore cross the region by the parallel routes known as the Icknield Way, the prehistoric highway that had once taken Neolithic axes from the mines of Grimes Graves to the rich cultures of Wessex. This region was covered in grassland, probably from

prehistoric times, and was famous for extensive sheepwalks until well into the 19th century. Because it was a natural highway, at times of war it was advantageous to cut communications along it, and so the Dykes were built.

Prehistoric

Land near to the Ouse is now being recognised as one of the few areas in Britain where, despite intervening ice-ages, deposits buried deep beneath river gravels have been undisturbed for as much as 250,000 years. As a result, artefacts such as hand-axes and chopping tools of flint, as well as fossilised animal remains of the Palaeolithic period are being discovered in large numbers in active gravel quarries.

Sites close to water attracted seasonal encampments by nomadic hunter-gatherers in the Mesolithic period, and tools such as axes and the tiny blades useful for setting into harpoons etc, typical of flint-working at this time, are quite commonly found around the fen-edge and in river valleys. These people camped on higher ground at other times in the year, and uplands near Wandlebury, for example, contain an occupation site identified by numerous tools and waste materials.

With the introduction of farming in the Neolithic period, from after about 3000BC, evidence for settlement and land-use becomes more widespread, particularly along river valleys and near to the fens. The fen-edge is particularly notable for the number of polished stone axes found without other signs of human activity, and it is likely that these were lost in undergrowth while timber was gathered. Like arrowheads, therefore, they are a good indication of

Paleolithic tools found at Fen Drayton in 1997.

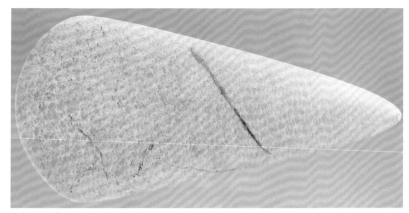

Jadeite axe from Histon, length: 15cms.

land that was still forested. Some Neolithic axes were used for ceremonial purposes, such as the three fine jadeite examples found at Histon, but most were work-a-day tools that would be re-sharpened as they wore out and would be used for innumerable carpentry tasks. A Neolithic settlement has been excavated at Fen Drayton, and traces of many others are known, usually recognisable from the flakes of flint left lying around when tools were being made. At Great Wilbraham there is an important monument of this date, a causewayed camp, which would have been used for a variety of social and ceremonial purposes.

The transition to the Bronze Age, very approximately 2000BC, was not marked by any sudden changes, but instead the trends to occupy more and more of the habitable land make finds of this period, now including bronze tools, more prolific. Amongst many settlements known the most interesting site was at Cottenham, where wooden artefacts were preserved in wet fen soils. Burial rituals were more elaborate and common at this time, and the round barrows that covered graves became a notable feature of the landscape, many of them surviving until sheepwalks on chalk downland were ploughed in recent times. Surviving examples, all somewhat disturbed, can still be seen at Balsham and at Mutlow Hill in Fulbourn, and there is one rare survival of a barrow in a river valley at Fen Drayton. Where excavated,

these barrows have all contained cremations in urns, accompanied by signs of flint-working.

Iron Age farming, after about 700BC, became so well developed that, by the end of this period, huge tracts of land, especially where there is a gravel subsoil, were covered with ditched fields and enclosed homesteads. Typical farming settlements, with small fields and sub-rectangular enclosures around circular houses that were thatched with reeds and had walls of wattle and daub, have been excavated at Fen Ditton, Fen Drayton, Longstanton, Teversham, Linton and Milton. At Swavesey, evidence for pottery manufacture and occupation has been excavated. Near the fens, which were very wet at this period, signs of occupation

are scarce, although close inspection of Roman sites has revealed that slightly higher areas in parishes such as Willingham, Cottenham, Over and Waterbeach were already in use at this time.

Hill forts were important monuments of this period, when a growing population, increased wealth and more sophisticated social and political organisation often led to open warfare. A line of distinctive circular forts, roughly separating the territories of the Iceni and the Catuvellauni, controlled strategic points. Belsars Hill in Willingham blocks one of the few approaches to South Cambridgeshire from the Isle of Ely, Arbury Camp in Impington protects a route into Cambridge, Wandlebury is on a high point that controls both the Icknield Way and traffic along the Cam, and Borough Mill in Sawston lies on an important ford across the Cam used by the Icknield Way.

Iron Age burial sites are not often recognisable, but in the latest years of this period an ostentatious ritual was introduced from Europe into south-east England. This ritual involved cremation and subsequent burial in urns, accompanied by symbols of rich feasting such as amphorae and vessels to hold food and drink, usually imported from the Roman Empire. Some of these burials were covered by mounds. This rite is particularly interesting

Belsars Hill in Willingham, 1988.

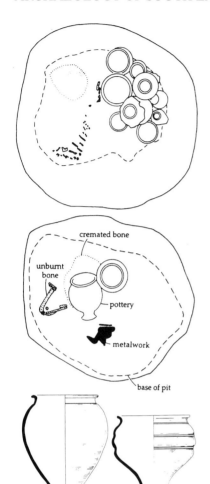

Iron Age cremation pits at Hinxton and two of the pots found in them. Maximum height 26cms.

Roman

The best preserved Roman settlement is at Bullock's Haste in Cottenham. This site was originally so large and has produced such fine artefacts that it seems more like a town than a village, even in terms of the extensive fen-edge sites in which this region is so rich. Similar earthworks, though on a smaller scale, can be seen in Waterbeach. Elsewhere, villas are known at Babraham, Bartlow, Horningsea, Horseheath, Linton, Teversham and Great Wilbraham. These villas were an important part of the Romanisation of the countryside. Their construction, with stone foundations, tiled roofs, plastered walls, mosaic floors, heated bath-houses and neat rectangular layout were a great contrast to the round thatched huts of the Iron Age, which were still used by much of the population. More significantly, they were the centres for the management of extensive estates, worked by wage and slave labour rather than by owner-occupiers, where advanced and large-scale farming techniques might be used. Most land, however, was still farmed by peasant farmers, living in many ways as their fore-bears had done, except that new fruit and vegetable crops were now available, enforced peace brought stability,

and markets developed with the use of coins, roads and a growing demand for agricultural produce in towns and for the army. These changes brought improved living conditions and therefore the population expanded. The old Iron Age farmsteads grew and additional land was settled, sometimes in areas that had been too damp or heavily wooded to be chosen in earlier times. There are particularly extensive settlements along the Cam valley, particularly at Hinxton, and close to the fen-edge at Cottenham, Landbeach, Waterbeach and Willingham. Temples and other religious sites are often found, particularly in fen-edge locations. A hoard of priestly regalia found at Willingham, with its mixture of Roman and Celtic symbolism, is an outstanding discovery of this period, and re-use of a Bronze Age burial mound at Mutlow Hill as a Roman temple is also fascinating. Amongst the gods we see worshipped are deified emperors, classical gods such as Venus, Mars and Jupiter, and the eastern gods Sol and Luna. At the end of this period Christianity was becoming important. A collection of pewter plates from Willingham, one inscribed with the Christian symbol of the chi-rho, is a clear indication of this religion.

because it continued in a similar form after the Roman Conquest, culminating in the finest of all Romano-British burials, those beneath the huge mounds at Bartlow. The rite was presumably the prerogative of a distinct upper class, perhaps best described as 'princely natives', who may have derived their wealth from trade rather than political power, and who were able to enjoy imported Roman luxury goods before the Conquest, and the traditional wealth associated with Iron Age chieftains after it. In this region, their burials have been found at Hinxton and Milton.

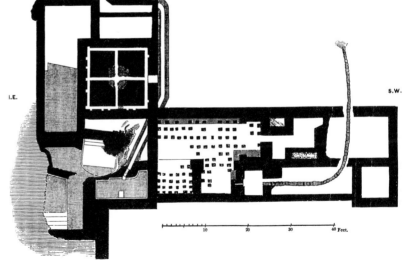

Plan of a Roman villa excavated at Linton in 1849

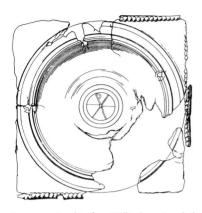

Roman pewter plate from Willingham, inscribed with a Chi-Rho symbol.

The Roman period is well known for its innovative industrial processes and for the high standard of its communication systems. Principal routes, where roads were made with layers of chalk and gravel and had ditches on either side, were those now known as Worsted Street and Akeman Street, but elsewhere there were innumerable thoroughfares that became more fixed in their routes than they had been in former centuries. Many tracks of the Icknield Way, following natural and man-made landmarks across open countryside, were unchanged, but some of its major routes, such as one running close to the present A11, were now more formalised.

Canals, which also served to drain neighbouring land, were another important element in the Roman programme of providing an efficient infrastructure to support economic and military objectives. Car Dyke, visible at Cottenham, Landbeach and, best of all, at Waterbeach, links stretches of natural waterway and may have enabled traffic to travel by boat from Waterbeach to the north of England, though its use for this purpose north of Peterborough is debatable. An important function of this canal was the transport of food-stuffs and other animal products such as leather from the agricultural regions of southern Cambridgeshire to the army stationed in Northern Britain. In later years it was also used to move the products of the

pottery industries of Horningsea and Milton. Numerous kilns in those areas were involved in turning out large and rather crude storage jars, which presumably acted as containers for the export trade in grain. Apart from large-scale processing of grain, which is apparent near to Car Dyke, and hints of bronze working and coin production at Bartlow, these kilns are the only evidence of industrialisation so far discovered in our region.

Anglo-Saxon

The best known sites of the early Anglo-Saxon period are cemeteries and defensive Dykes, although at last, thanks to an increasing amount of excavation work, we are also start-ing to find houses and even complete settlements from these years. Huts and halls, with pits, wells, ovens and boundary ditches have been fully investigated at Hinxton, and other sites of the early period were found at two sites at Linton and also at Cottenham, Waterbeach, Pampisford and Great Wilbraham. Settlements from the middle Saxon period are known at Hinxton and Willingham. There is also an increasing amount of archaeological evidence for late Saxon settlement within medieval

The Car Dyke at Waterbeach in 1988, now cut by the railway but once extending to the Cam.

villages, notably Cottenham, Hinxton, Little Linton and Barham, Swavesey, West Wickham and Willingham.

Cemeteries give a valuable insight into the lives of Anglo-Saxons of the 5th, 6th and 7th centuries, before adoption of Christian customs eventually changed the rituals of burial, and grave-goods were no longer commonly given. Single or small groups of burials are known from Fen Ditton, Hildersham, Hinxton, Horseheath, Sawston, Pampisford, Stapleford, Waterbeach and West Wickham, and magnificent cemeteries have been excavated at Linton, Oakington, Little Wilbraham and Shudy Camps. Of these large cemeteries, Linton and Little Wilbraham, both of which are notable for extreme wealth in the form of swords and imported luxury goods, are close to Roman villas, and were in use from the 5th century. There is little doubt that those who were buried within these cemeteries were able to take over a cultivated landscape complete with road systems from their predecessors, just as they collected and re-used many of their artefacts. Oakington, a 6th century cemetery which is not close to any known Roman site or road, also con-tains many grave-goods, but these suggest a more modest status for the inhabitants, with no swords and few imported items, and it may be that at this time settlers had to work harder to farm their land. The cemetery at Shudy Camps, sited on the later boundary between that parish and Castle Camps, dates to the 7th century. It is in an area where there are many indications of Roman presence, although there are no significant settlement sites nearby. Grave-goods found here show that jewellery was still important for demonstrating wealth and status, but weapons were no longer necessary.

Of the four great Anglo-Saxon dykes in Cambridgeshire, two lie within the area covered by this book. All appear to have the same function, to protect land in the east by preventing easy access along the Icknield Way, and all are built to a similar pattern, with wide, flat-

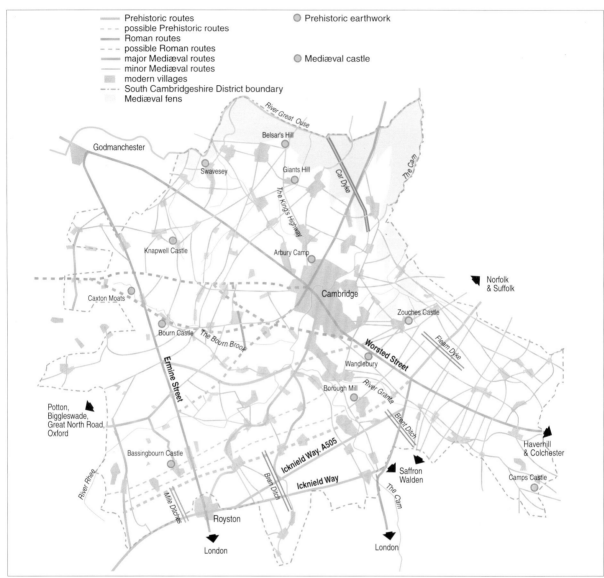

Prehistoric routes
possible Prehistoric routes
Roman routes
possible Roman routes
major Mediæval routes
minor Mediæval routes
modern villages
South Cambridgeshire District boundary
Mediæval fens

Prehistoric earthwork

Mediæval castle

bottomed and straight sided ditches on the western side. Fleam Dyke is an impressive bank and ditch that stretches for 2.5 miles from the fen-edge at Shardelowes Well in Fulbourn to the junction between chalk and clay in Balsham. It is much shorter than Devils Dyke and now appears to have a smaller bank and ditch, but excavations have shown that originally it was similarly massive and was much longer-lived, playing an important part in political geography throughout Anglo-Saxon times. Cyril Fox excavated five trenches through Fleam Dyke in the 1920's, showing that the ditch was cut at least twice, once with a V-shaped and once with a flat-bottomed ditch, and that there were several phases of construction separated by periods of inactivity. The most recent section through this dyke was dug in 1991 when part of it was removed to widen the A11. This confirmed that the original ditch was V-shaped, 6m wide and 3m deep. After many years of weathering, the ditch was recut on a massive scale, 7-8m wide and at least 4m deep, with a flat bottom and steep sides, in the style of Devils, Heydon and Bran Ditch. This phase was constructed probably in the 6th, later 7th or even 8th century. The resulting bank was raised higher on at least one occasion and the defences were kept in repair for many years. Cyril Fox's labourers told him that skeletons had been found within Fleam Dyke, and two shield bosses and spears of 6th century type come from here.

The first phase of Fleam Dyke, however, with a low bank and V-shaped ditch, must have been considerably earlier, for it had filled up before the final dyke was constructed. It was also much longer, for crop marks, hedge lines and the 1836 Ordnance Survey map show that this slighter feature extended north to Great Wilbraham and south towards West Wratting. Elsewhere, excavators of Bran and Brent Ditches often mention low 'marking-out' banks, earlier V-shaped ditches and the presence of Iron Age and Roman items, and it is quite possible that all the Dykes which we now see in their final Saxon form were originally built as much earlier boundary markers, perhaps belonging to the Iron Age, contemporary with similar monuments in Hertfordshire, Essex, Norfolk and Suffolk.

Brent Ditch is the shortest of the dykes but, although it looks insignificant today, excavations of part now destroyed by the A11 in Pampisford show that originally it was a formidable feature, more than 3m wide and 2m deep, with the characteristic steep sides and flat bottom. Though short, it cut off the routes of two Roman roads and the whole width of the chalk downland used by the Icknield Way, and was therefore a valuable defence for those on its eastern side. At the bottom of the ditch were four

Visitors to an excavation of a Saxon village at Hinxton in 1993.

An Anglo-Saxon necklace from Linton. A string of beads made of amber, crystal, glass and jet was fastened at the woman's shoulders with circular gilded brooches, and her cloak was pinned with another massive gilded brooch.

Roman coins and a fragment of Iron Age human bone, and there were several earlier ditches in the area investigated, probably including a side-ditch of the Roman road. An earlier ditch was also noted else-where beneath the dyke's bank, near Pampisford Hall.

Medieval

The location of medieval villages, all of which were in existence by the end of the Saxon period, was often strongly influenced by the long-distance routeways and drove roads which passed through them, especially where these tracks crossed either rivers or other routes. As the village economies grew other routes were developed, but in a well-farmed landscape with fiercely defended property rights and many physical constraints traditional thoroughfares are generally extremely long-lived. Villages needed an adequate water supply but had to be sited where flooding was not too common an occurrence. In several villages, there-fore, we see careful location of dwellings and the church just above the flood-plain or fen. Villagers, however, needed the benefits of as many natural environments as possible, and the care with which parishes were organised from Saxon

times, and in some cases perhaps even earlier, to include areas of woodland, downland, reasonable soils for arable agriculture and access to the fens, is striking.

Most villages in this volume are situated either at river crossings, close to the fen-edge, or in areas of woodland, and the villages in these three locations tended to develop in different ways. Villages that lie where tracks crossed the Cam or Granta originated in several centres but, during the years of expansion and contraction of the Middle Ages, these were usually reorganised into two main areas based on manor houses and village greens. Fen-edge villages were generally more compact. Little of their land might be suitable for housing, and their economies continually expanded, so house-plots had to be squeezed into a higher density. Villages on wooded clay soils near the Suffolk and Essex borders also had distinctive characters which most of them have retained. Here the villages have numerous widely-spaced centres, and the church is not necessarily in the largest of these. The scattered populations in villages of this kind were usually as large as those in more conventional nucleated settle-ments in medieval times, and there is sufficient evidence to prove they were in existence at an early date, but for some reason neither the villagers nor the lords of the manors saw a need to reorganise them into a centralised design. They probably represent an older pattern of Saxon settlement which was altered elsewhere by planned reorganisation and the other forces that led to the nucleated villages that we see more commonly today.

In the later years of the medieval period some villages were able to take advantage of their locations on navigable waterways to develop as ports for local and international trade. Fen Ditton, Fen Drayton and Horningsea were successful in this respect. At Swavesey canals were dug, first by monks and then by the lord of the manor, a major factor in the village's development into a town and a port. Other changes within villages in the Middle Ages were caused by lords of the manor deciding to take in hand land around their house for agricultural reasons or to lay out a park, so pushing development into a new area or restricting it to another existing centre. This process could occur at any time from the 14th century, and it affected about half the villages in our area. It was most dramatic where great houses were built in the 18th century, for example the halls at Great Abington, Babraham, Horseheath and Impington. In exceptional cases villages might move in order to be better placed to profit from a new market. This seems to have happened at Rampton, where the market must have quickly failed, and at Linton, where it was successful.

None of the villages described in this book were deserted during the Middle Ages, but a few were reorganised, so signs of contraction can be seen. Apart from areas that were cleared around manor houses, two original hamlets at Linton, (Little Linton and Barham), were virtually deserted as their populations moved to the central settlement, and the hamlet of Westwick almost disappeared. In Landbeach, drastic and controversial action by the lord of the manor for economic motives in the 16th century led to permanent desertion of one area, although the remainder of the village was unaffected. Elsewhere, especially on villages on clay soils, a succession of cold, wet summers in the early 14th century led to famine conditions, and the weakened population was later much affected by the Black Death. In these areas populations fell considerably from the high figures reached in the late 13th century. Fen-edge villages, with more varied economies, were less affected, and probably took in migrants from other areas. In the 16th and 17th centuries, too, these were the only settlements that flourished, as generous common rights provided free grazing for stock, and incomes were improved by use of natural resources from the fens. These villages also enjoyed comparative freedom from manorial control.

Some villages, (Balsham, Great Abington, Linton, Rampton and Swavesey), were granted the right to hold fairs and markets in the Middle Ages and, with the exception of Rampton, of which we hear no more, these continued for considerable periods. At Linton and Swavesey, both a suitable distance from Cambridge, they were extremely successful, and these became virtually towns. Linton, which at one time had three markets, had a population that included numerous craftspeople, and it developed a minor industrial base and various professional services for its surrounding area. Sawston became an industrial centre from the 17th century, but otherwise it was not until the 19th century that villages in this area began to change their reliance on agricultural employment.

Warfare scarcely seems to have touched South Cambridgeshire at the Norman Conquest, although the castle at Camps Castle was built by a follower of William, Aubrey de Vere, to secure control over his extensive possessions, and it is also likely that Belsars Hill at Willingham was brought into use again in the campaign against Hereward on the Isle of Ely. Fen-edge villages, however, were vulnerable to raiding parties at any time when dissidents controlled the Isle and could retreat quickly out of the reach of royal forces. In the mid 12th century there was a period known as the Anarchy, when Stephen and Matilda, nephew and daughter respectively of Henry II, fought for eighteen years for the Crown of England. At one stage Stephen ordered a ring of forts be built around the southern fen-edge to control a particularly troublesome baron, Geoffrey de Mandeville. Giants Hill at Rampton is a good example of a small, temporary castle built for this purpose. Defences at Swavesey may have been built at the same time, but is more likely that the castle there, and Zouches Castle at Fulbourn, were part of a similar campaign in the 13th century, when Simon de Montfort was in revolt and the fens were again used as a rebel retreat.

Religious houses were also built in a few parishes, though it is only at Denny in Waterbeach that significant remains can still be seen. A pre-Conquest priory at Swavesey was refounded as a possession of a French abbey, but was always small and poor and has left no physical traces except for indeterminate earthworks north of the church. There were also two small priories at Linton. Fragments of one of these can be seen at Barham Hall, but nothing survives of the priory in the village. Denny, however, used successively by monks from Ely, by the Knights Templar and by Franciscan Poor Clares, was still active when Henry VIII seized all monastic possessions, and some of its handsome buildings were merely hidden beneath brick to give them a more modern appearance, and so survived into the 20th century. They have now been restored by English Heritage and are open to the public. At Great Wilbraham the Knights Templar and later the Knights Hospitaller had a preceptory, or administrative centre, and at Balsham and Fen Ditton the bishops of Ely had palaces where they often resided and which also served as centres for running their vast estates. Of these, only the Biggin at Fen

The Biggin at Fen Ditton in the early 19th century.

Ditton still stands, and that is very much altered.

In the 17th century the controversial decision to attempt drainage of the whole of the fens by cutting canals that would take excess water straight out to sea was put into effect. There were many problems in the following centuries, for as the peat fens that had developed from Neolithic times lost moisture they shrank, leaving land below sea-level, from which water could not drain without artificial assistance. Windmills, and later steam, diesel and electric pumps were eventually developed to solve this problem. In the meantime the fenland landscape changed to farmland that was owned by the investors who had paid for the drainage works. Most of the habitats once used for hunting and fishing were lost, though in some areas these survived into the 19th century, and the way of life became very different. However, the rich farm-

land that was created, much of it suitable for labour-intensive fruit and vegetable crops, still supported a large population, and villages in the fen-edge region continued to expand.

The 19th century saw enormous changes in village life. Due to the Enclosure movement, the huge medieval open fields that had been farmed in narrow strips and owned by many villagers were divided amongst a few landowners, sometimes only one or two in a village, and were made into small fields surrounded by hedges or ditches. Landowning villagers were awarded some of this land, but legal and fencing costs were high, and most of their fields were soon sold. At the same time, many common rights to grazing and gathering fuel were lost, and most of the countryside became private property. At the same time, chalk downlands that had been sheepwalks throughout the Middle

Ages, and probably from Bronze Age times, were ploughed for arable farming.

The population rose rapidly at this time, and until the middle of the century there were few opportunities for employment except for poorly paid farm labour. Social discontent sometimes reached extreme levels, leading to rioting and outbreaks of arson. Fire had always been a hazard for thatched cottages and farmyards with hayricks and loose straw, and serious losses are recorded. Hinxton, for example, lost about half its houses in a fire in the 17th century. More crowded conditions would have made the situation worse in any case in the 19th century, but it was the deliberate firing of farmyards as protests against individual landowners that had the greatest impact on the village scene. Large compact villages on the fen-edge, with farmyards set amidst housing which was usually of the cheapest and most

ARCHAEOLOGY OF SOUTH EAST CAMBRIDGESHIRE

Even with a fire-engine stationed in the village, losses of this kind, photographed in Swavesey in 1913, had a lasting effect on fen-edge villages.

flammable kind, and a population that was traditionally more rebellious than most, were particularly vulnerable. Newspaper reports in the mid 19th century record devastation on a huge scale when rick fires got out of control, and villages such as Cottenham, Over, Swavesey, Waterbeach and Willingham lost between a third and a half of their houses on more than one occasion. The lasting effect of these arson attacks and accidental blazes was the loss of most of the picturesque cottages that are common in many South Cambridgeshire villages, and their replacement with plain houses of the local white brick.

By the late 19th century a railway network had developed which made it possible for several villages to send their produce, mainly fresh fruit and vegetables, to markets in Cambridge, London and the Midlands. Histon and Impington, where Chivers brought factory production to maximise profits from soft fruit farming, grew substantially, partly as a result of this new service, and the populations of fruit-producing villages around the fens also increased to more than a thousand inhabitants. These developed many of the local services, crafts and shops suitable for large settlements. Water transport in the fens also remained important well into the 19th century, when it was largely killed by the railways. Balsham and the industrial village of Sawston also expanded substantially at this time.

In the 20th century some of these centres, especially those in easy reach of Cambridge, expanded rapidly to provide homes for workers in towns, and Village Colleges were built at Cottenham, Impington, Linton, Sawston and Swavesey in order to give better educational opportunities to village people. When planners started to look for settlements that could relieve the pressure for growth on Cambridge, large villages with good facilities and few claims to status as Conservation Areas were often selected for deliberate expansion. Histon, Impington and Milton were chosen for growth in 1957, and Cottenham, Linton and Sawston in 1965. At the same time it was agreed that new estates would be permitted in Balsham, the Abingtons, Longstanton, Oakington, Over, Swavesey and Willingham. The first Structure Plan, approved in 1980, tried to keep expansion for new employment and housing to a few centres, principally Milton. Pressure on Cambridge remained relentless however, especially with improved communications by road and rail and the growth of high technology industries. In 1989 several more villages were accepted as 'Rural Growth Areas', mostly those to the north of Cambridge in order to protect the attractive landscape to the south, and by 1996 Cottenham, Fulbourn, Histon, Linton, Milton, Sawston and Waterbeach all had populations of more than 4000. Within these, however, as within the less developed villages in the south of Cambridgeshire, there can usually be found an older core, and the patterns left by earlier inhabitants still leave visible traces for the observant to discover.

Palaeolithic	Mesolithic	Neolithic	Bronze Age	Iron Age	Roman	Saxon	Mediaeval	Modern
7500		3500	2000	700	43	410	1066	1500

The Abingtons

Great and Little Abington are small parishes of 661 and 545 hectares respectively, lying on either side of the Granta, the boundary which separates them. They both lie on a somewhat hilly band of chalk which rises to 100m above sea level. At about 50m this chalk is followed by a major route of the Icknield Way, which became in turn a Roman road, important medieval highway, turnpike road and the modern A11, leading from Great Chesterford into Norfolk. Both villages were built away from this road on low-lying ground (about 30m), each on a patch of alluvium and river gravels around churches that are about 100m from the river. Both parishes include areas of glacial gravel and also chalky boulder clay, especially in the southern part of Great Abington, abutting Brent Ditch. The Granta divides the two parishes, and they are also bounded by two Roman roads, Worsted Street to the north of Little Abington and the successor to an Icknield Way route (A11) to the east of them both. Great Abington's southern border is also the County boundary with Essex. The common fields of Great Abington were enclosed following an Award made in 1804, and those of Little Abington in 1807. In Domesday Book they are *Abintone*, or 'Abba's farm', and they acquired their separate names by the 14th century.

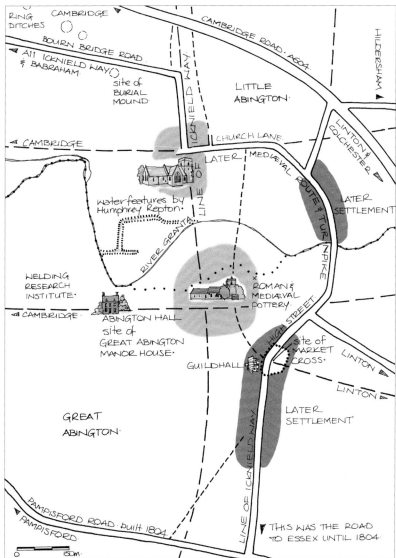

Prehistoric

Groups of round barrows were built along the main route of Icknield Way, including two clusters in Little Abington, some of which were upstanding mounds until the late 20th century. All are now ploughed, and low rises in a field and dark circles in the growing crop are the only indications of their positions. Several pieces of waste flakes from flint-working and tools such as scrapers were found on and around the more northerly barrow group and, when excavation trenches were dug through the southerly group in 1994, an exceptional number

of flint flakes and cores were found. The ditch around one of the mounds was more than 2m deep, though the ditch of the other mound examined was only 1m. Analysis of snails found on this site showed that the mounds had originally stood in pasture. A few artefacts and a small amount of human bone from one of the burials were found here. Pieces of Early and Middle-Late Bronze Age pottery had been ploughed into the ditches and there were also occasional sherds of Iron Age pottery, some of it with decoration, perhaps connected with

the Iron Age cemetery found nearby in Pampisford.

Roman

There are two Roman sites in Great Abington. In the south-east corner of the parish are crop marks of an aisled barn, round huts and rectangular enclosures. Pottery and tile have been collected from the surface. Within the village, close to the church and river, more Roman pottery has been found, and it is likely that this too was an area of habitation.

The church at Little Abington, with its blocked Anglo-Saxon door.

Anglo-Saxon

Part of Brent Ditch, one of Cambridgeshire's four defensive dykes, runs into Great Abington. Its ditch, with scarcely any trace of bank surviving, runs north-west from the tongue of chalky boulder clay that stretches westwards to Abington Park, up to the A11 and then across to the wooded park of Pampisford Hall, ending at the springs in Dickman's Grove.

The church in Little Abington is older than that in Great Abington. Its nave, two doors (one of which is now blocked) and north window are of late Anglo-Saxon type, though they may date to the years immediately after the Conquest.

Medieval

After the Conquest the whole of the manor of Great Abington was given to the de Veres, later created earls of Oxford, whose principal residence was Castle Hedingham in Essex and who had a large Cambridgeshire estate based on their castle at Castle Camps. The village was owned by this family until the 16th century. Their manor house was on the site of Abington Hall and was often used as a dower house for the widows of the earls of Oxford. In the early 15th century a hall and two rooms of this house were demolished by the resident countess, presumably to be rebuilt on a larger scale. There seems to have been a small deer park belonging to the manor in the south of the parish, where curving ditches marking the boundary pale near Bush Park are visible as crop marks. This park is not mentioned after about 1300, and probably by that time the earls of Oxford had replaced it with another at Castle Camps. Little Abington was a separate manor at the time of the Conquest, and it remained this way. It never had a resident lord, and there was no manor house in the parish.

Great Abington manor house was sold with the rest of the estate in the late 16th century, and in the 17th century it was a very substantial dwelling with 24 hearths. In about 1712 it was rebuilt, with new out-buildings and landscaping of the grounds by Humphrey Repton, including construction of an ornamental canal. Parts of this house were incorporated in a mansion built in about 1800, which still stands. Also in the 19th century, the river was straightened by residents of the Hall. Since World War II this mansion has been part of the Welding Research Institute and has been converted to flats and offices.

Village Development

The original villages were sited, like most settlements in the Cam and Granta valleys, on routeways that took advantage of crossing-places of the river. Two such tracks also crossed two old river edge routes from Cambridge to Linton on either side of the water, leading to the development of centres at their crossing-places. Later on, both villages were moved away from the churches and the manor house to the eastern of the north-south routes, and the main east-west road entered Little Abington to the north of the older road, winding through both villages and across the river before heading for Linton. This dislocation of the original routes led to awkward bends in the village streets and further shifts in the settlement pattern. The park around Abington Hall prevented growth of the village in that direction, and settlement was pushed still further away when the park was enlarged in the 19th century. Earthworks of two of the medieval villages can still be seen near the churches.

At the point where the village street of Great Abington was crossed by a road from the church to Linton there was a market place, marked by a stone cross until at least 1816. The grant to hold a weekly market and a three day annual fair was given in the 13th century. As the east-west route from Cambridge to Colchester

A hollow-way in Little Abington churchyard marks an old route between the two churches.

became more important, sharp bends were needed in the villages to negotiate the main north-south village street. This road was made a turnpike in 1766. The village has now been bypassed by a new line of the A604, to the north.

There is a separate small settlement at Bourn Bridge, where the A11 crosses the river. In medieval and later times this was renowned for its inns. In the 18th century County balls were held here for the gentry of Cambridgeshire and Suffolk, there were archery and other sporting contests, and various University clubs had their dinners here. One inn was notorious for smuggling, and this eventually led to its closure. With the coming of the railways in the 19th century the need to change coach horses disappeared, and the second inn was also closed.

Both villages had small populations in 1086, 20 in Little Abington and only 14 in Great Abington, and they remained modest in size. Great Abington's population of about 48 tenants in 1279 fell to 96 adults over 14 in 1377. By 1801 this had grown to 272 in total, and reached a peak of 382 in 1831, but it declined for a century after this, and in the mid 19th century was described as 'small but respectable'. In 1936 the Land Settlement Association, which was set up after World War I to give unemployed men a chance to begin a life in farming, bought land, divided it into 46 holdings of 10 acres each and settled smallholders there. New housing was built near the village after 1950, and by 1996 the population had risen to 840. Little Abington had about 35 tenants in the 13th century and 45 adults in 1377. In the 17th century 21 families lived here, growing to 339 in 1871, at which time it was the larger village. Subsequent decline was reversed when new housing was built after 1930, and in 1996 there were 500 residents.

Babraham

Babraham, a moderate sized parish of 970 hectares, lies mostly on chalk, with alluvium and gravels near the river, where the village is situated. The village and much of the parish are fairly low lying, less than 30m above sea level, but to the north the chalk rises steeply, in places up to 60m. The Roman road, Worsted Street, the parish's northern border, is mostly about 45m, with wide views to north and south. A branch of the Icknield Way that became a Roman road (A11) is the eastern parish boundary. The Granta flows through the village and forms only a small part of the southern boundary. In the early 19th century the open fields were enclosed without an official award being made, as all the land was in one ownership. In Domesday Book Babraham is *Badburgham*, or 'the village of a woman named Beaduburh'.

Prehistoric

A stray flint tool of the Palaeolithic period was found in Babraham Park, and several later prehistoric implements are scattered around the parish. However, despite extensive chalk downland and at least two important routes of the Icknield Way in this parish, no occupation areas can be identified and the crop marks of only one burial mound have been found. This is close to the A11, near to a group of four mounds in Little Abington. A chalk knoll known as Copley Hill, adjacent to Worsted Street, is often described as an outstanding Bronze Age barrow, and occasionally pieces of flint tools are found on it, but it is in fact almost certainly a natural rounded outcrop of chalk, although it is of course possible that such a feature would be used in prehistoric times as a ready-made site.

Roman

Worsted Street, known locally simply as the Roman Road, is a well-preserved feature now used as a green way where walkers can appreciate the character of a Roman highway running in a straight line on an agger or low bank flanked by side-ditches, between recognised destinations. The road is part of the route which seems to run in various sections from Chester to Colchester, including the road from Cambridge to Godmanchester that is now the A14. By no means all of this route

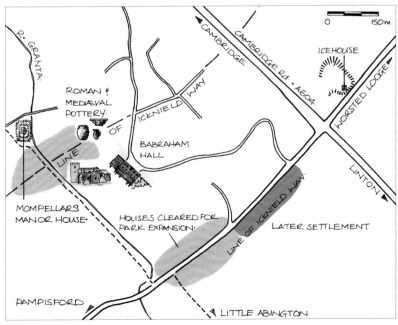

was constructed as the fully Roman-ised highway that we see in the stretch in Babraham, and much of it has lost its archaeological character because of later use as a turnpike road and modern highway. This particular stretch extends from the Iron Age hill fort at Wandlebury to Worsted Lodge, where it meets and crosses the Romanised line of the Icknield Way, now the A11. There would have been many benefits for the small town of Cambridge in being linked to this major through-route, which perhaps explains why construction of this section was so thorough. Several archaeological sections have been excavated through it, the latest in 1991 at the site now destroyed by the dualling of the A11. As in previous work, it was shown that earth and turf from the surrounding area was piled over natural chalk, and this layer was covered with chalk principally quarried from side-ditches. Over this was spread a mounded layer of gravel that had been brought from further afield. This particular layer has been added to in medieval and modern times, as the surface needed patch-ing to preserve a dry surface. Where excavated, this road surface was 1m high, 10m wide, with an overall width, including the side-ditches, of 15m. The ditches were 1m deep.

The Romans lived in several places in Babraham. Close to Worsted Street is a villa, including an aisled building and a granary, set in a square enclosure. Foundations of a stone and clunch building measuring approximately 10 by 6m, with pottery and other artefacts, were noticed when common land in the south-east corner of the parish was ploughed, and Roman artefacts have been found in Babraham Park, including iron barrel-locks.

Medieval

North-west of the church is a moated site that was presumably the manor house for Mompellers manor, a Saxon estate that was held by the King in 1086 but was granted to the Hamelin family of Babraham in 1166. The house was described as ruinous in the mid 14th century, but was obviously repaired or rebuilt, for it was lived in by the lord of this manor at the beginning of the 16th century, and in the middle of that century, when it had passed to absentee owners, one of them, Edward Wood, was accused of taking materials away from the house, including glass, ceilings and tiles, suggesting there was a respectable building up to that time. Late medieval pottery, tile and food debris have been noted on the surface of this site.

Another of Babraham's many manors was given to the de Scalers family, who gave the church to Waltham Abbey and later passed the rest of the estate to Bruisyard Abbey in Suffolk. This estate was taken over by the Crown at the dissolution of the monasteries. By the late 16th century it was owned by Robert Taylor, a wealthy servant of the Crown who bought up much of the rest of the village and built a new house before losing his fortune through massive embezzlement by one of his own servants. He sold Babraham to the colourful Horatio Palavacino, who came from Genoa, made part of his fortune as foreign financial agent and spy for the Crown and commanded a ship against the Spanish Armada. He was particularly popular because of the way he cheated the Pope in favour of Elizabeth after the death of Queen Mary - 'He was a thief; A thiefe? thou lyest, For whie? he robbed but Anti-Christ' was one contemporary comment. His son Tobias was another interesting character, but was better at spending money than making it, and was forced to sell the estate after carrying out many alterations to the 16th century hall. The antiquarian William Cole visited this Hall regularly during his child-hood in Little Abington and was upset when it was pulled down in the 18th century. He noted in his manuscript:

Being on the water May 25th 1768, I saw with grief and concern a great part of the columns and coin stones which came from Baberham Place lying on the shore near Chesterton Sluice, (Cambridge) which is next week going to be repaired with them. and referred to Robert Jones, who pulled the Hall down, as 'a low bred East India Director'. He also left a useful description of the Hall, with its Gothic-style courtyard and a long gallery that ran the length of the house, together with a portico and large hall with several bow-fronted windows that must have been Palavacino additions.

Village Development

Like the Abingtons, Babraham originally consisted of settlements based on wide converging tracks that cross the river quite close together. The eastern track, now the High Street, was on a route of the Icknield Way that was still an important high-way when the Ordnance Survey mapped Cambridgeshire in 1836, branching from the present route of the A505 north of Pampisford and joining the A11 at Worsted Lodge. The westernmost settlement, where the church and manor house were situated in an area of Roman occupation, shrank after the mid-14th century fall in the village population, although pits and ditches containing occupation debris dating from about 1200 to 1550 were noted in service trenches about 100m north of Babraham Hall and illustrate continued use of the settlement until the Taylor's hall was built. For the next three centuries Babraham was dominated by the families who owned the Hall and who expanded and landscaped the park, particularly in the 18th century when the hall was rebuilt on a grand scale and when works in the park included cutting of canals and creation of watermeadows. These works involved clearance of one side of the village street and construction of the wall that still bounds the Park here.

The Hall was inherited by the daughter of Robert Jones, who married into the Adeane family. In the 19th century the Hall was pulled down yet again and was rebuilt as a red brick mansion which in 1948 was sold to the Agricultural Research Council, its present occupants. In the mid 19th century it was described

Statue of Jonas Webb and the wall separating Babraham Park from the High Street.

rather charitably as 'a handsome modern mansion... situated in a small but beautiful park... surrounded with groves, pleasure grounds and tastefully laid down gardens'. The Adeanes continued to be a prominent family who were responsible for building many of the cottages and lodges in the village. Agriculture in the parish, and in fact in much of the world, was dramatically affected by Jonas Webb, resident at Church Farm from 1820-62, who imported Sussex Southdown sheep to the area and then greatly improved the breed. He ran a very large flock in Babraham, and breeding stock from here was sold to Australia, North and South America and many parts of Europe.

Babraham had a population of 38 in 1086, and this figure grew to at least 60 tenants, a minimum of 300 people, in the 13th century. It continued to grow until the mid 14th century but then fell substantially, and in the 16th, 17th and 18th centuries had little more than 30 families. In 1801 the total population was 196, which grew to 304 in 1861. This figure fell to about 200 in the early 20th century and, despite new building at the north end of the village and a housing estate in the Park, the population in 1996 was still only 250.

Balsham

Balsham is one of the area's largest parishes, covering 1831 hectares. The village and the eastern part of the parish lie on chalky boulder clay, but underlying chalk is exposed at the western end. The land is fairly high and undulating, with the village on a plateau over 100m above sea level. Roman roads form the western and southern borders. Fleam Dyke is an impressive earthwork along most of the northern parish boundary, following a ridge between 30 and 100m above sea level. The configuration of the parishes suggests that Balsham and West Wickham were originally one unit, in which case the division between them was made at an early date, for settlements are recorded in them both by the end of the 10th century. There are no rivers or streams in the parish, but the boulder clay retains water naturally and there were many ponds here until recent years, when water levels fell. Balsham's open fields were enclosed after an Award was made in 1806. In Domesday Book it is known as *Balesham* or 'the village of Baelli'.

Prehistoric

The Ordnance Survey map of 1836 shows the positions of three Bronze Age burial mounds on the eastern side of Balsham, of which there is no longer any trace, but the low mounds of four more can still be seen on the ground. Three of these are alongside the A11, originally a major line of the Icknield Way. Two were opened in the mid 19th century. One contained two large urns in shallow pits, inverted over cremated bones. The bones of one burial had been wrapped in cloth which was fastened with a bronze pin. A large urn with finger-nail decoration at the centre of the other mound also held a cremation which was accompanied by several freshly-flaked blades of the best quality black flint. Similar flints were found within the mound, and there was a pile of six more near the edge. It seems that flint-knapping at the grave-side was part of the ritual of burial. A fourth barrow survives where it lies in a belt of woodland, but part of the mound that extends into a field has been ploughed flat. In two other areas of chalk there are groups of ring-ditches that mark the sites of more burial mounds of this period.

In quarries just east of the village early Iron Age pits were found which contained pottery and animal bone, and some crop marks in the parish might point to habitation in this period, though a Roman date is probably more likely.

Roman

Crop marks close to the Roman road to Colchester suggest a large Roman farmstead or villa with square, round and aisled buildings, and other sites in the parish have rectangular buildings and field enclosures.

Anglo-Saxon

At the beginning of the 11th century the Danes defeated English forces and overran East Anglia, raiding the countryside from Suffolk to Oxfordshire. These events are described in the Anglo-Saxon Chronicle for the year 1010, and Henry of Huntingdon, who was born in the fens and was Archdeacon of Huntingdon in the early 12th century, made use of oral traditions to add local details.

Anglo-Saxon grave-slab in Balsham church.

They... burnt Cambridge; and retreating thence over the hills, through a very pleasant country near Balsham, they massacred all whom they found in that place, tossing the children on the points of their spears. One man... mounted the steps to the top of a church tower, which is still standing there, and... he defended himself single-handed against the enemy.

The estate of Balsham was given to Ely by Leofflaed, the daughter of Earl Brihtnoth, hero of the Battle of Maldon and himself a major bene-factor of the Abbey. This estate must have already included the church of the above story. Within the church can now be seen two decorative stone fragments, parts of a grave slab and a cross shaft. Both have inter-laced carving on them and date to the early 11th century.

Medieval

Balsham passed to the bishop of Ely in 1109, and remained in this ownership until it was taken by the

Crown in 1600. Shortly afterwards the new owner, Thomas Sutton, gave it to Charterhouse, the school that he founded, and it stayed in this ownership until the 20th century. The manor house, Balsham Hall, described as ruinous in 1356, had been built on a grand scale, probably by Bishop Hugh de Balsham, founder of Peterhouse College, who entertained Edward I here on at least three occasions. Fifty years later its ruins still included a chapel, gatehouse, two large halls with chambers above them, stables, granary, dairy, brewhouse and dove-cote, and other farm buildings and offices. These buildings were attacked during the Peasants Revolt, when documents were burnt and damage done. Bishops and their retinues were often resident in Balsham, and stone coffins of priests from their staff stand in the church-yard. The site of the manor house was given to build a school in the 19th century. During the short time that Balsham was in private hands, Thomas Sutton lived in the village, probably building himself a large house of which Nine Chimneys House is one surviving wing. Other smaller estates in Balsham included one held by the de Scalers, whose manor house was on the site that became Balsham Place.

Village Development

Balsham became a linear settle-ment spreading along the High Street for nearly a mile, with the church and manor house near the eastern end, but much of this development probably dates to medieval and later expansion, when the east-west High Street became an important highway and a fair and market flourished. The earlier village was based on numerous north-south routes and consisted of several small settlements and a larger one in the centre, south of the church. A curving road

The present tower of Balsham church (above) dates to the 13th century, with buttress added in the 16th century. (Below) The graves of medieval priests in the churchyard.

enclosing this central site probably marks a diversion of the road that once ran straight past the church and manor, following expansion of the grounds around the bishop's manor house. Because the land enclosed by this road remained the home farm and a residence for Ely and later institutional owners, housing for the villagers was kept elsewhere, and this, the oldest part of the village, was left undeveloped.

In the mid 13th century the bishop was granted a weekly market and annual three-day fair. These were presumably held on the green in front of the manor house. It seems likely that both did well as the village grew, and the fair was still held in the 19th century, though the market had ceased fifty years earlier.

For its size, Balsham only a modest population of 26 in 1086, perhaps not having fully recovered from the Danish attacks. This grew to 93 tenants, nearly 500 people in all, in 1251, but the figure fell in the 14th century, and in 1377 there were 255 payers of the poll tax. In the 16th and 17th centuries Balsham was a considerable settlement, with 80 households in 1563 and 104 in 1664. Many cottages and farmhouses set in long medieval closes along the High Street were built at this time. This

population was maintained through the 18th century, and in 1801 there were 542 people counted in the census. In the 19th century there was no local squire to prevent people moving into the village and there was great expansion, to a maximum of 1352 in 1851, most of them living in poverty. This population subsequently fell by half in the 20th century. New buildings after 1950 allowed an increase in size and rapid growth to about 1970, and slower expansion thereafter, and the population in 1996 was 1400.

Chalk heathland in the north-west of the parish, which was open country used for grazing when Fleam Dyke was built, was used for sheep until the fields were enclosed and plough-ed after 1806. In the south-east, parts of the landscape were wooded in 1086, with Ely, for example, having woodland for 200 pigs. Woodland continued to be important in the lord's estate, and the present Balsham Wood may be a survival from medieval times.

Most of the old roads to Balsham led to the part of the village near the church, where there were paths to Linton, Weston Colville, West Wratting, West Wickham and Fleam Dyke. The road from Newmarket to Linton, which originally only passed

the west end of the village, later moved to the east and therefore had to run the length of Balsham High Street. A 17th century coaching inn, now the Black Bull, was one result of this shifted road.

Nine Chimneys in 1997 and (above) before 1930.

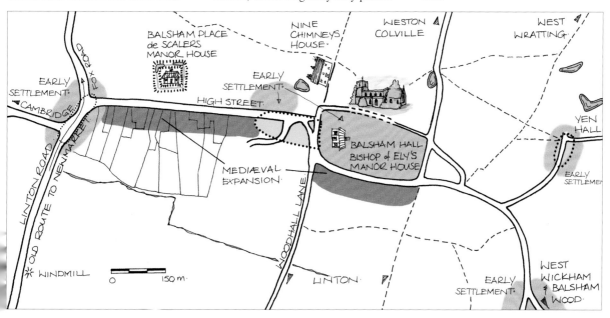

Bartlow

Bartlow is an extremely small parish of only 218 hectares even including areas that were added to the medieval parish in 1965 and 1990. It lies mostly on chalk apart from a narrow band of alluvium and gravels near the three streams which join within the village to form the River Granta. The countryside slopes gently from about 100m in the north-east down to 50m where the village sits within a valley, and then rises again to the south. Roman burial mounds which dominate the village are on this rising slope, and overlook the land to the north and east. Parish boundaries include a stream that is followed by the road to the east and a low bank known as Bartlow Broad Balk to the north. There have been several changes to the southern border, which is also the County boundary. It seems that parishes in this area were less stable entities than in most areas, and their flexible boundaries contained several small scattered hamlets in medieval times. Bartlow itself was not included in Domesday Book, and its earliest recorded name in 1232 is *Berklawe*, 'the mounds of the birch trees', commemorating the burial mounds. Open fields of the parish were finally enclosed in 1863.

Prehistoric

Within the gravel soils near the Granta two Palaeolithic hand-axes and a collection of Mesolithic tools, an axe and six flaked blades, have been recorded. Flint tools of Neolithic and Bronze Age date were found during excavations of the Roman mounds, and ring-ditches on a slope to the east of the village presumably represent Bronze Age burial mounds, although searches of the ploughed soil of this field produced scarcely any artefacts.

Roman

There were originally at least six, and possibly seven, conical mounds in two parallel lines close to the church in Bartlow, of which four survive. The largest is 15m high, taller than any other Roman mounds in Western Europe. All six were investigated in the early 19th century, and in each one there was a cremated body with rich feasting regalia. The cremations were in glass vessels within large iron-bound locked wooden chests in five mounds, and in a brick cist in the sixth. Lamps of iron or bronze had been left burning when each burial was sealed, and when excavated they still contained a 'fatty substance' and a partially burnt wick. Objects left with the dead were mostly exotic vessels of decorated bronze, glass and pottery, some of which contained food and drink. These included ornate bronze flagons for wine, sets of samian

Drawing of the Bartlow Hills in 1821 and (above) the highest mound, 1992.

Copy of a small enamelled cauldron and (above) a bronze wine flagon and patera, from Bartlow Hills.

were an élite class that moved easily to and fro across the Channel, probably making money from trade as well as owning large estates, and able to continue an even more lavish life-style under Roman rule than they had as leaders of Iron Age society.

Little is known about how the cemetery was actually used. Each mound was apparently intended for one individual, but many other skeletons were found in the area when the railway was constructed later in the 19th century. Burials have also been reported from Bartlow Park, and one had an iron shield boss, so it is also possible that the Anglo-Saxons later made use of the site, as they did so many monuments. A sherd of 4th century pottery found on the highest mound suggests that the barrows were raised higher in later centuries, and were perhaps still venerated then by descendants of the dead. Today only four mounds survive, one

of which is in Bartlow Park. All the artefacts were lost in a fire apart from some of the humbler items from the first excavation, which can be seen in Saffron Walden Museum.

The most likely residence for the barrow-builders was a villa that was excavated a few years after the mounds in Bartlow Park, for we know from cemeteries such as Guilden Morden and Litlington that the dead were not moved far. However, more wealthy residences have also been found at Linton and Ashdon, within one mile of the site, and their owners too could have been involved in construction of the mounds. The villa excavated at Bartlow was a modest building about 20m wide, with walls of flint and chalk decorated with painted plaster, a hypocaust, and a well more than 10m deep, down which much building material had been thrown and which had an infant burial in its top

tableware, cups, phials and bottles of clear and coloured glass, and one amphora. Dry and air-tight conditions in the chalk mounds preserved many organic remains. A wreath of box leaves, flower petals, a piece of sponge, incense that smelt of frankincense or myrrh, a wicker-work bottle and a wooden tankard were found, and some of the vessels held liquids that scientists of the time identified as wine mixed with honey, and blood and milk. The most unusual item of all was an iron folding chair with a seat of leather straps.

The burials dated to the late 1st and early 2nd century AD. Many of the items had been imported from the Rhineland and Northern Gaul, which is the only area outside Eastern England where this kind of burial is found, and it seems likely that the families who built them

Iron folding chair with bronze ornaments and a seat of leather straps found in Bartlow Hills.

layer. The site was in use over a long period, at least from the early 2nd to the 4th century to judge from the finds that are mentioned, and later buildings were of inferior workmanship to the earlier ones. A significant aspect of this site was the later discovery of many coin moulds and lumps of bronze, which supports the idea that this area was commercially important, for although in theory all coins were minted in Rome, it was not at all unknown for them to be locally produced.

Medieval

The parish of Bartlow was a late creation that incorporated parts of Ashdon and Castle Camps, from where it was perhaps colonised and with whom it was jointly owned by the de Vere family after the Conquest. The population was very small and scattered, the village is not known by name until the 13th century, and it is only the existence of an undoubtedly early church, built around 1100, that confirms there was a settlement here at this time. The present village is compactly clustered around the junctions of five roads, with the church and Park occupying a large area on the eastern side, but,

Wall-painting in Bartlow church, recorded in 1928.

as is common in North Essex villages, it originally included other hamlets, with few houses within the village. The original manor house may have been on the site of the building now known as the Old Hall, near the river. It was recorded in 1279, when it was said to stand in a small park of 5 acres, and was used as a farmhouse for Bartlow estate from the 15th century. The present house dates to the 16th century, with additions made in the 17th, 18th, and 19th centuries. Bartlow Hall was built in 1962, on the site of a 19th century house that had been destroyed by fire.

In 1279 there were only 32 tenants, about 160 people, the lowest population in this region. By 1377 this figure had fallen to a total population of about 42, and there were only eight families recorded at one stage in the 17th century. In 1801 there were 83 people here, and Bartlow estate ensured that few newcomers were admitted in the 19th century. Labourers from outside the parish were used on some farms, and the maximum population never exceeded 123. It fell considerably in the 20th century, and despite a slight recent rise it was still only 90 in 1996.

The railway which passed between two of the Roman mounds came to Bartlow in 1865, and, as the junction between the line from Audley End

Bartlow church, dated c.1100, has one of only two round towers in Cambridgeshire.

and the Haverhill to Great Shelford route it had a busy station, with a siding for goods trains. The Great Eastern Railway line closed in 1923, and the branch line to Audley End in 1965. The lines were taken up, and the route sold back to Bartlow Estate.

Carlton

Carlton is a parish of 974 hectares, lying on chalky boulder clay except for a small patch in the extreme north-west where underlying chalk is exposed. The clay soils supported considerable woodland in 1086 and throughout the Middle Ages, and in the mid 19th century the countryside was described as 'richly wooded and cultivated'. Some of this woodland survives today in Carlton Wood and Lopham's Wood. The land rises and falls between about 30 and 130m above sea level, with a narrow valley where the River

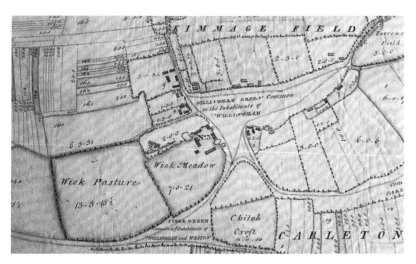

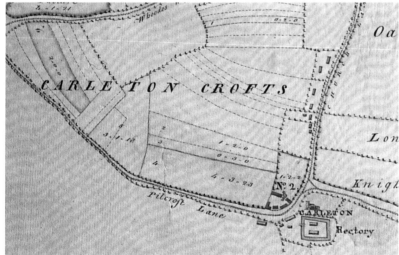

Carlton and (above) Willingham Green, in 1767.

Willingham. The manor house for this estate, which Lewes held until the dissolution of the monasteries in 1537, was at Hall Farm and stood within a rectangular moat, of which there are now only slight traces. On a map of 1767, however, it was an almost complete circuit, with one curving side, and contained three buildings, with three more outside the moat. The manor of Little Carlton was also a Saxon estate, which in the late 14th and early 15th century was owned by the Lopham family. The oval moat in which the manor house stood could conceivably have originated in Saxon times, but its final form is likely to be a result of landscaping, for it was sold to the Fyndernes in the 15th century and that family built a new house here beside the moat, surrounding it with a garden and a park. Their house was altered in the 16th century, when it was used as a farmhouse, and was enlarged in the 17th century. There are further doubts over this site, as in the 1767 map no moat is shown here, only a three-sided building, despite the careful representations of water-filled moats around Carlton Hall and Rectory. The house has now been restored, but the moat is filled in.

Village Development

Carlton is an example of a parish with several small centres which, because growth was limited and the manors stayed quite separate, has retained this pattern to the present day. The wooded landscape was probably not cleared until quite late in Saxon times, and fields were still being enclosed from woods around the small settlements in the Middle Ages. In the 18th century there were four distinct settlements, each with its own village green. At Carlton, a tiny village of five houses clustered on the opposite side of the road to the church, which was sited at the point where four roads met. A rectory stood in a moated site adjacent to the church. A narrow green ran south-east from the village, along the road to Carlton Green. Willingham, sometimes known as Willingham Green, was larger at this

Stour rises. The villages of Carlton and Willingham are on two of the highest places, and their churches were sited on particularly prominent points. This long thin parish, none of whose boundaries are ancient features, includes the medieval settlement at Willingham, which was the centre of an independent parish until the 15th century, and scattered settlements such as Carlton Hall, Lopham's Hall (once known as Little Carlton), Cocksedge Farm and Carlton Green. Its open fields were enclosed following an Award made in 1800, but before this time there were already many small hedged

fields. In 1086 Carlton was *Carletona*, or 'the village of free men or peasants'.

Prehistoric and Roman

In three areas crop marks show rectangular and circular enclosures that are likely to be settlements from these periods.

Medieval

Land in Carlton was willed to the wife of Alfhelm Polga in the late 10th century. This Saxon estate later passed to William the Conqueror's wife, who gave it to Lewes Priory, and they also received land in time and had 33 houses in groups around a triangular green on the 1767 map. At Enclosure, shortly after this, the green was divided up and houses were built upon it. Its church is depicted on the same map, but this (and probably much of the rest of the plan) must have been taken without correction from a map of 1612, for in 1750 William Cole had sketched the ruins and said that the church:

...stands in an open field, with a few houses at some distance to the east of it... The building never was large, consisting only of one small room, with a turret at the West end.

In a mid-19th century description of Carlton the ruins had lately been removed. The moated site at Carlton Hall also had a few houses nearby and a long narrow green stretching along the road to the west. Carlton Green, now in the parish of Weston Colville but at that time mainly on the Carlton side of the border, had already shrunk considerably from its size in 1612, when houses had stretched to Lopham's Hall, and there were only four houses and a large triangular green depicted, with one field labelled 'ruins'.

The population in 1086 was given as 24, which included 6 at Willingham. In 1377 there were 71 tax-payers, but at times in the 15th and 16th centuries only 8 households were counted. The settlements expanded from the late 16th century onwards, and there were often as many as 200 people here in the 17th and 18th centuries, divided between at least three settlements and the isolated farmsteads. An estate map of 1767 shows 50 buildings, but it looks as if Willingham in particular was copied from an earlier map, and had in fact shrunk further by this time. In 1801 there were 229 people here, some living in subdivided and crowded cottages. Growth continued in the 19th century, to a peak of 469 in 1871, and new housing was built along Brinkley Road. Since then the population has generally fallen, and in 1996 there were only 190 people within the parish.

Castle Camps

Castle Camps is a large parish of 1256 hectares, mostly lying on chalky boulder clay, but with underlying chalk coming to the surface in the west. Much of the parish was still heavily wooded in early medieval times and the population was scattered in hamlets, without any nucleated village. Extensive tracts of land were used as a deer park, possibly from late in the Saxon period, and this too has affected the settlement pattern and created unusual field shapes in some areas. Two sides of the triangular parish are also the County boundary, adjusted several times in some places. Its smooth line on the eastern side was probably the fenced edge of the deer park, while the irregular western edge reflects the uncertain parochial status of portions that were taken out of woodland during the Middle Ages. The border with Shudy Camps to the north, however, follows divisions between fields. Tributaries of the Granta rise near Camps Castle and flow to Bartlow. Castle Camps contains some of the highest land in Cambridgeshire, with a ridge nearly 130m above sea level on the east, and the Castle itself on a similar high promontory. The few remaining open fields of the parish were enclosed after an Award was made in 1863, but there were already many hedged fields that were taken in from woodland, from which the name *Camps*, meaning 'enclosed fields' derives. The parish was at one time Great Camps, differentiating it from Little, or Shudy, Camps, with Castlecampes first recorded in 1384.

Prehistoric

A Mesolithic 'mace-head', or perforated stone, and a Neolithic axe were found north of the castle, and a small collection of waste flint flakes came from the site of a ring-ditch near to Camps Green. Elsewhere in the parish there are a few sites where rectangular or circular crop marks show there must have been prehistoric habitation in the area, and flint tools are occasionally found. The first real evidence for prehistoric settlement was not found until 1996, when a site on a gravel terrace near the junction of two of the streams was examined as part of systematic investigations in the parish. Here there was a dense concentration of flint artefacts which included a pick, scrapers and many sharp blades, and also waste flakes and discarded cores of flint which showed where tools had been made. Many heat-crazed flints were evidence for cooking in the area. This site dates to the late Mesolithic and early Neolithic periods.

Camps Castle from the air, 1993.

Roman figurines of a frog and a goddess (maximum height 3cms).

Roman

A major Roman site, perhaps a villa with a small temple, has been found near the Castle. Roof and flue tiles, nails, an iron spear-head, brooches, bracelets, lead weights, harness fittings, a lead gaming dice and miniature frog, the small bronze head of a goddess and a clay statuette of another were found, together with much pottery that mostly dated to the 3rd and 4th century AD. Geophysical prospecting has located the foundations of some substantial buildings. A fragment of what may be either part of a lead coffin or a large decorated vat used in christening rituals, was found nearby.

Medieval

A large Saxon estate was given to Aubrey de Vere, one of William's foremost Norman followers, after the Conquest, and he built the original castle on a promontory of land, a highly strategic situation that may well have been used for many centuries before the Normans arrived. The castle was designed like his principal residence at Castle Hedingham and the King's castle at Cambridge as a motte and bailey. Its large motte was surmounted with a wooden keep and surrounded with a wide ditch and a small bailey, and it was used as the administrative centre of the extensive Cambridgeshire estates of the de Veres, or the earls of Oxford as they became. It was held by this family until it was sold in 1584. During that time a village grew up around the castle, developing from one of the many hamlets that were scattered through the parish, and the small bailey was replaced

with a much larger one which enclosed some of the medieval village. In the 15th century a church was built abutting the original castle ditch, which must have been filled in by this time. There had been a church in Castle Camps much earlier than this, which was given to Abingdon Abbey in 1111. Later in the Middle Ages villagers moved away, perhaps because the importance of the castle declined, leaving only the earthwork remains of their houses and crofts in areas of pasture within the castle's bailey, and scatters of pottery in ploughed fields around.

The Castle was sometimes used as a residence by the earls, and their economic and sporting activities affected much of the countryside around. In particular, they had a deer park which extended from the Castle eastwards to the parish boundary and which was expanded to include the Little Park in the north-east of the parish, abutting Camps Green. Deer were kept until the whole estate was sold, after which the land was used for pasture.

A four-storey brick tower was built on the motte in the late 15th century, with a house attached. This tower was intended to be effective as

a defence, for at this time the earls were involved in the last stages of the Wars of the Roses. One earl was executed, and the castle was seized twice by Richard III, though later restored. However, it did not actually see any action until 1526 when a new earl forced out the dowager countess and defied the Justices of the Peace with force of arms when they came to restore order. Excavations in the mid 19th century found masonry that was described as 27 inches thick and of 'very solid construction', which was probably part of this late medieval structure, and some rubble was still standing in the 1920s. When the farmyard was re-surfaced in 1997 the foundations of this tower were exposed and recorded. In 1584 the estate was sold by an impoverished earl to a London merchant who rebuilt the house, and it is his mansion that we see in a print made in 1730, just before it fell down. The brick tower survived for some years before it too collapsed. In 1611 Castle Camps was owned by Thomas Sutton, who bequeathed it to Charterhouse, the school he had founded. After this the Castle was leased out and was later used as a farmhouse.

Camps Castle, about 1810, drawn by R. Relhan.

The manor of Westoe, now a farm in the north-west of the parish, was held separately from the de Vere's estate, and had a manor house that was last recorded in the 17th century. Olmstead, in the south-east of the parish was also a separate manor, though held under the de Veres. At the end of the 15th century this manor passed to Queens' College, and the manor house was leased as a farmhouse. Olmstead Hall is a 16th century timber-framed building with many later alterations that still stands within a water-filled moat. The nearby hamlet of Olmstead Green had a group of tenants living around a triangular green from at least the 13th to the 16th century, though it shrank to just a few houses after this. The hamlet also contains three moated sites. Pottery dating to the 13th, 14th and 15th centuries has been found on the surface of the small rectangular moat on the south side of the road, and this may have been the site of the manor house before it was moved to Olmstead Hall. Fragments of a moated site on the opposite side of the road, now Greenhouse Farm, were once within the grounds of a large late 16th century house, the centre of an estate held by the Reynolds family. In the early 18th century Sir James Reynolds was a prominent public official, and he replaced the house with a summer residence known as the Green House, which was demolished in 1969.

Two other interesting buildings in the southern extremity of the parish are Brownings Farm and Charlwood Farm. Charlwood Farm is a massive timber-framed building that stands beside a drove road on one of the highest points in East Anglia. Tree-ring dating shows that timber for the main post was felled in 1588, and there were additions and repairs during the 17th century. It may originally have been a warehouse for storing fleeces. Brownings Farm, standing a short distance north of a moat which it perhaps succeeded, has been dated by the tree-rings of its timbers to 1461, with other timbers added until 1555. In the mid

16th century some of its rooms were decorated with wall-paintings.

Village Development

Historically, Castle Camps has closer links with adjoining areas of Suffolk and Essex than it has with Cambridgeshire, a tradition that continues today. The desertion of the village that once surrounded the church and castle left the parish without a recognisable centre in later centuries, and instead there was a large hamlet at Camps Green and smaller ones at Olmstead Hall, Olmstead Green, Brownings Farm, Camps Hall, Camps End and Westoe. Interestingly, the name Castle Camps is nowadays often used for Camps Green, suggesting that this hamlet is in the process of becoming accepted as the centre of the parish. Within the hamlets there are at least six moated sites, and many slight earthworks and scatters of pottery, showing that medieval populations were larger than those found in the countryside now.

In 1086 there were 27 peasants recorded, and this figure grew very substantially to 87 tenants, at least 435 people, in 1279. There was then a sharp drop to 113, perhaps 147 in total, a century later, which was perhaps when most people left the village near the castle. The population of this large parish stayed fairly small for its area in the 16th century, with a short period of temporary growth in the 17th and more sustained expansion in the 18th century. In 1801 there were 546 people counted in the census and, as labouring families were able to move freely into the parish, this figure went up to 949 in 1851. After this the population steadily fell, and was down to about 400 in the late 20th century, though new housing, mostly in Camps Green, led to a rise to 640 in 1996.

Cottenham

Cottenham is an extremely large parish of 2914 hectares whose position on the edge of the fens has been the major factor in its development since prehistoric times. The village itself lies on a ridge of greensand that forms a promontory about 7-10m above sea level, but around it are fen soils, underlain by clay to the south and gravel and alluvium to the north, and here the land falls below sea level in places, though there are islands that are as much as 2-3m high. These lower areas were once covered with rich fen soil which has now virtually disappeared. Many of the watercourses in the parish are artificial, including the Roman Car Dyke, medieval Beach Ditch, (which forms the eastern parish boundary), medieval Cottenham Lode, and its 17th century replacement. The River Ouse, otherwise known as the Old West River, is the northern boundary, and some natural watercourses still exist, such as the Beck Brook along the Rampton border. Other watercourses that are now extinct are occasionally visible as roddons, or lines of silt where streams once wound through the marshy landscape. The boundaries were mostly fixed in the 13th century, when common land shared with Landbeach and Histon was divided and the Beach Ditch was cut. There was piecemeal enclosure of land in the Middle Ages, and some common

Excavating a Bronze Age wheel in Lingwood Fen.

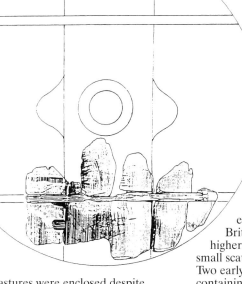

Bronze Age wheel, diameter: 95cms.

pastures were enclosed despite furious complaints in the 16th century. The remaining land was enclosed following an Award made in 1847. In 1086 Cottenham was *Cotenham*, 'the village of Cotta'.

Prehistoric

Many areas of the southern fen-edge are rich in prehistoric finds, but Cottenham is slightly too far south of the junction of deep fen and high land, and its scatter of sites of these periods is more representative of the type of settlement and land-use that we see in upland areas. One Meso-lithic axe has been found in the village, and shallow pits with Meso-lithic flint flakes have recently been excavated near Crowlands Moat. A few Neolithic and Bronze Age axes have been found in the parish, and numerous Neolithic and Bronze Age flint blades and waste flakes are found whenever Cottenham Lode is dredged and undisturbed layers of soil are exposed.

In the fens to the north-east of the village a Bronze Age burial mound was visible when the peat around it shrank, leaving a slight gravel rise where flint flakes have been found. The most impressive site is a Late Bronze Age settlement at Lingwood Farm near the River Ouse. Excavations which followed the discovery of pottery on the field surface uncovered a building, granaries, several pits, fence-lines and waterlogged wells. Many pieces

of worked and coppiced timber were found in the wells, including an object that looks like the bowl of a ladle.

The most interesting find was a wheel made from three planks of ash fixed together with dowels of oak, one of the earliest wheels found in Britain. On some of the slightly higher points in the fens there are small scatters of Iron Age pottery. Two early Iron Age pits, one of them containing a complete pot that had been deliberately damaged and buried, presumably for ritual reasons, were found in excavations near Crowlands Moat. Although the fens were becoming wetter at this time, they were obviously not uninhabitable.

Roman

In Roman times the fen-edge was further south than it had been in prehistoric times, and the northern and eastern parts of the parish were ideally situated to take advantage of an environment that provided rich soils for farming, all the fenland resources such as fish, wildfowl, turves and reeds, and good communications to north and south by road and water. The fens were

considered an important area by the Roman authorities, and they invested heavily in their development, both for agriculture and industry. A new town was built on a grand scale at Stonea, near March, and innumer-able farmsteads were founded wherever there was firm soil that was far enough above sea level not to be flooded too regularly. Major roads were laid across the fens, one of which is approximately followed by the A10. It is now known as Akeman Street, and ran from Cambridge to Norfolk, passing just to the east of Cottenham.

The most important investment in the fens was an attempt at drain-age by means of the Car Dyke. This also acted as a canal that linked stretches of natural watercourse so that it was possible to travel by water from Cambridge through the fens to the Peterborough region and from there on to the north of England. Markets provided by the needs of the Army were therefore opened up to the agricultural producers and pottery manufacturers of the fenland areas, bringing prosperity and activity on an exceptional scale. One indication that these changes were due to direct government action rather than private investment is that there are no villas and few signs of personal wealth within the fens, though there are plenty in the surrounding regions. However, there was a dense population that was well

Bullocks Haste Roman settlement and canal from the air, 1988.

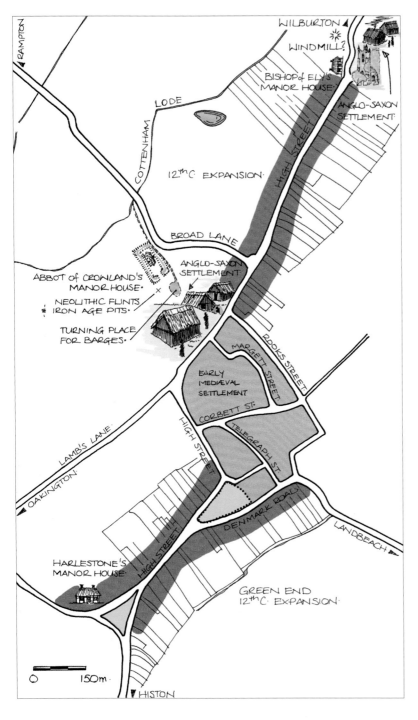

provided with transport systems, carefully laid-out farmsteads and many places for worship.

An excavation of Car Dyke at Bullocks Haste to the north of the village in 1947 showed that it was originally about 2.5m deep, 10m wide at the bottom and 17m wide at the top, with a profile rather like that of an 18th century canal. There was a wide foot- or tow-path on either side, with banks made from the up-cast of the ditch. In places the Dyke could be forded, and in these places gaps were left in the banks. Construct-ion seems to have been in the early 2nd century, its immediate purpose in this area being to link the Cam and the Ouse. It seems to have fallen out of use in the mid 4th century.

Bullocks Haste itself was a large and elaborate settlement and port, possibly even a small town, equipped with many shrines and temples. It is about a mile north of the present village, lying on either side of Car Dyke where it commanded access to important fenland transport from the Cambridge area and presumably acted as a commercial centre. Some of the metal finds from the site also suggest there was a military presence here. Masonry remains have been seen in plough soil, and there have been numerous important finds. Close examination of the earthworks that remain shows that there were clusters of small irregular enclosures and tracks on the site before Car Dyke was dug, and there was sub-sequently a more regular layout of features on either side of the dyke. Interesting earthworks are regularly spaced ridges and ditches which resulted from spade-dug cultivation in Roman times for some horticultur-al purpose. The site was common land until Enclosure and so was not damaged by ploughing until the 1960s, and even now one field still has the earthwork remains of hollow-ways, house and garden sites, small enclosures and the ridges of garden-scale agriculture. Elsewhere in Cottenham there were at least seven other centres of Roman occupation, where crop marks, surface finds and remains exposed during gravel extraction show that there were not

The Emperor Commodus, height: 20cms.

only extensive farming settlements but also metalworking areas and numerous religious sites.

A bust of the emperor Commodus from Bullocks Haste shows that the Imperial cult was followed there, and there were also small figurines of classical Mercury and the eastern gods Sol and Luna. and several brooches and other decorative objects with religious motifs. Elsewhere in the parish a small double-ditched temple where votive objects such as a miniature axe and many low-value coins had been deposited was noted briefly when it was quarried away in 1980, and many items found by metal-detecting show that Cottenham, like its neighbour Willingham, was an area which attracted an abnormal level of religious activity, perhaps because of the peculiar natural characteristics of its fen-edge environment. A hoard of over 5000 coins of the late 3rd century, found in a pot in a Roman field-ditch in 1986, however, was probably someone's savings that were buried for safety and never recovered, perhaps during the political struggles of that time.

Anglo-Saxon

After the exceptional level of settlement and development in the Roman period it seemed until recently that the parish was almost deserted in the Anglo-Saxon period, with only occasional artefacts such as fragments of brooches being found. Then, in 1995, excavations in the centre of the village, next to Crowlands Moat, uncovered a sunken-floored dwelling of early Anglo-Saxon date, and square middle Saxon timber buildings, set within ditched compounds. Iron slag that was found in some of the features shows that metal was being worked on this site. There were also large ditched enclosures later in the Saxon and early medieval periods.

In the late Saxon period much of Cottenham was given to the abbeys of Crowland and Ely. Soon afterwards, early in the 11th century, the Crowland estate was looted and burnt by the Danes. It was rebuilt by Abbot Brihtmer after the accession of Cnut. The manorial centres of the two abbeys at this time were probably near the site that was later known as Crowlands Moat and around the church, about half a mile to the north.

Medieval

Crowland Abbey also owned much of Oakington and Dry Drayton, and their manor house in Cottenham was the collection and despatch point for the products of these manors. A waterway here linked the moat to Cottenham Lode, and thence to the Ouse, so boats could travel by water to Crowland. A circular pond that was visible until recent years was the terminus where the barges could turn round. Fragments of medieval worked lime-stone found around the site are relics of this time. Cottenham was also the malting centre for the three manors, cheese was made and sent to the Abbey, there were huge numbers of sheep, and cattle were bred here for the three estates' plough-teams, so its economic importance was

Roman coin hoard from Cottenham, found in 1986.

Figurines of Sol and Luna, height: 5.5cms.

considerable. At one stage in the early 12th century it was used as a residence for some of the scholarly monks, after a fire at the Abbey. A tradition recorded in Crowland is that these monks came to Cambridge to earn money for restoration work by teaching. They attracted many students and so are credited as some of the founders of the University. The rectangular moat that still exists here was once part of a double moat, the larger enclosure being destroyed in the 20th century. A hall is recorded on the site in the 13th century, and in the mid 15th century there was extensive rebuilding, with a new hall, granary, kitchen, bakehouse, kilnhouse, barn and sheephouse, some or all of which may have been on sites nearer to the village street, perhaps including the present Crowland House. By the 15th century the Pepys family had already run the estate as bailiffs for many years, and at the dissolution of the monasteries they were able to buy it from the Crown. Later, the family more often lived in their house in Impington, but the last of the line in Cottenham, Katherine Pepys, died at Lordship House in 1703.

The other significant manor in Cottenham belonged to Ely from the late 10th century, made up from various bequests including one which left an estate to a son 'if he will take the advice of his friends', which apparently he failed to do, to the benefit of the Abbey. Ely's lands in Cottenham were not managed centrally in the Middle Ages, and no manor house is known, but a Saxon and Norman manor house may have stood near the Rectory, opposite the church, for the Rectory Manor was originally part of Ely's estate. The Rectory itself is a fine medieval building that was altered and enlarged at the end of the 17th century. Harlestones Manor, also originally part of Ely's estate, was held by the Burdeleys family jointly with land in Comberton. Their manor house, which included a chapel, stood in the south end of the village, on the western corner of the village green. During the Peasants Revolt of 1381 this house was demolished and its goods, including many animals, lead, timber and 20lbs of 'dirty blue wool' were sold by the rebels, and the Harlestones left the estate. Their successors built a new house which

was replaced by Manor Farm in the 19th century.

Village Development

Although Cottenham appears to be a continuously built-up village stretching for over a mile along the High Street, maps that were made just before Enclosure, and variations in property boundaries that are still apparent in places, show that the original pattern contained three widely-spaced centres. Two of these continued to be separate communities with their own Village Feasts well into the 20th century. The earliest settlement, as we have seen, was near the centre at Crowlands Moat, but land there was farmed in hand and it may be that the monks deliberately sited the village outside but close to their manorial centre, in a rectangular plot to the south-east. However, the church was built in a separate location much closer to the fen-edge, where there was also convenient access to Cottenham Lode for the import of building stone. This part of the village belonged to Ely, and property boundaries show that it too was never part of the open fields but was intended for settlement. Unusually, at Cottenham the parish church was not decisive in fixing the principal location of the medieval village, though a smaller settlement continued here.

After the Conquest Ely divided its Cottenham holdings into a number of manors and was no longer directly involved in village affairs. The Burdeleys family who held one of these manors, Harlestones, may have been responsible for establishing the southerly 'Green End' of Cottenham in the 12th century as a planned settlement. There, house-plots were laid out over the furlongs of the open fields and there was a triangular green with the manor house on one corner. Probably at about the same time similar house-plots were created in the long gap between the church and the main part of the village. In the 13th century a market grant was given to the Rectory manor and so was presumably held in the northern end of the village.

Largely due to the inhospitable nature of the surrounding fenlands, the parish's farmyards and all their outbuildings were kept with the expanding population within the village, and this pattern was maintained after Enclosure, so the frontages of the streets were solidly built up but there were long medieval-style closes behind most houses. The closely-packed houses were vulnerable to fire, one of which destroyed most of the village in 1676, and several outbreaks in the 19th century led to much rebuilding on the same house-plots, giving a deceptively Victorian appearance to the village.

Cottenham has always been one of Cambridgeshire's largest villages, and in terms of its size is almost a small town. There were 60 peasants recorded here in 1086, and a minimum of 134 tenants, about 670 people in 1279. More than half of Crowland's tenants died in the Black Death, but they were rapidly replaced and 121 families were taxed in the 16th century, and 230 in the 17th. This latter figure was nearly twice as high as even the other large fen-edge parishes of Willingham, Swavesey, Over and Waterbeach, and was more than the market town of Linton. With access to rich summer grazing for almost all families, virtually every home owned both cattle and sheep, and there were no restrictions on incomers, so the population grew to 1088 in 1801, all packed into 191 houses. In 1851 it had increased to 2300, after which it remained fairly stable, avoiding the decline seen in most other villages. In the 1960s Cottenham was chosen as a village that was suitable for growth because of the standard of its facilities and its convenient distance to Cambridge, and large areas have continued to be allocated for development. In 1996 the population was 4840, and further growth is planned.

Fen Ditton

Fen Ditton is a small parish of 600 hectares which lies mainly on chalk, with a strip of gravel and alluvium along the Cam and an area of gravel in the extreme south of the parish. Much of the present village makes use of a ridge about 15m above sea level, but almost all the rest of the parish is about 10m, apart from lower areas adjacent to the river where there are now attractive watermeadows. Its boundaries include the Cam, Quy Water and a drainage ditch known as Black Ditch. This Ditch roughly follows an ancient watercourse and marks the edge of a tongue of fenland that stretches down to the east of the parish. The irregular and peculiar boundary with Horningsea is due to division of the two parishes by the bishop of Ely in the 15th century. Previously, although Fen Ditton was a settlement from at least the 10th century, it does not seem to have been considered a separate parish, and it is not mentioned in Domesday Book or in the 13th century Hundred Rolls, for example. Some of the southern boundary with Cambridge has been adjusted in the 20th century. Much of the parish was enclosed in a piecemeal fashion linked to fenland drainage in the 17th and 18th centuries, and the remaining open fields were enclosed by the official Award made in 1807. Fen Ditton is *Dittone*, meaning 'the village by the (Fleam) Ditch' in a will made in about 950. By the late 13th century 'Fen' had been added to differentiate it from Woodditton.

Prehistoric

Early prehistoric finds are concentrated in fields at the margins of the parish, near Quy Water and Black Ditch where many Mesolithic and Neolithic flints occur at the junction of the fens and slightly drier land, and in Ditton Meadows, next to the Cam, where a collection of Mesolithic tools was found. At least four Neolithic polished stone axes come from this parish. These include one from The Biggin and a fine

ceremonial-style example from the Rectory garden, both of which may be collected examples that were subsequently lost. A Bronze Age cremation within an urn was found at Ditton Meadows as a result of 19th century coprolite mining and, as well as occasional scatters of flint flakes, several bronze implements have been found near to the fen-edge in the north of the parish, including a spear, rapier and two axes.

The parishes of Fen Ditton and Horningsea form a peninsula of higher ground between the river and the fens which was cut off from dry land to the south by the construction of a bank and ditch. This is called Fleam Dyke, although it has no other relationship with the Anglo-Saxon dyke of that name further to the south-east. It is not known when it was built, but early Anglo-Saxon bodies were buried in its ditch at a time when it must have been almost filled in, and is therefore considerably earlier than the 6th century. Though most defensive dykes in Cambridgeshire have been shown to be Anglo-Saxon in their final phase, they often seem to be preceded by Iron Age works, and elsewhere in East Anglia they are commonly Iron Age in date. This is therefore a strong possibility for the Fen Ditton example.

Immediately south of the dyke, on the opposite side to the area we would expect to be protected, a large middle Iron Age settlement site was excavated in 1996. There were about 300 pits here which contained animal bones and much pottery, some of it decorated, hearths and the curving ditches of enclosures for stock and perhaps for habitation. Otherwise, no other finds or sites of this date are known so far from the area. Another possibility is that the Dyke belongs to the very late Roman or post-Roman period, when there were many times when the population may have found it worthwhile to protect themselves within this enclave.

Roman

Compared to the wealth of Roman sites in neighbouring parishes such as Milton and Horningsea,

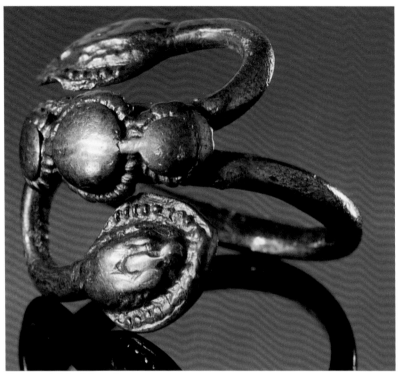

Roman snake's head finger-ring.

Later in the Saxon period, in the late 10th century, estates in Fen Ditton were bequeathed to Ely. In the 12th century these passed to the bishop rather than the Abbey, and they remained in this ownership until 1600, when they were taken over by the Crown.

Medieval

The Biggin was originally built by Hugh de Northwold, Bishop of Ely, in the mid 13th century in a palatial style, possibly using an earlier site. It was used by him as a residence, where he could observe events in Cambridge, and where he also had hunting rights. Royalty were often entertained and undertook official business here, with several visits by Henry III, Edward I and Edward II.

Fen Ditton seems surprisingly empty in the Roman period. A group of crop marks of enclosures with regular internal divisions at the south-eastern edge of the parish probably belong to this date, and there have been a few metal finds, including a silver finger-ring with snake's head decoration and other jewellery, suggesting a site of significance in the area.

Anglo-Saxon

As we have seen above, the section of Fleam Dyke in Fen Ditton must have been constructed before this period, and was already an historic feature of the landscape to which Anglo-Saxons paid respect as they did so often by burying their dead close by. In this case they buried skeletons within the ditch and accompanied them with a sword, eight spears, three shield-bosses, a knife, five brooches, a buckle and a pair of wrist-clasps, all of the finds dating to the 6th century. This was quite a sizeable cemetery, especially as the discoveries were only accidentally noticed in spoil dug during roadworks and a great many others must have been lost.

The Biggin drawn by William Cole in 1768 and (above) in 1997.

In the later 13th century the Bishop was granted a 'licence to crenellate' the house, which was probably when the moat around it was dug. In the mid 14th century the building included a hall, three chambers, a pantry, buttery, chapel, kitchen, stable, gatehouse, two barns, two dovecotes and a horse-mill, all of them in poor condition. The building that survives was mainly built in the later 14th century, when its use had declined to that of a manor house, and it was remodelled in the 17th century. Its walls are of clunch and stone, now covered in concrete. In the 17th century it was sold to the Willys family of Eye Hall in Horningsea. Sir Thomas Willys, at various times MP for Cambridge and the County and also Sheriff of the County, who lived to be 90, was probably responsible for the alterations and extensions to the building in the 17th century. In the mid 18th century it came into the ownership of Thomas Panton, Charles II's chief groom, and his son who was Sheriff of Cambridgeshire and Huntingdonshire. It was their house that William Cole sketched in 1768.

Several Fen Ditton merchants were involved in trade on a national and international basis. One of the manors, for example was held by the Muschet family who made their fortune as traders and money-lenders, often working on behalf of the king or the bishop. They held a manor in Fen Ditton throughout the early Middle Ages, with their manor house on the site of The Hall. In the early 15th century the manor passed to the Cheynes, who substantially rebuilt the Muschets' hall, and much of their house survives. In the 17th century the estate was bought by the Willys family, who already owned the Biggin. They carried out extensive alterations and additions to the house, and it was probably they who created elaborate water gardens in front of the Hall at the end of the century, fragments of whose sunken grounds and long shallow ponds remain.

Other important buildings in the village include the Barn, a massive 16th century structure that is now used for public events. It is two-storied, and seems to have been used both for storage connected with the wide-scale trading activities and as a village guildhall. One of the medieval wharves can still be seen between this building and the river, and there was another near the Plough Inn which was used by coal barges until recent years.

Village Development

The original settlement at Fen Ditton was principally a strip that ran parallel to the river, with the church at the extreme southern end, for much of the economic importance of Fen Ditton was due to river traffic and wharves were built between the Cam and the village. The northern end was later known as Green End and still contains the village green that was probably the site for a market granted to the bishop in the 13th century. Later in the Middle Ages, as it expanded, the village changed direction and moved to make use of the higher ground along the line of the filled-in Fleam Dyke, and the deserted plots of the earlier settlement can be seen as earthworks between the present village and Green End. The reason for this move was probably the increase in importance of the road from Cambridge to Newmarket, which originally turned east near the church in Fen Ditton and ran along this part of the Fleam Dyke.

There area no figures for early settlement at Fen Ditton but it clearly grew into a substantial village, for its population in the late 14th century, despite contractions in previous years when empty tenements were recorded, still included 330 adults. This dropped in the 16th and 17th centuries to less than 60 families, presumably due to loss of trading activities. In 1801 there were still only 337 people here in total, but this grew in the 19th century, reaching 680 in 1881. The old village streets have been infilled with new housing since the 1950s, some of it replacing buildings that were destroyed by bombing during World War II, but by 1996 the population had only grown to 730.

Fen Drayton

Fen Drayton is a small parish of 600 hectares and is flat and low lying, its maximum height of 10m above sea level being along the Roman road from Cambridge to Godmanchester. Near to the river much of the land is less than 4m high. It lies mainly on gravel and alluvial soils, with clay in its north-west and south-east corners, the gravel attracting large quarries which are now a major feature of the parish. Parish boundaries include the Roman road in the south and the River Ouse in the north. Two tributaries of the Ouse flow through the parish, one of which runs through the centre of the village. The open fields of the southern part of the parish and the meadows and commons to the north were enclosed in 1841. In 1086 Fen Drayton was known as *Draitone*, the meaning of which is not known. 'Fen' had been added by the late 12th century to differentiate it from Dry Drayton.

Prehistoric

The most interesting discoveries in Fen Drayton are the earliest in date. Palaeolithic flints have been collected during early gravel extraction on the western side of the parish and expansion of the quarries in the 1990s has led to many more coming to light, most of them in a fresh condition that shows they have not been rolled around during glacial activities but lay in the undisturbed sites where they were deposited in approximately 200,000BC. Many tools have been found here, including more than fifty hand-axes and tools

Giant-deer skull and mammoth bone found at Fen Drayton.

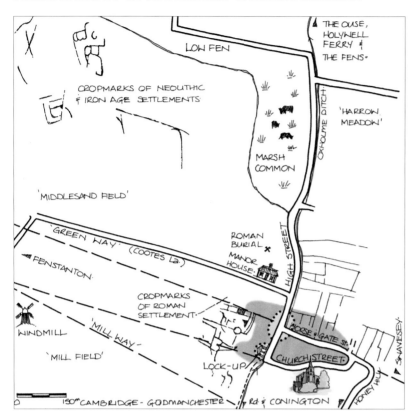

protected from the quarrying that now surrounds it.

In the Iron Age the sites discussed above were used again at various times. Large enclosure ditches were dug to surround two circular houses which had a well whose waterlogged fill contained seeds of soft fruits (blackberry, raspberry, elderberry and dewberry) and useful wild plants such as fat hen, sedge and nettle. There were also many cattle bones and one grain of wheat.

Roman

Fen Drayton is bounded by an important Roman road and a navigable river and it seems that the whole parish was used intensively in Roman times. There were very extensive settlements in areas near the river that have now been quarried away, where timber buildings, pits and ditches were excavated and huge quantities of pottery have been collected. Much of the dating evidence is 4th century, but there were also 2nd century samian wares and amphorae. There are many areas in the parish where crop marks show fields and farmsteads of Roman and earlier date, and these even underlie much of the present village. Within the village, too, a burial was found, two adults and a child with a pot that was made in the Nene Valley and decorated with a scroll pattern in applied white slip.

Roman ditches were found during excavations of the prehistoric sites described above. These included a series of shallow, parallel, straight-sided, flat-bottomed ditches set 4m apart that had only been opened for a short time. It is likely that these were dug for some horticultural purpose and are reminiscent of the earthwork ridges at Bullocks Haste at Cottenham. A vineyard has been suggested but the land seems too low lying for this.

Medieval

The village is sited roughly at the junction of low-lying land that was used for pasture until the mid 19th century and which was too wet to be attractive for settlement, and slightly higher and drier land that was used

designed for scraping skins. In addition to flint tools, mammoth tusks and picks made from antler, probably of the same date, were found nearby.

Investigations of a low-lying area at the junction of gravel soils and the fen to the north-west of the village uncovered settlements dated to Neolithic and Iron Age times. Early Neolithic features include ditches, pits and the posts of a fence and other indefinable structures. One of the pits contained a pot buried upside down. Neolithic flint tools and waste flakes were found in many later ditches on the site, showing that, although the area was occupied for only a short time, considerable rubbish was accumulated. Another excavation just to the east of this site revealed a later Neolithic settlement. The only features found were a cluster of pits that contained plain and decorated pottery, flint tools, cattle bones, hazel shells and grains

of wheat and oats. This must have been a temporary encampment for people making use of the fen-edge resources but normally living on higher ground, for their cultivated food-stuffs came from farming drier land, and there were few of the waste flakes that show where tools were being made and therefore where people were living.

At periods in the Bronze Age there seem to have been short episodes of casual occupation, probably also on a seasonal basis. Ditches, pits and fire-hollows were found, but no evidence for structures or collections of rubbish. An important site of Bronze Age date is close to the river, just to the north of this site, where an upstanding burial mound is a very rare survival of the kind of low barrow that was commonly built on the gravel soils of river valleys. These mounds have now usually been ploughed flat so that they can only be recognised as ring-ditches. This barrow has been for arable agriculture within open fields. Fen Drayton was a small compact settlement lying on a north-south track that links the Roman road and higher ground to the south with the fens. The track largely followed a stream and ran from Conington, across the Cambridge-Godmanchester Roman road as far as the village. At the south end of the village it was crossed by an east-west road which ran from Boxworth End in Swavesey, past Fen Drayton church and then on to Fenstanton. As it entered the village it split into Church Street and Horse Gate Street. The latter was the more important road, and there is still a small green and a 19th century lock-up where it met the High Street.

A manor house and other important medieval buildings are on the High Street, which in the Middle Ages and until the 19th century was the docking area for barges from the Ouse. The dock basin can still be seen next to the Three Tuns, and the Homestead is an 18th century merchant's house. When barge traffic ceased with the coming of the railway, the tow-path was incorporated into gardens of the properties on the eastern side, and bridges were built over the lode. As in other fen-edge settlements there do not appear to be any other medieval settlements in the parish.

The population of Fen Drayton grew from a moderate figure of 23 in 1086 to a minimum of 55 tenants in 1279. Sited between very small upland parishes such as Conington and very large fen-edge parishes such as Swavesey, Fen Drayton's growth was typically intermediate between these extremes. Its

Fen Drayton Green and lock-up.

Remains of the wharves near the Three Tuns.

population fell to 111 adults in the late 14th century and was still only about 40 families in the 16th century. The 17th century saw growth to 58 families, perhaps about 250 people, but there were still only 265 people here in 1801. There was the usual rapid growth to 450 in 1861, though

The Homestead and its barn, adjacent to the lode which connected the village to the Wash.

even then the village was described as 'small but pretty', before falling to about 200 in 1900. This figure was fairly static until 1936 when land was bought by the Land Settlement Association for use as small-holdings to help relieve unemployment, and 53 families were brought into the parish. An area of growth was allowed in the 1960s, and there was considerable expansion in the 1980s, so that the population in 1996 was 810.

Fulbourn

Fulbourn is an extremely large parish of 2124 hectares, mostly lying on chalk but with alluvial gravel soils beneath low-lying areas of fen in the north and east of the village. Its topography is varied, with much of the parish being dry and hilly, rising to about 50m above sea level along the Cambridge-Colchester Roman road and on other local high-points such as Limepit Hill, but with fenland that is only about 10m above sea level extending into the parish from the north. Fulbourn Fen itself is still an area of damp pasture that has limited development of the village in the east. The church, as in most fen-edge villages, is sited on the nearest high point above this fen. Parish boundaries include two Roman roads, (Worsted Street and a Romanised route of the Icknield Way, now the A11), a section of Fleam Dyke and two streams that flow into Quy Water. Land which still survived as open fields was finally enclosed after an Award was made in 1814. In 1086 Fulbourn was *Fuulburne*, or 'stream frequented by birds', an apt description of the fenny parts of the parish.

Prehistoric
Four Neolithic axes have been found in Fulbourn, three of them

Miniature Bronze Age urns from Mutlow Hill, maximum height 12cms.

Neolithic flint blades, found near Fleam Dyke.

near to the Icknield Way route and one in the fens. Close to the fen-edge, particularly near the terminal of Fleam Dyke, there are sites where ploughing of previously undisturbed areas has brought to light dense scatters of flint tools, showing how intensively the margins of dry land could be used. Higher areas of chalk-land were used to site burial mounds in the Bronze Age, and the ditches around at least twenty of these have been photographed from the air, including a cluster in the north-east of the parish around Mutlow Hill. Mutlow Hill itself was a Bronze Age burial mound that was venerated as a site of religious and social import-ance at many times in the past. When it was investigated in 1852, 'turning it over regularly from end to end', there were five cremations in

urns and three urns that were not directly associated with burials. One other cremation was found with worked flints, six paste beads, and a bone and a bronze pin and two more cremations had no grave-goods. The mound, which had been heightened during its use in the Bronze Age, was described as 'sixty-seven feet in dia-meter... Depth at greatest elevation, from nine to twelve feet', and had already been disturbed by shafts and tunnels that had been dug into it.

One early 19th century discovery in Fulbourn was a Late Bronze Age hoard of metal-work from Fulbourn Common on the edge of the fen. It included two swords, a spear and two ferrules that had protected the ends of the spear-shafts. A Bronze Age site was found in recent excavations at Fulbourn Hospital on the western edge of the parish, which may have been a settlement, although livestock management is perhaps more likely. A large circular ditched enclosure was surrounded with debris such as pot-sherds and waste flint flakes, and there were fences and structures that were probably used for controlling animals.

Roman

Close to Fulbourn Hospital an extensive site has been revealed in aerial photographs, with droveways and rectangular enclosures and buildings. Fulbourn village itself is immediately south of a major Roman site where there was a cemetery, an industrial area with massive kilns recorded but no evidence for their actual use, and indications of sub-stantial buildings, perhaps belonging to a villa. Numerous finds from this area include an unusual candle-holder in the form of cockerel. One of the graves found here in the mid 19th century was said to be in a 'square brick grave' with glass and pottery vessels. Elsewhere in the parish there is a small Roman temple near the Cambridge-Colchester Roman road, and another religious site was excavated next to Mutlow Hill. Here there was a metre-wide wall of chalk blocks and mortar that apparently formed a circle about 12m in diameter. With this building there was one burial with a bronze finger-ring, and also a collection of objects that are assumed to be votive offerings of some kind. These included about eighty Roman coins of the 1st to 4th century, an Iron Age coin, a decorated samian sherd, glass bead, fragments of two Neolithic axes, and Roman bronze brooches, buckles and writing implements. Later investigations of the area uncovered large quantities of pottery, some dating to the very late Iron Age.

Anglo-Saxon

Fleam Dyke, the massive bank and ditch that runs from Balsham and is used as a parish boundary all along its length, terminates as an upstanding earthwork in the wet areas of Fulbourn Fen, though a slighter defence once extended from

Roman candle-holder, height 5cms.

there to fenland in Great Wilbraham. Mutlow Hill was used again in late Saxon times as the moot or meeting-place and also the sheriff's court for the three major land divisions or hundreds that abut the site, and this use continued through the Middle Ages. Many former trackways still visible from the air led to the site, and the main Icknield Way route through Fleam Dyke, now the A11, probably crossed nearby.

Fulbourn had a very high population in the late Saxon period, and there were two major estates, one of which belonged to Ely. It is therefore likely that a church existed at this time, of which a carved Saxon cross, found beneath the floor of St. Vigor's church and now in the churchyard, is perhaps a relic.

Medieval

Fulbourn consisted of two parishes during the Middle Ages, based on the two churches which shared the present churchyard of St. Vigor's. The church of All Saints was allowed to fall down in 1766, after the parishioners had permission to re-use materials from it and the vicar was allowed to hold services in St. Vigor's. Medieval wall-paintings on boards were taken from this church before its collapse and are now in Trinity College library. William Cole visited All Saints in 1747 and described it as 'consisting of a square

tower, a spacious nave and chancell partly ribed and partly thatched, 2 sides and isles leaded, and ye new vestry dilapidated'.

These churches belonged to the two principal Saxon manors which were later known as Zouches and Manners, and were presumably built by the rival lords of these manors to serve the unusually high medieval population of the village.

Both manors were held by absentee lords who subdivided, reorganised and reunited the estates on many occasions. Zouches was given to Alan, Earl of Brittany, after the Norman Conquest, and was taken into the King's hands in the late 12th century. In the early 13th century it was exchanged for other lands by Roger de la Zouche of Ashby de la Zouche, and this family continued as overlords of the manor until the 15th century. The estate later passed to the Dockwra family who settled in the village in the 16th century, building themselves the house now known as the Old Manor. Another estate that the Dockwras acquired was a manor known as Dunmowes, which may originally also have been part of the Zouche's land.

Dunmowes manor house is thought to have stood in the defensive moated site known as Hall Orchard or Zouches Castle, which commands access to the village and the upland areas from the fens. It was probably built against attack from the fens

Fulbourn Old Manor, 1994.

during troubles such as the Barons War in the 13th century, when Fulbourn and St. Vigor's church are known to have been attacked. Alan de la Zouche was certainly involved in fighting and in seizing land at this time, and contemporary records speak of 'sheep and oxen, corn, malt ....they took and carried off to the island'. The site itself was later used as a residence by the Dalton family, when they were owners of the manor, and it is probably the debris of their house that is commonly found on the site. Fulbourn Manor was first built in the 17th century, and was surrounded by a small park. The house and park were both greatly enlarged in the early 19th century by the Townley family, who by this time held Zouches manor and most of the village. A new front to the house was added in the early 20th century.

The manor that became known as Manners was given to Ely by Brihtnoth in the 10th century, but the abbey lost it in the 12th century and it was held by the Manners family until 1311. It was taken over by Zouches manor some time before 1360. Two other medieval manors were Colvilles and Shardelowes. Despite the two churches in the village these both made provision for private worship on their own estates, Shardelowes in an oratory within their manor house and Colvilles in a chapel. Both manors were held by the Shardelowe family in the 14th century, and in the 15th century were acquired by Zouches manor.

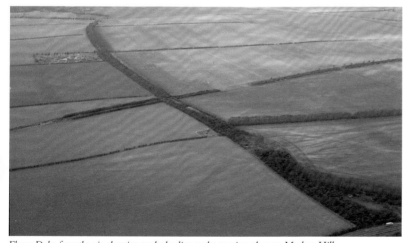

Fleam Dyke from the air, showing tracks leading to the meeting-place on Mutlow Hill.

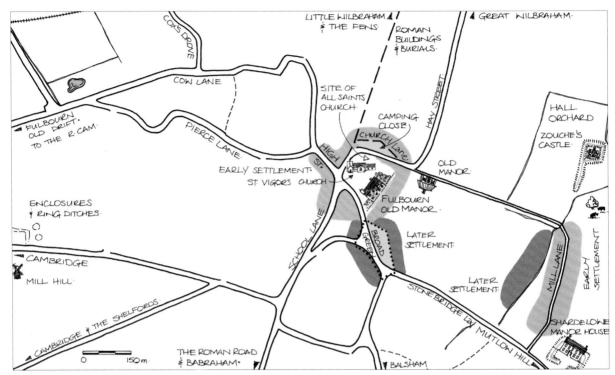

Shardelowes manor house stood in a moated site to the south-east of the Park, where a farmhouse surrounded by a moat still stood in 1808. This moated site was attacked and captured in 1378, and Shardelowe's widowed daughter-in-law was carried off. In 1825 part of it was pulled down in order to build the house now known as New Shardelowes, 'out in the fields'. Crop marks of a rectangular moat now mark the site.

Several watermills have been recorded in Fulbourn, the earliest being in the 11th century. Mill Cottage near Zouches Castle is the domestic portion of a watermill, and the L-shaped ponds and streams of old water channels can still be seen. The largest smock mill in the county is on Cambridge Road. It is marked on the 1806 Enclosure map, and has been restored by the Village Society.

Village Development

The two churches stood on a direct route from the Roman Road to the fens, at a junction where roads from Balsham, Trumpington, Cambridge, the Cam and Teversham

met and led down to the fens via several lanes. One early settlement was around this junction, where the Rectory and Camping Close (or medieval sports ground) were situated, perhaps with one of the original manors on the site of the present Fulbourn Manor. There may also have been another early settlement to the east of this area, nearer to the two moated manor houses and the fens, as there certainly was later in the Middle Ages. The 17th century park around Fulbourn Manor probably displaced some village houses near to the church and along Manor Walk, and it took in the sites of medieval houses that had stood to the east of the present village, some of which can be recognised as low platforms. Clunch foundations, tile and 15th century pottery have been found in this area. When the Enclosure map was prepared in 1806 housing had been moved away from this side of the village, apart from a small group near Shardelowes manor house, and was principally clustered around the roads just to the north of the church, on the western side of

Broad Green, and along the roads to Balsham and Cambridge. At Enclosure the park was extended, and later development has been on the western side of the village.

In 1845 the Asylums Act was passed, authorising local authorities to levy rates to build asylums for the insane, and in 1858 Fulbourn Hospital opened, with rooms for 250 patients, the patients themselves being expected to carry out most of the work of landscaping the grounds, infilling clunch pits, laying out paths, building a bowling green and preparing land for cultivation and gardens. Also in the mid 19th century the railway came to Fulbourn, though its station, to the north of the village, was, as usual, inconveniently placed for the villagers and the Hospital, and was said to be principally for the benefit of visitors to Newmarket races. It also served middle-class commuters into Cambridge. As produce could be sent into town, it also led to development of a nursery nearby.

In 1086 Fulbourn had an extremely large population of 91, the highest figure in South Cambridgeshire. This probably doubled in the next century but had fallen to 82 families in 1327. In 1377 there were 426 poll tax payers, again the highest population in the region. By the 16th century this figure had fallen to 52 house-holds, though it had started to recover in the 17th century, when 91 households were taxed, and there were 702 residents in 1801. It continued to grow through the 19th century, to 1807 in 1881, and after-wards fell. After 1950, when 1440 people lived here, its position close to Cambridge made development attractive, and Fulbourn doubled in size by the 1970s and had expanded to 4920 in 1996.

Hildersham

Hildersham, a small narrow parish of 616 hectares, straddles the valley of the Granta between the chalk uplands followed by the Cambridge-Colchester Roman road to the north and the Essex border to the south. These parish boundaries are respectively more than 80m and 100m above sea level but the village itself is on lower-lying gravel and alluvial soils at about 30m, built on either side of the small winding river. The parish included considerable areas of woodland in Domesday Book and throughout the Middle Ages, including Hildersham Wood which still exists on the Essex border. Close to the river are meadows that were used as common land. There are also a few high-points such as Furze Hill where the chalk is capped with clay and gravel. Hildersham was the last parish in Cambridgeshire to be enclosed, following an Act made in 1887. In 1086 it was known as *Hildricesham*, 'the village of Hildric'.

Prehistoric
A Palaeolithic hand-axe and another flint tool have been found on Furze Hill, there is a collection of Mesolithic flints from the parish, and from the high ground to the north of Furze Hill came a Neolithic axe and many flint flakes.
Roman

The low-lying meadowland between the church and the river appears to have been used in Roman times for substantial buildings, of which foundations and cobbled floors were found early in the 20th century. William Palmer was regularly finding Roman pottery there in the 1920s, and several cartloads of building stone were removed from here in the 19th century. Unfortunate-ly, one interesting feature on this piece of land, a possible Roman burial mound, was destroyed in the mid 19th century by the vicar, because he disapproved of the villagers using it as a maypole site, and we have no way of verifying its original purpose. In 1847, after an antiquarian visit to Hildersham, it was described as 'a decided mound, perhaps 6 or 8 feet in height, flat or rather sunken at the summit; in diameter 20 feet'. It was examined in 1852 before the mound was levelled, but it seemed to have already been disturbed and the only finds were fragments of Roman pottery, which could have originated from the surrounding settlement, and a hollow lined with puddled clay.

Anglo-Saxon
Furze Hill, as a prominent piece of waste ground, was used as a bombing range in World War II, and it was following this disturbance to

the ground that remains of a small Anglo-Saxon cemetery were

Two churches at Fulbourn, drawn by William Cole in 1747.

St Vigor's Church

All-Saints Church in Fulbone.

now a 17th century farmhouse, to the north of the river, and Netherhall Manor, now Hildersham Hall, to the south. A northern village green lay between the church and Overhall manor house and the southern one, on which stood the village forge, was near the Hall.

The two manors were united in the 14th century but the village remained in two parts. From the 15th to late 17th century their lord also held manors in Linton and Duxford, and Overhall was some-times used as a residence for the lords' widows. The two Hildersham estates each seem to have been farmed separately. There were also a few substantial local farmers from the 16th century who acquired most of the non-manorial land and com-mon rights. They enclosed land near to the village and built farmhouses that are set back from the village street, such as Burford's Farm. The land of the parish fell into fewer and fewer hands. It was in single owner-ship by 1800 and was sold to the manorial estate in 1865, so the whole parish was owned together before

discovered, though it seems that human bones had been known from this vicinity for some years. A spear, shield-boss, bucket-hoops and fragments of an ornate bronze hanging-bowl were collected. In the same area, but closer to the river, four Anglo-Saxon brooches, two of which looked as if they were a pair, were found recently, together with an 8th century coin and some Roman remains.

Village Development

An Anglo-Saxon hanging-bowl from Hildersham, diameter 22cms.

The village grew on either side of a fording-place, where a street that was part of a route from Great Chesterford to Balsham crossed the river. The church was built on a high point above the flood-plain on a site that was in use in Roman times. Originally there were two settle-ments, one on either side of the river, each with its own field system. By the time of the Norman Conquest there was only one manor, which was given to the de Vere family. Their tenant in the 12th century reverted to the older organisation and divided the estate between two heirs. Hildersham village remained as two centres, Overhall and Netherhall, although to judge from scatters of 12th century artefacts found in the meadows near the river and the church, the village at this time had become a more continuous settle-ment than we see today. The river had no bridge until 1886, and the two sides of the village remained as separate places in the Middle Ages, with the church and a manor house,

The ford across the Granta in Hildersham.

Enclosure, which was therefore accompanied by little reorganisation or new hedging of the open fields.

Hildersham was always a small village. It had 20 people listed in 1086, perhaps 100 inhabitants in total, and in the late 14th century there were only 47 adults here. This fell further, so that only 6 house-

Hinxton

Hildersham church in 1997 and (above) in the early 19th century.

holders were counted in the early 15th century, and 17 families were taxed in the 16th century. The population fluctuated after this and only rose steadily from the late 18th century. In 1801 there were 170 people in total, when 45 families were crammed into 26 houses, growing to 248 villagers in 1851, a modest expansion due to the owner of the parish refusing to build more cottages and preferring to employ labourers from less restrictive villages such as Balsham and Linton. This figure stayed fairly steady in the 19th century but fell thereafter. It recovered slowly from the 1950s, and despite new house building the population in 1996 was only 210.

Hinxton is a small parish of 632 hectares, mostly lying on chalk, except for gravel and alluvial soils along the river. Its boundaries include the Cam, the Roman road (A11) from Great Chesterford to Norfolk, and a route of the Icknield Way on the southern side. The village itself lies on a slight chalk rise adjacent to the flood plain, with the church in the highest place at about 30m above sea level. The Cam could be forded at several places in Hinxton, and these fords have influenced the areas used for settlement since prehistoric times. It was also liable to flood along some stretches. East of the floodplain the chalkland rises steadily to the eastern parish boundary, which is also the County boundary with Essex. Here the land is mostly over 60m. The open fields of the parish were enclosed after an Award was made in 1833. Hinxton's name in Domesday Book is *Hestitona*, or 'Hengest's Farm'.

Prehistoric

Mesolithic and Neolithic flint flakes were found on the northern route of the Icknield Way, and exten-

sive sites of Neolithic and Bronze Age date have been excavated on gravel soils near to the river in the north and south of the parish in the last few years. A prospective quarry near the A505 was investigated between 1991 and 1993 and was found to contain signs of habitation of several periods. The earliest were Neolithic, both early and late in that period, and consisted of quite dense scatters of waste flakes together with blades, scrapers, borers and two leaf-shaped arrowheads. Suitable large nodules of flint were being collected in this area and made into tools on the site.

Other collections of flint artefacts found in different areas within the same site were more crudely made and date to the Bronze Age. These were concentrated mainly on a burial mound which was visible as a ring-ditch and which was found to contain two secondary cremations in shallow pits. Not only was worked flint thickly scattered over the mound, as has been noted on similar sites such as Little Abington and Balsham, but much of the waste material had been dumped in the ditches before they had gradually been filled in.

South of this site, in the grounds of Hinxton Hall, many more worked flints of Mesolithic, Neolithic and Bronze Age date were found, most of which derived from debris washed down into the river valley from the surrounding slopes. They were then deposited in old stream beds and holes left by uprooted trees. There was, however, one important feature, a ritual shaft that had been dug to nearly 2m in depth and then deliberately filled in stages during the Early Bronze Age. It contained great quantities of decorated Beaker sherds in its upper layers, (about 150 sherds from 30 different pots), and there was rubbish in both its upper and lower layers. Some of the waste flints related to arrow manufacture, including two unfinished arrowheads.

An exceptional site excavated in the north of the parish was a late Iron Age cremation cemetery, dating to 50-10BC, where the funerary customs and artefacts are part of a tradition

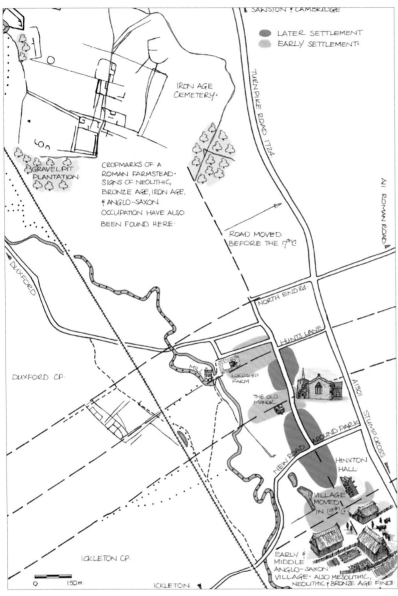

inhumations nearby, but these had no dating evidence and probably belonged with the Roman settlement that succeeded the cemetery.

Roman

Roman occupation was found on both of the sites discussed above, which is not surprising in light of the known importance of this area in Roman times. The Roman town of Great Chesterford, for example, is immediately south of Hinxton, and there are villas at Ickleton and Duxford to the east. On the northern site, which is in the river valley on the route of tracks which led to Duxford, crop marks indicated there was a well-organised farming settlement with droveways and regular rectangular fields, including gardens and paddocks and one corn-drier. There was plenty of occupation debris such as pottery and animal bone but the site was quite short lived, being only occupied in the 1st and 2nd centuries AD. Few of the ditches were cleared out or reorganised though agricultural use of the site may have continued later. Similar evidence for a farming settlement came from excavations at Hinxton Hall, and in the extreme south of the parish there was occupation with cobbled surfaces and a chalk floor adjacent to the river by the crossing-place from Brookhampton hamlet in Ickleton.

A Roman site discovered during dualling of the A11 had a very different character. It was on a locally high point adjacent to the Roman road, opposite a wealthy settlement in Great Abington. Three sides of a rectangular building with stone foundations, and evidence for a concrete floor and tiled roof were found, with many coins and metal artefacts, including a bronze chain, but little occupation debris, suggesting that it is likely to be a shrine or temple.

Anglo-Saxon

The Cam valley was widely settled in the early Anglo-Saxon period, but remains of actual houses sites are difficult to find unless large areas are being examined. Thanks to the scale of work recently undertaken, Hinx-

found in south-eastern England, and which in Roman times developed into 'princely native' customs, of which the finest examples are at Bartlow Hills. At Hinxton there were eight cremations, five of them surrounded by small ring-ditches and therefore presumably once marked by low mounds. The richest grave contained nine wheel-made pottery vessels, including urns, bowls and cups, another had a cup, urn and

bowl, and another an urn, bowl, a joint of meat and a bag filled with personal metal objects that had corroded and fused together. Using X-rays, the excavators were able to discern four brooches and parts of two others, tweezers, nail-cleaners, a chain, iron disc and a decorative bronze object of classical design. The remaining burials had single bowls or jars, and one of these also contained an iron brooch. There were three

An early Anglo-Saxon sunken-floored hut at Hinxton Hall.

well, a cess-pit, oven, fire-pit and other pits. Later in the 10th century there were three halls in one enclosure and two smaller buildings in another, all within a larger enclosure. In the 11th century two more halls were built, with a new well and cess-pit, and the enclosure ditch was repaired. Flax-processing was a feature of this period. The settlement was still used from the mid 11th to mid 12th centuries, but it seems that the centre was shifting elsewhere. One of the buildings was still occupied, and two ovens, a corn-drier, a fire-pit and a recut cess-pit were in use, but the enclosure ditch was allowed to fill up. Processing of cereals was an important activity on the site in all periods, with wheat as the major crop in addition to oats, rye, field peas and horse-beans.

Medieval

Much of the land in Hinxton was held by free peasants before the Conquest, but afterwards it was given to Picot, sheriff of Cambridge, when it was reckoned to be two manors. These manors were split in the 12th century but reunited in the 15th century when both were held by the earls of Oxford, who sold the estate in the late 16th century. Another manor in Hinxton, Barbedors, also became part of the larger estate in the early 15th century. By the 17th century there was only one manor house in Hinxton, the house now known as the Old Manor, which had been built as a court house in about 1500. A site at Lordship Farm which was strongly moated until the 19th century is situated close to the manorial mill and is presumably the site of the house for the manor which drew the village away from the Hall end. This is probably one of Picot's estates, as we know that he owned the church until he gave it to Barnwell Priory in 1092. There were three watermills in Hinxton in 1086, one of which was presumably on the site of the 17th century mill that has been restored to working order by Cambridge Preservation Society, and which was worked commercially until the 1950s.

ton has proved to be a particularly prolific area, with areas of settlement located in both the south and the north of the parish.

During the quarry investigations a 6th century brooch on the site of an early Anglo-Saxon sunken-floored hut filled with debris such as loom-weights, hand-made pottery and animal bone proved that there was a settlement on a routeway that crossed the north of the parish, while at Hinxton Hall, to the south of the village, a larger and more organised site of a similar date was found, the forerunner of prolonged settlement that lasted into the medieval period. Four of the typical sub-rectangular sunken-floored type of hut were found here. One of them contained a row of loom-weights and in all of them weaving and sewing equipment such as spindle-whorls, needles and pins as well as pottery, a comb and a 'girdle-hanger' were found. There were also two long halls, providing the main living quarters and social areas for the community, while the small huts were perhaps for industrial processes and private sleeping arrangements. A woman was buried just outside the settlement in this period, with a knife as her only grave-good. The early sites at both the quarry and Hinxton Hall were

also used in the middle Saxon period, though in both cases the evidence is quite slight, relying on small quantities of pottery.

The settlement at Hinxton Hall was moved a short distance to the north in the late Saxon period, and there was a substantial settlement on this site from the 10th century until the Middle Ages. This village was limited by a large ditch which survived from the 10th to the 19th century, and initially contained two large halls built on sill-beams, with a

A middle Saxon pot, excavated from a well at Hinxton Hall.

Hinxton watermill.

Most of the estates in Hinxton were in one ownership from the beginning of the 18th century, and at the time of Enclosure were held by Wedd William Nash. He concentrated all his parcels of land at that time and built a new house at Hinxton Grange.

Hinxton Hall itself was not built until the mid 18th century and was part of only a small estate. The first house was built earlier in the 18th century by a friend of William Cole, Joseph Richardson of Horseheath, as 'a private retreat and for fishing retirement' according to Cole, who also 'used to spend many happy days there'. Cole described it as 'a pretty neat box', and it was constructed on the site of or adjoining a cottage. Cole also stayed in the new Hall that was built when Richardson's house was demolished in the mid 18th century, and he described it as 'very elegant'. Later owners bought more land, enlarged the house, and in the 19th century created a park around it.

Village development

There were settlements in the north and south of the parish in the early and middle Saxon periods, both of them near to crossing-places with villages on the opposite side of the

river. It is highly likely that there were also early settlements on the routes which run past the church and the site of the manor house. The site of the northern settlement was still used for agriculture in later years, but it was the long-lived village in the south that we can see as the original Hinxton. Here, the excavation evidence shows there was a slight shift to the north, which

seems to have started in the 12th century, and the cluster of Saxon buildings was expanded into a linear planned village that ran straight along an old riverside route. A church, which was in existence by 1092 when it was given to Barnwell Priory by Picot, was built on a high point in the centre of this village, with a rectangular green separating it from the village street. Much of this green has now been built over. The area of the village near and to the north of the church was most significant in the Middle Ages, with a moated site and manorial mill. Regular narrow plots along the village street suggest that at one time it was quite densely built-up, but several serious fires, such as one which destroyed about half the village in the 17th century, left many gaps. In the 19th century villagers were moved from the old site at the southern end of the village when a park was created around the Hall.

The original village street continued south of the present High Street, passing between the Hall and the river, only being moved to go around the Hall's parkland setting in the mid 19th century. This road, whose route can also be traced to the north where it eventually turns to pass through the archaeological sites discussed

The surviving area of Hinxton's village green.

above before meeting the ford to Duxford, was an important north-south highway in the Middle Ages but was bypassed by the present A130 before the 17th century.

Hinxton was a substantial settlement in 1086, when 38 villagers were recorded. By 1279 there were about that number in just one of the two manors, but in 1377 only 115 adults were taxed. The population was stable in succeeding centuries, still with only 111 adults in 1676, growing in the 18th century to 270 in 1801. In 1851 the population reached its peak of 465, though even at that time Hinxton was described as having 'a very ancient and mean appearance', but then started to fall. There were some temporary increases in the 20th century, with new housing has been built in North End Road, on the old green, and along the High Street, but the population has generally been stable since the 1950s, and in 1996 was 270.

Histon church and manor house in 1820.

Histon

Histon is a small parish of 710 hectares which lies on a tongue of gravel surrounded on the east and west by clay soils. Though well above the fens, the parish was fairly low lying, sloping from about 15m above sea level south of the village to 8m in the north of the parish, where areas known as Great and Little Moor were used for rough grazing in the Middle Ages. Histon's soils were often described as particularly fertile and were able to support large populations despite the small size of the parish. A stream that flows through the village, a tributary of the Ouse, has been used to create a large pond on the village green, and elsewhere now runs mainly in culverts. There were also several springs in the parish. Histon's original parish boundaries mostly followed tracks and field edges, but these were revised in the 19th and 20th centuries, particularly where the medieval parish included built-up areas within the villages of Girton and Impington. The open fields were enclosed following an Award made in 1806. Histon's name in Domesday Book is *Histonona*, the meaning of which is not known.

Prehistoric, Roman and Anglo-Saxon

Evidence for prehistoric land-use in Histon is very slight. Traces of three ploughed-out Bronze Age barrows exist in the extreme west of the parish, and three exotic Neolithic polished axes made of jadeite and other imported stone are recorded though their find-spots are not known. Apart from crop marks of possible fields and a few coins no Roman sites are known in the parish, and the only Anglo-Saxon evidence is the discovery of a loom-weight on the site of the school.

Medieval

Almost all the parish was held by the bishop of Lincoln in 1086, though this estate counted as two manors. The bishop gave one of these manors to Eynsham Abbey in Oxfordshire, and it was held by them until the dissolution of the monasteries in 1539. It was on this estate that St. Etheldreda's church, one of two medieval churches with independent organisations that were used for worship in Histon until the late 16th century, was built. The site can now be seen in a pasture field at Abbey Farm as low banks, all that survives of a chancel, nave and tower. In the 16th century the manor was bought by the Hinde family of Madingley Hall, and the church, which was already falling out of use, was allowed to become ruinous. The two parishes were effectively united in 1588, following a request by the congregations, and St. Etheldreda's was subsequently pulled down by Francis Hinde. Some of the materials from the church were quarried for houses in the village and some were taken for use in Madingley Hall, although the fine medieval ceiling there, often reputed to come from Histon, is more likely to be from Anglesey Abbey, another building the family demolished. The reason why there should have been two medieval churches in Histon is not known.

Stone Corner Cottage.

and the manor house and grounds, and so most space for the growing population was organised around and eventually over the green, which therefore became much smaller. The village also developed to the north. Clay Street, which probably began as the northern side of the early street-grid, had crofts along both sides, and Stone Corner Cottage, a 14th century hall house, is a survivor of growth in this area. In the 16th and 17th centuries the High Street and the green were on the major thorough-fare and became the most thriving area of the village. Several surviving buildings date to this period, including the Rose and Crown. Away from the green the village remained large but thinly settled, and is described in the mid 19th century as 'much scattered'.

The population in 1086 was given as 75, about 375 people, one of the largest in South Cambridgeshire. By 1279 this had grown to 189 tenants, about 945 people and second only after Swavesey. Afterwards it declined, and only 54 families were taxed in the 16th century. By 1801 the population had grown again to 523, and in 1851 was at least 1000, similar to the 13th century figure. It stayed high throughout the 19th century, thanks to the development of horticulture which served the Cambridge market and also to Chivers jam factory, both of which

Perhaps it was the unusually high population early in the Middle Ages that made it worthwhile for the monks to found this second institution.

To the south-east of the site of St. Etheldreda's lies the other Histon church, St. Andrew's, standing close to its associated manor house, Histon Manor. This medieval build-ing was substantially rebuilt in the 17th century and again in the 18th, 19th and 20th centuries. In its grounds is a large rectangular water-filled moat in excellent condition. The park around the manor house, extended in the 19th and 20th centuries, has prevented develop-ment at this end of the village.

Village Development

The original village seems to have two centres, one around a large oval green and the other, Church End, near the two churches. Church End was the earliest settlement, perhaps planned by the bishop of Lincoln on a rough grid system, with Church Street as the main east-west road which divided the two later manors. At this time the most important route was probably the east-west road from Milton and Impington to the north end of Oakington, later the High Street and a route through the

park which was blocked by the moat. Later, the road to Rampton, now a track known as Gun Lane, was part of the King's Highway from Cambridge to Ely, and the road to Cottenham also became important as that village grew. By that time, however, the crofts and fields of Histon had been laid out and these later roads had to take right-angled bends which have persisted.

Development at Church End was not possible because much of the land was occupied by the churches

Fruit-picking for Chivers, 1895.

were helped by the opening of a railway station in 1847. In the 20th century the village continued to grow, with good road and rail communications, development of light industries and easy commuting into Cambridge. In 1957 it was designated as one of the villages which should grow in order to relieve pressure on Cambridge, and it has continued to be Rural Growth Village. There was therefore rapid growth from the 1950s, leading to a population of 4310 in 1996.

Horningsea

Horningsea is a small parish of 663 hectares, the village being sited close to the river. Much of its land is low lying, in places below 5m above sea level, rising to about 10m in the south-east. The southern half of the parish lies on chalk and the northern half on clay, both overlain in places by gravels. Patches of peat and alluvium still survive, especially near Clayhithe. In the east of the parish and extending into Stow-cum-Quy and Lode there are clay soils that contain coprolites, nodules of calcium phosphate that were extensively quarried for fertiliser in the late 19th century. Sites of some of these quarries are still visible. Near the Cam were areas of common meadow land that were also used for peat-digging. The long western boundary of Horningsea is the Cam, and the three original settlements of Horningsea, Eye and Clayhithe were all situated where they had easy access to the river. Horningsea's peculiar southern boundary interlocks with Fen Ditton, and is the result of them being a single parish until they were divided in 1412. To the north and east the parish is now bounded by Bottisham Lode and a drain. In the 18th century the fens

around Clayhithe were drained, and the open fields of Horningsea, of which there are still many traces of ridge and furrow, were enclosed after an Award was made in 1810. In 1086, Horningsea was *Horningsie*, 'island or marshy place of Horning'. Clayhithe was *Cleie*, in 975, and *Clayheth*, 'landing place on the clay' in 1268. Eye Hall was *Eie*, 'island' or 'wet place', in 870.

Prehistoric

Several individual finds and two scatters of flint flakes are known from Horningsea, mostly from the chalk soils in the south. One Palaeolithic, one Mesolithic and two Neolithic axes have been found. Bronze Age discoveries include three axes, a rapier and a spear made of bronze, and a knife and dagger of flint. The ploughed-down mounds of Bronze Age burial mounds have been identified south of the village. Worked flints have been found near to them and also near the border with Fen Ditton.

Roman

The evidence of a major Roman pottery industry at Horningsea has been known since the 19th century and was investigated on two occasions in the early 20th century. From the report on excavations around Eye Hall it is clear that a villa or similar building stood in this area, and samian and Nene Valley pottery, bronze and lead vessels, a glass perfume phial, spoons and jewellery were found here. On the west side of the road seven kilns were excavated in 1911, some of which were lifted and taken to museums in Cambridge. They used the local clay and seem to have been functioning in the 2nd and 3rd centuries, principally producing tall, thick-walled jars that were suitable for storage and transport of grain. These would have been much in demand in the fens, where it was far too wet to use storage-pits or even granaries, and they could have been used to transport produce on the Car Dyke, which adjoins the parish on the opposite side of the Cam. Other types of pottery found here, which

the excavator thought were also made on the site, were rather finer jars, bowls and beakers, some decorated with slip in the style used in Nene Valley kilns and some inscribed with geometric patterns, and also miniature pots less than 5cms high.

The sites of many more kilns were noted in plough soil when pasture near Eye Hall was ploughed for the first time in the 1970s, and kiln-debris has been recorded over an

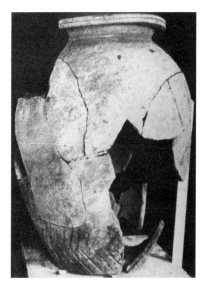

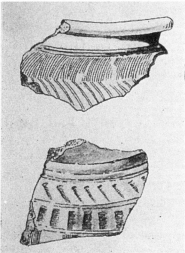

(Above) Roman jar with grooved base and (below) fragments of pottery with indented patterns, excavated from Horningsea kilns.

area of at least 8 hectares, with dumps of waste sherds found in many places. When further areas were ploughed between the kilns and the river human bones were found, possibly a cemetery linked to the industrial site. Elsewhere in Horningsea, mainly to the south of the village, small Roman farmsteads are known from aerial photographs and scatters of sherds on the field surface.

Anglo-Saxon

The parish of Horningsea was again a place of considerable importance by the middle Saxon period, when several coins and sherds of pottery are known from the area near the Roman kilns, indicating a commercial use of the riverside. With the arrival of Christianity, a monastic site was founded here. All we know of this religious house was that it had 'not a small congregation of monks', and that it was destroyed by the Danes when they overran East Anglia in 870. A century later, after most of the parish had been given to Ely by various gifts, another church was built here. A carved coffin-lid from this period survives in the church. Together with its twin parish Fen Ditton, Horningsea continued to be a single estate in the ownership of Ely, and it is even possible that these two parishes, cut off by the Cam, the fens and by the earthwork styled 'Fleam Dyke' in Fen Ditton, developed from Roman times without the dislocations of early Anglo-Saxon settlement experienced by most of Cambridgeshire.

Medieval

Eye Hall is on the site of the hamlet of Eye, which was in existence in 870 and was described as a separate settlement in 1279. Around the Hall there were, until recently, earthwork remains of the old village street which ran under the site of the Hall and of a small group of houses fronting onto this street. The estate was granted by the prior of Ely to the bishop's butler in the 12th century, and in the 13th century there were 19 houses here, and the hamlet was leased from Ely by the Pecche family. It passed to the nuns

of Denny in Waterbeach in the 14th century, and they held it until the dissolution of the monasteries. The Willys family, who already owned most of Fen Ditton, bought Eye Hall in the 16th century and built the house which substantially survives. The whole estate passed to the Pantons of Newmarket in the late 18th century, but after 1812 the estate was broken up and sold in separate lots. Eye Hall was bought by the Musgraves, who also acquired Clayhithe, and they added the south block to the house and may have been responsible for a landscaped garden with ditched enclosures and a small park that was created around the Hall. By this time no medieval houses survived.

Horningsea Church, which dates back to the 12th century, was previously a Saxon minster. In the 18th century William Cole, who made the sketch below, went over the river from Waterbeach in his carriage after some exceptionally dry weather, and described this church as 'a very large building, and in a deplorable nasty shattered condition'.

Clayhithe, also known from Saxon times, had five houses in 1279. The manor here was known as Sibills, and belonged to William Sibill of Cheveley in the 15th century. In the 16th century it passed to a

Horningsea family, and in the 17th century was combined with the Willys' estate. During the 14th century Peasants Revolt Clayhithe was the only area attacked in Horningsea. Timber was cut and houses were pulled down.

Village Development

The original village of Horningsea, like Fen Ditton, Eye and Clayhithe, probably lay along the north-south road running parallel to the river from Cambridge to Waterbeach, much as it does today, with the church on a local high point on one short lane to the west and a medieval hall and Manor Farm, now a 17th and 19th century building, on another. As river trade became more important in the Middle Ages, these two lanes were extended down to the river, where they ended in wharves, and some of the older houses in the village were built along them. Later, when road traffic was again more

Horningsea church, as sketched in 1779, and (above) in 1997.

important than river trade, the main road became the focus of the village once more. Buildings along this road, such as the 17th century public house, the Crown and Punchbowl, often have long plots behind them which run down to the river, to where many of their goods were delivered.

Eye occupied a patch of higher ground, and the house-sites that can be recognised there are aligned north-south along the village street, but it too had access to the river, and it is likely that the settlement extended in that direction. At Enclosure, the two tracks which led to the north were replaced with the present road. The settlement at Clayhithe always clustered by the river.

Horningsea had a high population of 51 in 1086, and this grew to more than 86 villagers by 1279, split between the three settlements. In the 16th century it was only a small village of 32 households, growing modestly to 57 families taxed in 1664, and a total of only 293 people in 1801. In the mid 19th century the village was described as 'small but neat... and contains a few very good houses'. Its highest population in the 19th century was 435, in 1881, after which it fell considerably. It has risen again in recent years, but in 1996 still only had a population of 320.

Medieval hall on Dock Lane, which leads down to the wharves.

Horseheath

Horseheath is a small parish of 777 hectares, mostly lying on chalky boulder clay, with chalk on its western side. The village itself is about 100m above sea level, and the whole parish is on high undulating ground which rises to as much as 120m on the eastern side near the border with Suffolk. Its long boundary on the north is part of the Roman road that runs from Cambridge towards Colchester. Other boundaries are field edges and a road from Bartlow to West Wratting. There were several ponds and springs in Horseheath, but only one very small stream. The parish was well wooded in 1086 and for much of the Middle Ages. These woods and trees planted within the park have now been lost, but some old woodland survives to the north. The parish was in one ownership in the 19th century, and so no Enclosure Award was made. In 1086 its name was *Horseda*, which probably just means 'horse heath'.

Prehistoric

There are two ring-ditches on chalkland near the western boundary where waste flakes from flint working have been found, and there was much late Iron Age pottery on a large Roman site excavated on the Roman road.

Roman

A settlement on the Roman road was investigated by digging some small holes in the 1920s and clearly contained substantial buildings and the debris of a wealthy household, though the methods of excavation makes it difficult to understand much about the site. Pebble paving was uncovered, and great quantities of pottery, vessel-glass, a lamp, bone pins, keys, bricks, tiles, nails, and coins dating from the early 2nd to the mid 4th centuries were found. Collections of animal bone included several boars tusks and ox horn cores. Roman finds, including more pebble paving, pottery and a barrel lock were also found in the centre of the village, and, in the south of the

The Roman Road at Horseheath.

by the mid 15th century. Members of the family held high government offices, and several are buried in the church. Their original hall, where Elizabeth I was entertained, was near to the village. In 1448 William Alington, Sheriff of Cambridgeshire and Huntingdonshire, created a park around his hall, with a licence to surround arable land, meadow and woodland with walls, fences, hedges and ditches, and the right to hunt. A deer park was added in the next century, and in the 18th century parkland covered over 300 hectares, half in Horseheath and the rest in surrounding parishes.

The new Horseheath Hall was built at the highest point in the parish in the late 17th century, one of only five houses designed by the influential architect, Sir Roger Pratt, who also laid out the gardens here. It was lavishly altered and extended in the next century, after the estate had been sold to the Bromleys, who often served as MPs for the County. Buildings on the estate included a menagerie, an orangery which cost £1300 to build and held 150 orange trees, a summer house, ice house and many statues. A large pond was stocked with fish, and there was a wilderness area. These later gardens were designed by William Kent. William Cole spent many holidays

parish, a hoard of Roman silver coins was found in a pot.

Anglo-Saxon

An unexpected discovery when a cable was being laid near the Roman settlement described above was the burial of a 6th century woman buried with a pair of bronze brooches and amber and blue glass beads.

Medieval

Horseheath Hall, once a Saxon estate, was the principal manor in Horseheath, and was held by the Alington family from the late 14th century to 1700. This family acquired all the other manors in Horseheath by 1550. They were resident in the parish and had built a hall there, after which the manor was named,

Horseheath Hall in the 18th century.

here and was a good friend of the family, often attending wild all-night balls and parties, though, as a clergy-man, he always claimed he only drank water himself. The Bromleys finally bankrupted themselves with this expenditure, and the new owners soon emptied and then demolished the Hall. When Vancouver, the contemporary writer on agriculture, visited Horseheath in 1794 he wrote that 'Many of the farm houses and offices appear in a very ruinous condition: the hall, in particular, a very elegant and modern building, is now levelling with the ground'. Later owners lived at Horseheath Lodge. The parkland, too, was returned to agriculture. Final traces of the gardens were bulldozed in 1991. Wrought iron gates from the park were taken to Trinity and St. John's colleges and to Cheveley rectory when the Hall was demolished.

Other manors in Horseheath included Carbonells, or Cardinals, whose manor house stood in two successive moated sites, now very fragmentary and overgrown, at Cardinals Farm, and whose estate was principally in the neighbouring parish of Shudy Camps. The heiress of this estate married Giles Alington, uniting the estates. Another manor that was distant from the village was Limburys, which had a manor house at Limberhurst Farm, virtually on the border with Suffolk. Only part of one arm of its moated site survives. The

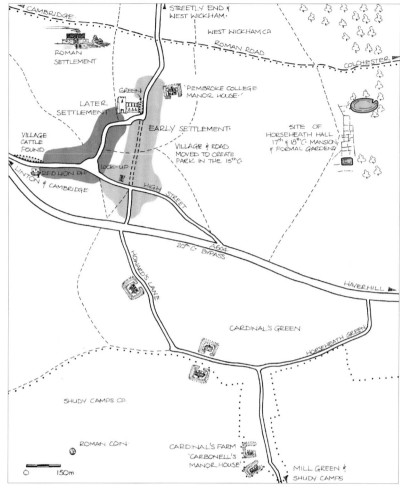

The Alington memorial in Horseheath church.

manor was purchased by the Alingtons in the mid 15th century.

Another small estate was sold to Pembroke College who held it until its sale to the heirs of Horseheath Hall in the 19th century. The manor house probably stood within the moated site at College Farm, near the church.

Village Development

Like other parishes on the south-eastern edge of Cambridgeshire, Horseheath was made up of several distinct centres. Some of these are sited where the parish boundary had to be extended to include them, and some manors had land outside the parish, both of which are indications that, unusually, the manors are more ancient than the parish. Limberhurst

Farm, Cardinal's Farm, Cardinal's Green, Lower Cardinal's Farm and College Farm, each of which has at least one moated site, are relics of this scattered settlement. The village itself is sited on a crossroad where the north-south road from West Wickham to Shudy Camps crossed the Linton to Haverhill route. It was pushed sideways by the creation of the park in the 15th century, and the High Street was re-aligned further south in the 18th century, when the park was enlarged. The Roman road, which forms the northern parish boundary, is recorded as being in use until this time, but was then said to be impassable. Later growth of the settlement was prevented on the eastern side of the High Street by the existence of the park.

There was a village green on the east side of the church, on which the stocks stood. Elsewhere in the village was a pound, sited within the curve in the road near the Red Lion, and a lock-up to the south-west of the village, on the line of the original village street. The socket stone of a village cross has been moved to the churchyard.

Horseheath has always stayed quite a small village. In 1086, 29 villagers were recorded, and this figure grew to 80 tenants, perhaps about 400 people, in 1279. By the late 14th century many holdings were said to be empty, and the population was taxed at 121 adults, about 157 people. It stayed low in succeeding centuries, slowly rising to 342 in total in 1801. At its maximum size in the 19th century, Horseheath housed 578 inhabitants, this figure subsequently falling to 328 in 1951. It grew again to 440 in 1996, with one small estate of houses and considerable infilling between the previously widely-spaced houses of the village centre.

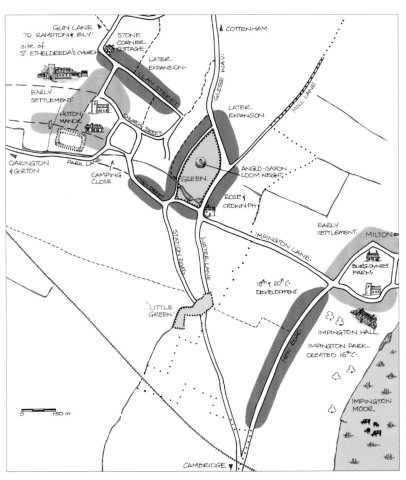

Impington

Impington, a small parish of 736 hectares, lies mainly on gravel soils, with heavier clays on the western and north-western sides of the parish. It is fairly low lying, rising from about 8m near the fens in the north to over 20m in the south where it adjoins Cambridge. The long straight eastern boundary is the Roman road known as Akeman Street or Mere Way, and the zigzag northern boundary with Landbeach follows field edges. The boundaries with Histon, Milton and Chesterton partly lie in built-up areas and have been adjusted several times in recent years, the medieval parish having extended into Girton as far as the

Cambridge-Godmanchester Roman road and including part of Howes hamlet. To the east of the village there was an area of meadow, Impington Moor, that was flooded in the 14th century and was considered shamefully neglected in the 18th century. This was used as common land for cattle, sheep being excluded. A large part of it was taken for the park around the Hall in the 16th century. The need for additional grazing land in the 16th century, which had already caused many quarrels with villagers from Histon who claimed rights over Impington Moor, led to enclosure of small fields near the village. Otherwise, the open fields were enclosed with those of Histon in 1806. Impington is *Impintune* in Domesday Book, 'the village of Impa'.

Prehistoric and Roman

Despite the Roman road and important Roman sites close by in Arbury and Milton, the only early finds from Impington are a few scatters of prehistoric worked flints and Roman pottery. Arbury Camp, half of which lies in this parish, is an important exception. This is a large late Iron Age circular fortified site of about 5 hectares, surrounded by a bank and ditch, which commands one of the approaches to Cambridge. Its earthworks have been levelled by ploughing, but when trenches were cut through the defences in 1990 it was shown that these included a massive timber gateway at the entrance. The ditch was deep and still waterlogged, and in it were preserved many fragments of leather, of which over 200 were recovered. The

Camp was also used in the Roman period, possibly as a stock enclosure.

Medieval

The earliest reference to Impington is in 991, when a manor was given to Ely by Brihtnoth. This manor, which included about half the parish, was in the hands of the Colville family who also had estates in Histon and Longstanton by the late 13th century. It was farmed jointly with the Histon manor until the 19th century. The other main manor, Burgoynes, was held by the de Lisle family from the early 13th century and by a courtier, Peter de Chauvent, from 1269. De Chauvent was granted the right to hold a weekly market and annual fair, and must have built himself a substantial residence for he entertained Edward I and was given hunting rights here. His house may have been built in a new location, leaving the old manor house as a farmhouse, which is how it remained. The present Burgoynes Farm is a 19th century building, probably still using the original site.

In 1574 this manor was divided into Manor Place Part, later known again as Burgoynes, and Farm Part, which became the Impington Hall estate. Farm Part was bought by the Pepys family of Cottenham who pulled down de Chauvent's house and began building a mansion which they surrounded by an ornamental park. During the 17th and 18th centuries the house was enlarged and altered, and formal and then landscaped gardens were created, including a lake, avenue and canals. Samuel Pepys, the diarist, stayed with his relations here on several occasions. There were extensive alterations to the house in the 19th century but some 16th century features remained. In the 20th century it was bought by the Chivers family and fell out of use, being demolished in 1953.

Village Development

The original village was near the church, probably within a rectangular enclosure made by the roads to Milton, Histon and Chesterton

The South East front of Impington Hall, in the late 19th century.

(Cambridge). Burgoynes Manor house was on the northern edge of the rectangle and the church on the south. A village pound lies to the south. Medieval crofts were arranged around the streets, some of which survived to be mapped in the 19th century although the southern side was destroyed when Impington Park was laid out in the 16th century, a time when the whole village was extremely small and many houses must have been derelict. Apart from the out-lying hamlet of Howes, this seems to be the only early settlement in the parish, but there were dwellings at Little Green from the 16th century.

Before the 19th century a few houses were being built along the Cambridge Road and Impington Lane, and this trend increased so much that these became the main parts of the village. With the opening of a railway station and the increasing importance of communications with Cambridge the fast-growing village developed almost entirely in that direction, becoming merged with its equally fast-growing neighbour, Histon. The church end of the village remained very rural until the 1990s, when a new estate was built. In the 19th century farmhouses and cottages were built on farmland outside the village for the first time.

Impington was a small village right up until the late 19th century. There were 24 villagers recorded in Domesday Book, about 45 tenants in 1279 and only 57 adults in 1377. It continued to shrink, and in the 16th century there were just 14 families. Although this rose in the 17th century, there were only 92 people living here in 1801. This increased to 273 in the first half of the 19th century and then rose steeply, like its twin-village Histon, thanks to Chivers jam factory in Histon which provided much employment, the coming of the railway, fruit and vegetable production linked to the factory and the Cambridge market, and easy commuting travel. In 1901 there were about 600 people here. Impington was chosen for growth after the 1950s as one of Cambridge's necklace villages and was given facilities such as a large Village College. The Village College itself is a much-admired modern building, designed by Walter Gropius (founder-director of the Bauhaus school) and Maxwell Fry in 1938, and is still at the forefront of Cambridgeshire's policy of providing good educational resources for village communities. This population went on growing, reaching 3230 in 1996.

Landbeach

Landbeach is a medium sized parish of 932 hectares that lies immediately to the south of the fen-edge, mostly on gravel soils but with heavy clay along its higher south-western edge. It is low lying, the land rising from less than 5m above sea level in the long triangle to the north of the parish, an area occupied by High Fen and Frith Fen, to about 7m in the village, which was normally above flood levels, and 10m in the south and west. Until the 13th century, when Beach Lode was dug and used as a boundary, Landbeach was part of Waterbeach parish. Beach Ditch was dug a few years earlier and was agreed as the boundary with Cottenham. Other boundaries include stretches of Car Dyke, the Roman road known as Akeman Street, and field edges on the Milton border. The fens in the north were often marshy until they were drained in the 17th and 18th centuries, and were used for common pasture. Land across the centre of the parish was flooded less often and was used for sheepwalks, only the south of the parish being suitable for arable agriculture. The open fields were enclosed following an Award made in 1813. Like Waterbeach, Landbeach is simply *Beche*, or 'Stream', in Domesday Book.

Crop marks of a Roman road and farming settlement at Landbeach.

Prehistoric

As in other parishes on slightly higher ground south of the Old West River, prehistoric finds are rare in Landbeach and no settlement sites are so far known. Only one Mesolithic pick and two polished stone Neolithic axes have been found and even reports of worked flint flakes are scarce, despite systematic field-walking as part of the Fenland Project.

Roman

In Roman times, however, areas that were close to the fen-edge but above the level of flooding at that time (about 2m) were densely settled, and virtually all the land on gravel soil in Landbeach contains signs of occupation, usually crop marks and find scatters. This does not apply to the clay soils, which seem to be empty. Important monuments include the Roman canal, Car Dyke, much of which is still used as a drain and therefore is kept scoured, which means that it is less well-preserved than sections in Cottenham and Waterbeach. Where Akeman Street has been used as a parish boundary it is covered by modern roads and cannot be seen, but where it runs across the parish, to the west of the High Street, it is exposed in the arable soil as a slight straight bank of gravel. Excavations across the road and its adjoining area in 1996 showed that the road was about 10m wide, made of gravelly soil excavated from quarries next to the site, with side-ditches nearly 2m wide and 60cms deep. Pottery evidence suggested it was built in the 2nd century and was still in use in the 4th, and it was preceded by a track that ran towards a farmstead, suggesting that local needs were met before national communications were in place.

Other settlement sites are connected by trackways to Car Dyke and Akeman Street and usually consist of rectangular enclosures, some of which were field-ditches and some surrounded dwellings and industrial sites. Domestic debris and soil blackened by burning are abundant on the field surfaces, and kiln-bars and large quantities of quern fragments are often noted. However, the only possible buildings that have been noted as crop marks or found on excavations are shallow circular ditches that could have been rather crude huts. This seems to confirm theories that, though the use of the fens was planned by the Roman government and a sophisticated infrastructure of transport and drainage provided, peasants were settled on a rent-paying basis that prevented them accumulating much individual wealth. Some groups of small enclosures have the appearance of paddocks with associated drove-ways and may well have been used for cattle-ranching while others were suitable for arable crops. The exist-ence of mixed farming is confirmed by pollen and charred cereal remains found in excavations of the road side-ditches.

Anglo-Saxon

Only one artefact of this date has been found in Landbeach, although there is plentiful settlement evidence nearby in Waterbeach. This is a 6th century brooch found during quarry-ing adjacent to Car Dyke at the point it crosses Akeman Street, and may represent a burial site which was otherwise unnoticed.

Medieval

There were two main manors, each with a house defended by a moated enclosure. The principal manor was Chamberlains, situated close to the church. This had been created after the Conquest by Picot, sheriff of Cambridge, from various Saxon land-holdings. In the mid 13th century it was acquired by William le Chamberlain, apparently after he had arranged the murder of another claimant, and his successors were often resident in the parish. It was probably they who built their manor house within a moated site that is still a well-defined feature with adjoining ditched paddocks in a pasture field at the northern end of the High Street. In the late 14th century the manor passed, with many disputed claims, to Corpus Christi College, and resident lords of the manor were then the rectors, a college appointment. The moated site went out of use, and instead the Rectory was built. This building is the oldest in the village, its 14th century cellar being carved with coats of arms. The present house was originally an aisled hall that was con-verted into a building suitable for a rector and curate by William Sowode, a rector in the early 16th century, with a farmhouse added on. This was

Cattle now graze Worts Meadow, once part of the medieval village and manor. The moat is within the trees on the left.

the house that was used by Matthew Parker, also the Master of Corpus Christi and later Archbishop of Canterbury, the first clergyman to have a family here. From the 18th century the rectors adapted the building in line with the needs of a country gentleman.

The other significant manor in Landbeach was Bray's, whose house stood within a moated site surrounded with traces of the original village in a pasture field that is now a public park, in the centre of the village. The estate was given to two king's carpenters after the Norman Conquest, and was held by the de Brays from the early 12th-14th centuries. In the 16th century it was inherited by Robert Kirkby. His son Richard was a notorious character whose policies had immediate and lasting effects on the village. Conversion of common land and enclosure of open fields for sheep grazing was highly profitable at this time, but was only legal if common rights were extinguished. Kirkby enclosed some land illegally, greatly overstocked the sheepwalks with his own flocks, harassed the villagers by impounding their animals and even physically assaulting individuals, and, most significantly of all, he evicted tenants from fourteen crofts that had been part of the medieval village so that he could take over their grazing

rights. These crofts were never inhabited again. His effect on the common rights of villagers would have been more extreme but for Matthew Parker, who defended the villagers case in courts up to the Star Chamber, England's highest jurisdic-tion. Kirkby even quarrelled with his own family, and the estate was split before his death. In the late 18th century it was reconstituted by William Worts, whose son bequeath-ed it to the Worts Charity for the benefit of, amongst other institutions, Cambridge University Library. In the early 20th century it was bought by Cambridgeshire County Council.

Village Development

Landbeach has been studied in depth by local historian Jack Ravensdale, who lived in the village

Landbeach High Street still contains many empty areas.

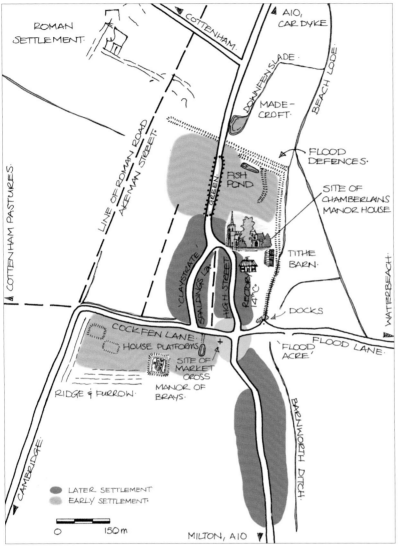

The medieval tithe barn near the docks at Landbeach.

the later village having the appearance of a straggling linear settlement.

South of the village were the docks where boats approaching the village along Beach Lode could load grain and other cargoes. These docks are still apparent as broad shallow hollows in pasture. Adjoining them is Landbeach's tithe barn, a magnificent thatched late medieval barn that is preserved by the Village Society

In 1086 Landbeach was a moderate sized village of 32 villagers, growing to at least 55 tenants in 1279. It is known that the village was severely affected by the Black Death, losing half its inhabitants, and in 1377 there were 114 tax-payers, less than the Domesday population. It stayed low in the 16th century, receiving little encouragement from the lords of the manors, and grew slightly in the 17th century, staying fairly stable at about 55 families until the 19th century. In 1801 there were 235 people living here, and this figure grew to a peak of 526 in 1851, though even then it was described as 'small but pretty, and contains several good houses'. After this it slowly declined. It has grown again steadily through most of the 20th century, and in 1996 had a population of 790.

for many years, and its development is discussed at length in his publications. The early village had two centres, with the church, Chamberlains Manor house and associated buildings in the north and Brays Manor house in the south. At the crossroads, where the road widened into a southern village green, roads from Waterbeach, Cottenham pastures, Milton and Ely met, and there was a stone market cross. The Roman road to the west of the High Street formed the back lane. Beach Lode bounded the eastern edge. In the early 14th century

periods of wetter weather led to flooding, and banks and ditches were created across the northern end of the village as protection from rising waters. Also at the northern end, a green was created in the 15th century when a plot had fallen vacant.

Expansion towards higher ground along the road to Cambridge was encouraged by the clearance and fossilisation of the southern area of the village by Kirkby and his heirs, the land being too wet for expansion in other directions. This had probably started to happen before the late medieval contraction and has led to

Linton

Linton, now a large parish of 1600 hectares, comprises the three Domesday townships of Linton, Little Linton and Barham. It straddles the valley of the Granta, and the land rises to high ground on either side. Near to the river there are alluvial and gravel soils about 40m above sea level, and to the north and south are chalk uplands, rising to ridges at about 100m and hills that are up to 125m, the highest points being topped with clay or glacial gravels. The river is crossed in the village by routes of the Icknield Way, there are significant east-west routes along the river valley, above its flood-plain, and the Roman road from Cambridge forms the northern parish boundary. Linton High Street was part of the main road from Cambridge to Haverhill until a bypass was built, and was a turnpike road from 1765 to 1876. Linton's southern boundary, which is also the county boundary, was changed in 1965 and now follows a railway line that was opened in 1865 and closed in 1967.

The Granta, separating the two halves of Linton, is still liable to flood, and William Cole recorded that even in the 18th century it was difficult for carriages to cross it in the winter. It was still famous for its trout in the mid 19th century, and was used for boating and bathing well into the 20th century. There was only a wooden footbridge until 1867, when a iron bridge was built

The parish contained much woodland in 1086 and in medieval times, most of which was felled in the 18th and 19th centuries. There were also heaths, especially in Barham, and Barham was unusual in Cambridgeshire in having goats included in its Domesday entry. Most of Linton's open fields, which were mixed with areas of pasture, were enclosed after an Award was made in 1840, though Little Linton had been enclosed some time earlier and there were already many closes around Barham and the main village. The two

Linton's were *Lintone* and *Alia Lintone* in Domesday Book, meaning 'flax-farm', and Barham was *Bercheham*, or 'enclosure on the hill'. Later in the Middle Ages the settlements were known as Great Linton, Little Linton and Barham.

Prehistoric

Prehistoric artefacts and evidence for settlement are found in many areas around the parish, particularly to the west of the village. Palaeolithic flint flakes have been reported from near the Hadstock border. Neolithic flints are commonly discovered, and two Neolithic axes and two Bronze Age spear-heads are known. An Anglo-Saxon cemetery re-used a Bronze Age burial mound which contained two urned cremations, and in his excavation report RC Neville says that he examined four other mounds on the area known as Linton Heath, but found nothing. There is still the ring-ditch of one such mound visible as a crop mark, and presumably this area was significant for Bronze Age burials, of which we have lost almost all trace.

Several pits belonging to an early Iron Age settlement were excavated when they were discovered in a chalk pit in 1948. There were large amounts of pottery, much of it decorated, and

bone tools including a needle, three awls, three gouges and a spindle-whorl. A barbed spear-head made from whale-bone was also collected, though there is doubt if this belongs with the other material. Another Iron Age settlement, probably belonging to the middle of that period, was found during investigations near a Roman villa just to the south of the village in 1990. Grain storage pits containing pottery and the charred remains of wheat and the weeds that grew with it were excavated. Elsewhere in the parish were found an iron reaping hook with bone handle, a bone weaving comb, and Iron Age coins.

Roman

Many Roman sites are known in Linton, which is adjacent to the Bartlow Hills and an area of north Essex rich in villas and other buildings. One villa was excavated in 1846-50 in a field that was at that time in the parish of Hadstock. It had several mosaic floors, painted wall-plaster, bathhouses and hypocausts. Stones from the walls had already been taken for road-building, but in excavations that were carried out in 1990 it was found that some areas of collapsed masonry survived, and there was also a range of small

Roman artefacts from Linton.

Gilded brooch from Linton, height 17cms.

storage rooms with flint walls. In the same field was a small cemetery. Four burials were found with nails and one spear. Nearby was a cremation of the 1st century AD, accompanied by a set of table-ware that included a flagon, beaker, two samian platters and one bowl, as well as an amphora, brooch and a bronze stud in the form of a lion's head, indicating there was a wooden box here, finds which are reminiscent of Bartlow Hills, less than a mile away.

Scatters of Roman pottery have been found across the river from this site at Barham, and more Roman sites are known at Little Linton, at Chilford in the north of the parish, within the village itself and next to Linton Village College. At this last site 2nd century burials were excavated, consisting of three children and two women. One child's grave-goods included five bracelets, 148 jet beads, the neck of a glass bottle, a shale armlet and two pots. Close to these burials, which lay by the course of a track leading to a ford across the Granta, were pits, ditches and other settlement remains. Further Roman finds reported from Linton are a hoard of some 200 coins and the figurine of a satyr. The account of Anglo-Saxon cemetery excavations in a Bronze Age barrow suggests that at least one Roman cremation was found with an urn in the mound, and Roman pot sherds were found throughout the excavation. Several coins, too, were included in the mound, many of which were used as Anglo-Saxon grave-goods.

Anglo-Saxon

Following on from this wealth of Roman sites was a comparable spread of early Anglo-Saxon settlements and cemeteries. The most spectacular of these was a cemetery based on the Bronze Age barrow, which was enlarged in Anglo-Saxon times into a large oval mound. As at the Hadstock villa, the excavation was by RC Neville in the mid 19th century. His discoveries, in addition to many burials which he said were damaged by agriculture, included 104 burials that dated to the 5th and 6th centuries, the men, as usual, often buried with weapons and the women with jewellery, but there are several unusual aspects to this site. One is the large number of Roman objects that had been used as grave-goods, including ten coins, mostly pierced for suspension, earrings, writing implements, armlets, Roman-style brooches and a comb in a case. Several of these objects must have been collected from the rich Roman sites round about. It also noticeable that some items were used in a way more typical of Roman than Anglo-Saxon styles. For example, the excavation report describes brooches occurring in male graves, generally near the head or foot, and the comb was also with a man. Finger-rings, earrings and bracelets are also more often found with Roman bodies, though several pairs of wrist-clasps and the way most of the brooches were worn were very much in the East Anglian tradition. The grave-goods illustrate an uncommonly wealthy community, for they include two swords, and of the 42 brooches at least five were gilded and several were set with garnets or coloured paste. There were 740 beads in total, mostly amber, with many of glass or paste in varied colours, and some of

Giant cowrie shell, 7cms in length, from Linton.

jet, crystal and bronze. Other links with the wider world are demonstrated by finds of a glass beaker and a giant cowrie shell, the earliest one of this kind in Britain. Though no horse bones were found, grave-goods included a spur and a bridle in different graves, in the Frankish style. Five bronze-bound buckets and twelve pots were placed in graves, but many of the types of item often found in later graves, such as ivory bag-rings, 'girdle-hangers' and collections of small items, were missing.

Another Anglo-Saxon cemetery, obviously much smaller and poorer, has been noted on three separate occasions in the centre of Linton. At one time a burial with a spear turned up in a trench, and at other times two cremations and then two skeletons, one of which wore two silver finger-rings, were accidentally found.

A hut-site of similar early 6th century date has also been found at Barham, immediately across the river from the excavated villa. It was of the sunken-floored type, with remains of a clay-daub wall and a hearth. Finds on its floor included decorated pottery and a bone comb, needle and awl. On the opposite side of the parish, at Little Linton, there was more early Anglo-Saxon settlement evidence on the site that became a medieval village, in the form of pottery dating to the 5th and 6th centuries. Similarly, in the late Saxon or early Norman period, there were settlements that left scatters of pottery in many locations, such as the fields at Barham, the centre of Linton and sites to the west of Little Linton.

Medieval

Great Linton's manor house stood within the village, near to the

market place between the High Street and Church Lane. In the 13th century it was held by the de Say and then the Northwood family. It ceased to be used as a manor house at an early date for, from the 16th century, when the Parys family held this manor, they stayed at Little Linton manor house when visiting the parish. In about 1600 the Paryses built a house on the hill at Catley Park that was developed into a mansion surrounded by a large park in the 18th century. This building was mostly demolished in 1772 when its owner was bankrupted by gambling debts, and some of its lavish furnishings were taken to the Bishop's Palace in Ely. One wing survived as a farmhouse, and was pulled down in 1978.

The manor house for Little Linton stood in the moated site near the river. The manor was united with Great Linton in the 14th century, both being held by the Parys family, who used the house in the moat as their residence until Catley Park was built. This moated house was described as having a chapel in 1517, and it is sketched on the map of the parish made in 1600. Next to the moat is another moat that is apparently somewhat similar but contains a rectangular arrangement of ponds and has been identified as a medieval or 16th century water garden, probably built by the Parys family. In later centuries the site was again used as a garden feature, with yews planted in the 16th or 17th century and with summer houses and boat houses in the 18th and 19th century. A short distance downstream of the moats stood a water-mill that was first recorded in Domesday Book and was used until the late 19th century.

In 1086 there were two manors at Barham, but they were both held by the de Furneaux family in the 13th and 14th century. Part of their manor house, at Barham Hall, was used by Robert de Furneaux to endow a small friary known as Barham Priory in the late 13th century. When the religious house was dissolved in 1539 the new owners, the Millicents, again used the site to

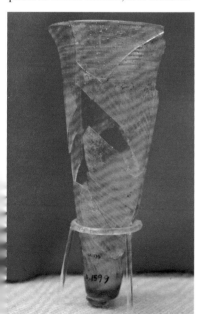

Anglo-Saxon glass beaker from Linton.

Barham Hall in the early 19th century.

Linton, obtained a grant for a weekly market and annual fair, and made a market place near to his manor house at the junction of High Street and Church Lane. Around this he leased small plots to numerous craftspeople and traders. In 1279 his tenants included several merchants, tailors, bakers, tanners, falconers, millers, smiths, ale-wives, potters, and a drummer, clerk, chaplain, cobbler and money-lender.

Noting the economic success of this venture, Simon de Furneaux, lord of Barham manor, acquired a similar grant to hold a market and fair in 1282, and made a large rectangular market place at Green Lane. He must, in fact, have begun commercial activities before the grant was made, for in 1279 many of his tenants were already involved in trade. Soon afterwards yet another market place was created, this time south of the river. The settlement around it looks very much as if it has been deliberately planned in regularly spaced plots, and it seems as though the villagers of Little Linton, which was deserted by all but the residents of the moat at this time, moved to this new location to enjoy its economic advantages, either by their own choice or at the wish of their lord. During the Middle Ages, therefore, the settlements at Little Linton and Barham Hall were reduced to a manor house and a friary respectively, whilst those at

rebuild the friary as their own residence, incorporating part of the friary buildings, of which fragments still remain. In the early 19th century the estate was left to Pembroke College, and the house was allowed to fall into disrepair. Most of it was demolished later in the 19th century.

There was also a priory within the village. This was built for a prior who was appointed by the Breton abbey of St. Jacut de la Mer to look after property that it had been given in Linton, which included the church. Its buildings had gone by the 17th century, apart from a tithe barn which survived to the early 20th century. Linton's 16th century guild-hall stands near the site. As a foreign institution, the priory was taken over by the Crown during the wars with France in the 15th century, and was given to Pembroke College.

Village Development

Domesday Linton consisted of four separate holdings, Great and Little Linton, Barham and Barham Hall, and archaeological evidence confirms that there were settlements in all these areas in the 11th century. Each of these settlements made use of sites where the river was forded by Icknield Way routes, as is found in

many villages in the Cam and Granta valleys. By the late 13th century, however, a combination of good communications at points where the Icknield Way routes crossed the east-west routes and the ambitions of the lords of two manors, Great Linton and Barham, made Linton into the foremost commercial settlement in Cambridgeshire outside Cambridge, and the settlement pattern had been changed for the benefit of this new order.

Changes began in 1246 when William de Say, lord of Great

One of the three fording places across the Granta in Linton.

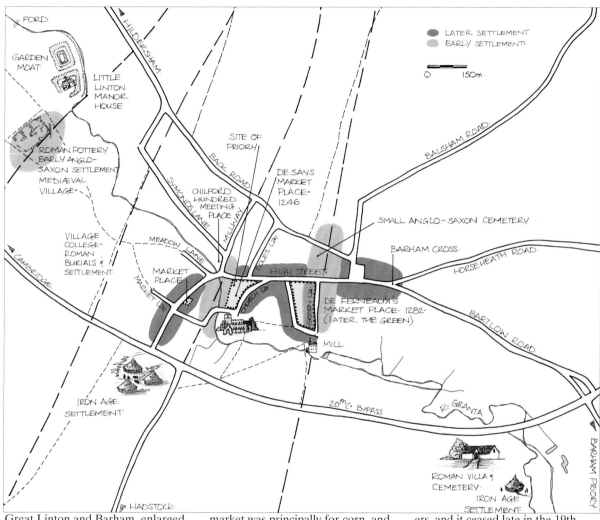

Great Linton and Barham, enlarged by the addition of new houses south of the river, came to be seen as one market town.

In the end it was the market south of the river that was most successful, and it was still in use when a map of the parish was made in 1600. A market house, demolished in the 1950s, was built here in the early 16th century, and in that century there were rows of stalls dedicated to single provisions such as bread and meat. In the 17th century rows were named after woollen and linen drapers, and there were stalls for tanners, shoemakers and glovers. A Rental of 1633 records 41 shops and ten stalls. In the 18th century the market was principally for corn, and in the 19th century it declined and ceased. However, Linton remained an important local commercial centre, with a wide range of shops in the 19th and 20th century, and the site of the market itself was largely covered by a general store. When this store was converted into apartments in the 1980s it was discovered that the Dragon Inn still incorporated an 18th century rebuilding of the market hall. In the mid 19th century Linton was described as 'formerly of considerable importance, but now much fallen into decay... The general appearance of the town is indifferent...' The annual fair became partly a hiring fair for servants and labourers, and it ceased late in the 19th century.

The fair that had been granted to Barham was revived in the 17th century as a lambing fair, held near Barham Cross. In the 19th century it was the largest sheep fair in Cambridgeshire. Elsewhere in the village many craftsman and traders are recorded in the 17th and 18th centuries. In many cases these were related to the wood products and animal hides that were produced locally, and sites in the town were used for processing these products. For example, there was a saw-pit on the former site of de Furneaux's market place, and there was also a tanyard here, with a tanner who

Linton Guildhall.

could spread the bark he used on the village green. Elsewhere in the parish industrial processes included tile, lime and brick kilns, a chalk pit was worked until the 1960s, there was an attempt at coal-mining, and a great many people involved in building trades were based in Linton. Professions included auctioneers and land-surveyors. There were several boarding schools, one of which was attended by William Cole, and doctors are recorded from the 18th century, of whom the best known is the local historian WM Palmer, who lived in the village and worked here from 1900 to 1925.

In 1086 the various settlements at Linton had a large population of 61, and this grew to at least 172 tenants in 1279, about 860 people, much the largest settlement in Cambridgeshire away from the fen-edge, and already recognised as a town. By 1377 it had collapsed to 155 tax payers, only about 200 people, but was up to 92 families in the 16th and to 166 families in the 17th century. In the 18th century the population grew steadily, and in 1801 was 1157 in total. It increased in the 19th century to a peak of 1858 in 1851, and it then fell until about 1920. During the 1960s and '70s new housing estates were built, and large industrial estates were established south of the

bypass. Linton already had one of the earliest Village Colleges, opened in 1938, and many other facilities, even including a zoo, and in the County's Development Plan of 1965 it was selected as a centre where growth was to be encouraged. This policy has since become more restrictive, but the population was able to rise to 4310 in 1996.

Longstanton

Longstanton is a moderate sized parish of 1120 hectares. Most of it, including the two original villages, lies on a north-south ridge of gravel running towards the fens, with heavier clay soil to the west. There is a patch of low-lying marshy ground, Cow Common, near Swavesey, which produced more than 3000 eels a year in 1086, but otherwise the parish was well above land liable to flood, rising from about 6m above sea level near the fens in the north, to 7-9m in the villages and nearly 20m on the southern boundary, which is the Roman

road from Cambridge to Godmanchester. It was therefore well placed to take advantage of the natural wealth of the fens while enjoying the easily-cultivated soils and good communications of upland areas. Cow Common, Great Moor near Rampton and Great Meadow, which followed a stream from Childerley flowing through Longstanton All Saints and then on to the Ouse, provided plentiful grazing, principally for sheep. The two parishes of Long Stanton All Saints and Long Stanton St. Michael were separate by the 13th century, possibly much earlier, and were united in 1953. However, their fields were always farmed in common, and in most ways they were one settlement, though consisting of scattered centres. Some open field strips were being consolidated and sometimes enclosed before 1600, and closes were made near the villages. The remaining common fields were enclosed after an Award was made in 1816. In 1086 Longstanton was *Stantune*, which is supposed to mean 'Stone-farm enclosure'.

Prehistoric

A scatter of Mesolithic flints found at Slate Hall Farm near the Cambridge-Godmanchester road shows there was early occupation in this corner of the parish, but generally finds dating before the Iron Age are very rare, despite several programmes of field-work. Only one Neolithic axe has been found, in the centre of Longstanton All Saints, for example, and even large-scale excavations have produced very small quantities of struck flint flakes. There were, however, two important Iron Age settlements. Close to the Cambridge-Godmanchester road is a group of crop marks which show small ditched fields and a 'banjo enclosure', so called because of its shape, which is a type of Iron Age enclosed house commonly found in Wessex but little known in Eastern England. Scatters of pottery sherds have been found on the field surface.

At Hatton's Farm, to the north-east of the village, on a site that has been changed from arable land to a golf course, late Iron Age occupation has been excavated over an 80 hectare site. Several round huts were found, most of them within sub-rectangular enclosures, and also droveways and large enclosures. Some of the huts had been protected from later ploughing because they were covered with a windmill mound in the Middle Ages. Pottery recovered was all locally made, which showed that this farming settlement had little wealth and limited contact with the outside world.

Roman

The Iron Age site at Hatton's Farm continued to be used for farming in Roman times, particularly in the 3rd and 4th centuries, and there must have been a centre nearby. As in the Iron Age the pottery was generally locally made in quite crude fabrics, an exception being some late sherds from the Nene Valley kilns. Unusual features of the animal bones from this site were the number of horse bones found, occasional deer, and the butchery of many of the food bones (cattle, sheep, pig) into small pieces with metal cleavers.

Medieval

There were four medieval manors in Longstanton, each with a home farm, although the lords normally lived elsewhere. In the early 13th century, Colville's manor house was in the south-east of Longstanton St. Michael, near Oakington Barracks, on a site often wrongly called a Bishop's Palace. In the mid 19th century a moat enclosing about two acres and part of a fishpond were recorded here, but these have not

Longstanton All Saints in 1820.

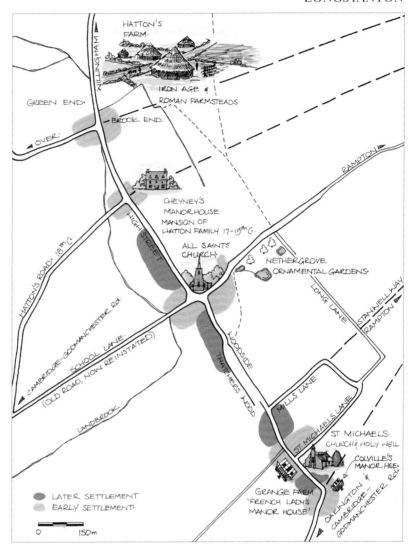

survived. Another manor in Longstanton St. Michael was called French Lady's Manor, after Eleanor of Aquitaine who held it for a short time as guardian of a young heir. In later years the manor house for this estate was the 17th century Grange opposite St. Michael's church. The site of Walwyn's manor house, which is known to have existed in the 13th and 14th centuries, is not known for sure. The manor was amalgamated with Cheyneys in the 15th century and is not recorded afterwards.

Cheyneys manor house was probably on the High Street just to the north of All Saints church where it certainly existed in the 16th century and where the Hattons lived from the 17th to the 19th century. 'The Manor-house, a spacious ancient mansion, is about to be pulled down', was noted in Gardner's Directory for 1851. Sir Christopher Hatton of Kirby Hall in Northamptonshire, who had already bought Colvilles Manor, bought Cheyneys Manor together with Walwyns, in 1617, and then sold them to a relative, whose descendants lived in Longstanton and dominated its development until the 19th century. The estate was finally sold in 1874.

Holy Well, in the churchyard of St Michael's.

Village Development

Originally, Longstanton consisted of a group of separate settlements along the road from Oakington to Over and Willingham, each forming where minor drove roads crossed the main route. One was around St. Michael's church, another near All Saints, another near Cheyneys manor house, and there was possibly another at Hatton's Farm. The first parish church would have been St. Michael's, probably built on a very ancient site. Its holy well is still maintained. Subsequently, with the early growth of the village, another church was built, and the village became a continuous linear settlement along the High Street and its southern extension. In the late Middle Ages, as the manors were amalgamated and the population shrank, the pattern of settlement became broken up again, and this was accentuated from the 16th century by the many changes made by the Hatton family. These particularly affected St. Michael's, which became a shrunken settlement, much of its area enclosed as small hedged fields, preserving ridge and furrow and other features of the medieval estates in pasture.

In the late 18th century the old field roads were replaced by a private road built by Sir Thomas Hatton directly to his mansion, and this became a major road. Longstanton All Saints grew into much the most important settlement, and this was emphasised when the Hattons treated parts of St. Michael's hedged fields as the parkland setting for their mansion. Nowadays one of the older routes has been reinstated, most traffic entering on this route then turning left at All Saints church towards Over and the other growing fen-edge villages.

Longstanton was one of the largest villages in South Cambridgeshire in 1086, with 67 villagers recorded, about 335 people, and it is likely that this figure doubled in the next two centuries, the population being spread between two villages. In

Longstanton St Michael's in 1800.

1377 the population was down to 267 adults as settlements nearer the fen-edge became more attractive, and later became dramatically smaller. In the 16th century 42 families were recorded, only 8 of which were in Longstanton St. Michael, and its southern end was deserted. There was some growth from the 17th century, but St. Michael always stayed much smaller, and in 1801 there was a total population of 400. This figure grew to a maximum of about 600 in 1851 and then shrank considerably. It was after World War II that the population grew suddenly with the creation of Oakington Barracks, which are situated in Longstanton. Including servicemen and families, the population expanded to 1300 in 1951, and new housing estates were added in the 1960s and 1970s. In 1996 there were 2370 people living here.

Milton

Milton is now a moderate sized parish of 800 hectares, after several 20th century changes which included addition of substantial areas previously part of Chesterton. The village and most of the parish lie on gravel soils, with alluvium near the river and a wide band of very heavy clay on the western side. It is all low lying, less than 10m above sea level, being much lower close to the river. There, marshy land was divided into Baitsbite Fen, Lug Fen and Land Fen and in the late 18th century was still 'greatly injured by occasional overflowings of that river'. There were osier holts near the river, and renders of eels were due from these areas. Parish boundaries include the Cam, a well-used navigation route in Roman and medieval times, and the route of the Roman road known as Akeman Street or Mere Way, which survives as a raised bank and green-way along the western edge of the parish. The southern boundary with Cambridge has been reorganised at various times. Milton's gravel soils have been extensively quarried in the 20th century. Considerable areas near the village were made into small hedged fields in the 16th century, and the remaining open fields were enclosed following an Award made in 1802. In 1086 Milton was Middeltuna, 'the middle farm'.

Prehistoric

The river valley in this area was too low lying to be attractive for early settlement in the way the Cam valley to the south of Cambridge was, and Milton is not close enough to the fen-edge to benefit to any great extent from that attractive environment. Evidence for pre-historic settlement is therefore not common, although there are indications that a low level of casual and intermittent land-use may have been fairly widespread. Recent field-walking exercises in several areas in the parish have revealed thin scatters of burnt stones and waste flint flakes, with very few recognisable tools. One Mesolithic blade was found near to Akeman Street, all other flakes

Excavating an Iron Age cremation at Milton.

Small Roman flagons found with a Roman crematio, heights 14 and 15cms..

being Neolithic or later. Fields in the north-east of the parish close to the river contained scatters of worked flints that had been deeply buried by later alluvium caused by flooding of the river from Iron Age times onwards. These deposits are only visible in deep and carefully cut trenches and probably occur in many locations where they cannot yet be explored.

Late Bronze Age remains and a large Iron Age site were found in other recent excavations in the south-west of the parish in an area of more than 100 hectares which is being dug out for disposal of Cambridge's waste. Part of this site falls on a gravel ridge although most is on the clay soil. In one part of the site there were at least four round Iron Age huts set within enclosures and surrounded by further ditched agricultural boundaries. A few years later, rectangular timber buildings were constructed and the old farm ditches were replaced with a better organised system of fields. In one of the enclosures a timber mortuary was made in which were placed four cremations, all in urns and accom-panied by three other pots. Closer to Akeman Street another group of round huts was found, consisting of three pairs with one large and one

small hut each, once more surround-ed with ditched enclosures. Three cremations were found in some of the field ditches in this area.

Roman

The Roman pottery industry centred at Horningsea also extended across to the western banks of the Cam and through much of the parish of Milton, most of the evidence being discovered and destroyed in great quantities when extensive quarries were dug for the post-World War II building boom. One enthusiast in the village collected 'several hundred-weight' of pottery and building materials and described seeing pits and ditches in the quarries south of the village over many years. He collected kiln-bars and sufficient 'wasters' that had been spoiled dur-ing firing, usually pottery resembling the Horningsea wares, to be con-fident that the industrial area extended along much of the river valley. Habitation accompanying these sites seems to have been impoverished, and a group of burials that he found had no grave-goods. Finds recorded in the late 19th century give a similar picture.

Recent work in the north of the parish close to the river also showed that there were simple dwellings

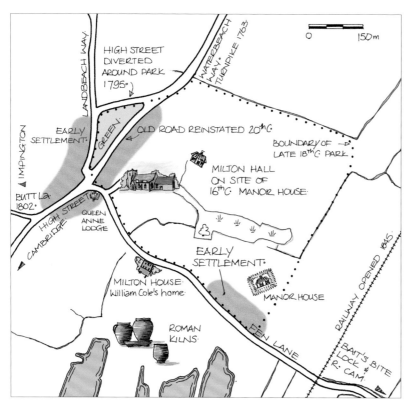

along the edge of the gravel ridge, with occasional fragments of roof and flue tile hinting at a more elaborate structure in one place. Adjacent areas on the landward side were divided by ditches and fences into small paddocks. A group of burials was found here too, also without grave-goods.

The Iron Age settlement on the waste disposal site discussed above was used again from the 2nd century onwards for a highly organised farming estate. The layout of the estate was changed around on at least three occasions, which usually involved dismantling old buildings and filling in field ditches and quarries. On the last occasion, a pond that had formed over old ditches was used to dump broken pottery, material from a corn drier and an old boot. Structures belonging to this Roman estate included a timber barn, corn drier, smithy, oven and cattle trough. In one corner of the site was a particularly interesting cemetery arranged within and around a low

mound, later ploughed flat. There were three 2nd century cremations, one of them in a box with a storage vessel that contained the bones, and two small flagons for wine. All these vessels had been deliberately spoiled or 'killed' with holes made in their sides. This tradition of barrow-burial with cremations and feasting regalia in a box fits in with the 'princely native' customs we have seen in the Iron Age at Hinxton and in the Roman period at Bartlow and which occurs elsewhere in South Cambridgeshire and surrounding regions. Around the mound were buried nineteen inhumations belonging to the 3rd and 4th centuries. One had a broken Nene Valley cup at his feet and another was accompanied by a bone comb.

A trench cut through Akeman Street where it survives as a greenway between Milton and Impington showed that the modern embanked track has shifted slightly to the west of the Roman road. Its agger, or raised bank, was 10m wide, 45cms

high, and made up of hard-packed clay. Its side-ditches were nearly 70cms deep.

Medieval

Most of Milton belonged to Ely at the Conquest, but this estate was disputed by Picot and his heirs, and although some dues were paid to Ely it passed to lay landowners through the Middle Ages. In the 13th century it belonged to Henry III's steward, Godfrey of Crowcombe. He is a likely candidate for building the moated manor house at Fen End. In 1948 there were still slight traces of a rectangular moated site here, though it has now been ploughed flat. The King presented him with timbers suitable for building and also granted him hunting rights and an annual

Excavating a Roman inhumation and (above) a cremation.

fair. This estate was plundered and burnt later in the 13th century by rebels supporting Simon de Montfort. William Cole, whose own house was nearby, described finding foundations, fishponds and ditches on the site. In the 16th century the estate was sold to William Cook of Chesterton, a dignitary who was probably the owner who replaced the old moated manor house with a larger home near the church. A brass for him, his wife and five children is in the church. In the late 18th century the new rector, Samuel Knight, also owned much of the parish, and he rebuilt parts of the Elizabethan house, though it was his son who built Milton Hall and created parkland, designed by Humphrey Repton, around it.

Village Development

The original village was well away from the Roman road, on a route from Cambridge which forked in the centre of the village into roads to Landbeach and to Waterbeach. The Waterbeach road was also the principal route from Cambridge to Ely, and became a turnpike road in 1763. There was a triangular green where the roads met, with the church to the east and a manor house along Fen Lane, where, judging from crop marks around the moated site and later use of the name Fen End there may also have been a separate part of the village. In the late 18th century the manor house was rebuilt as Milton Hall and was surrounded with a formal park, for which the village High Street was replaced with a right-angled turn to the north of the green. Most houses of the small village were on either the High Street or Fen Lane at this time.

A few old cottages survive near the junction of these roads, including the picturesque Queen Anne Lodge, which has a late medieval plan though the present building is substantially 17th century. Another attractive house whose interest lies particularly in its ownership by the antiquarian William Cole in the 18th century is Milton House. Cole's principal contributions to local studies are the sketches he made of

churches in Cambridgeshire before they were altered in Victorian times, but he also transcribed reams of medieval documents and minutely recorded epitaphs and memorials in every church he visited. Though he served as a curate in Waterbeach, he chose to rent a farmhouse in Milton. It was in a bad state of repair when he moved in, and he carried out extensive alterations and additions in a Gothic style which has been followed by later occupants.

There were 36 villagers counted in Milton in 1086, and in 1279 this had grown to 75, representing at least 375 people. In 1377 this figure had fallen to 146 adults, and afterwards was fairly stable with about 160 inhabitants until it grew slightly towards the end of the 18th century. In 1801 there were 273 residents, and this had grown to 576 in 1871, the village being described as 'exceedingly pretty'. There was some loss of population after this, but otherwise it generally increased steadily until after 1950, when the position of the village near Cambridge meant that it was chosen for rapid growth, and several new estates were built. In 1980 the village was again selected for major expansion, and, despite much local opposition, by 1996 the population was 4320. By this time the parish, which is crossed by the Cambridge Northern Bypass (A14), included the Cambridge Science Park, a major superstore, the Children's Hospice, and a Country Park created on old gravel pits.

Oakington and Westwick

Oakington and Westwick combined now make a medium sized parish of 883 hectares. This includes areas previously in Histon added in 1953, when Oakington was officially combined with Westwick, and in Longstanton, added in 1985 when the boundary was straightened to the railway line. The village itself is situated where a greensand ridge crosses a tongue of gravel and alluvium that projects from Histon, following the Beck Brook. North and south of this ridge the soil is mainly clay. The parish extends from the Cambridge-Godmanchester Roman road, which is about 15m above sea level and forms the south-western parish boundary, to a medieval route known as the King's Highway, later Rampton Drift. This is about 14m above sea level and forms Westwick's north-eastern boundary. The two villages are lower lying at about 10m, and the extreme north of Westwick near to the fen-edge is about 6m, but otherwise there is little height variation within the parishes. Oakington Brook flows from near the Cambridge-Godmanchester road, along the southern side of the village and then joins Beck Brook, the boundary which separates Westwick from Oakington. Small fields were made near to the villages from the late 15th century, and the remaining open fields were enclosed following Awards made in 1834 in Oakington and 1856 in Westwick. In 1086 Oakington is *Hochintone*, or 'the farm of Hocca', and Westwick is *Westuuiche*, or 'west dairy farm', suggesting that it was originally settled from the east, i.e. from Cottenham.

Palaeolithic hand-axe from Oakington.

ARCHAEOLOGY OF SOUTH EAST CAMBRIDGESHIRE

Prehistoric and Roman

Two Palaeolithic hand-axes are known from Oakington and, during a programme of field-walking near the Cambridge-Godmanchester road, a dense scatter of Mesolithic waste flint flakes were found, suggesting there was a chipping-floor here. A few flint flakes of Mesolithic and Neolithic date were found in a prehistoric ditch when an Anglo-Saxon cemetery was excavated on the village recreation ground in 1994. Roman pottery, though with few fine wares, has been found several times in gardens and in neighbouring fields, sufficient to indicate occupation of some sort here from the 2nd to the 4th century, and occasional Roman coins have been reported from near the Roman road.

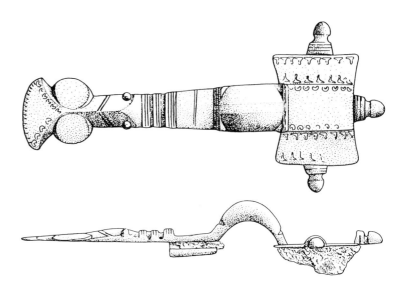

Anglo-Saxon brooch from Oakington, length 12cms.

Anglo-Saxon

An Early Anglo-Saxon cemetery has been known at Oakington since 1938, when four skeletons, one with a spear and shield and another with three glass beads, were found after a pasture field was ploughed for a nursery garden. This field later became the village recreation ground, and when holes were dug for new play equipment in 1993 more skeletons came to light, leading to an archaeological excavation. In all, 25 inhumations and one cremation in a pot were found, of whom five were men, seven were women and eleven were children. Other bodies were too fragmentary to tell their sex. The children were unusually well equipped with grave-goods, one young girl wearing a magnificent gilded brooch and another having two brooches and a long string of amber and coloured glass beads, though very small children only had pots which presumably held food. Women, both young and old, were well dressed, wearing bronze brooches, bead necklaces, buckles, pins and, in one case, an ivory-fitted bag holding three keys. There were only four men, and these were equipped plainly with weapons, having two shield-bosses and one spear, as well as knives and one pair of tweezers between them. This affluent population seems to have been well fed and was unusually tall. Three of the men were over 6ft, one being 6ft 3ins, and most of the women were between 5ft 6ins and 5ft 8ins.

A gilded Anglo-Saxon brooch from Oakington.

Recording an Anglo-Saxon grave at Oakington.

Many of the skeletons showed that they were related to each other, and even in a normally well-built Anglo-Saxon population these families must have stood out for their size.

Medieval

The largest manor in Oakington belonged to the Abbot of Crowland from Saxon times, and it was farmed by the monks along with their estates in Cottenham and Dry Drayton. Their manor house was opposite the church at Manor Farm. It is known

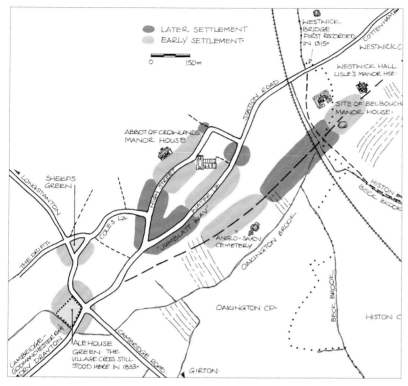

LATER SETTLEMENT
EARLY SETTLEMENT·

0   150m

WESTWICK BRIDGE FIRST RECORDED IN 1315·

WESTWICK C

WESTWICK HALL LISLE'S MANOR HSE·

STATION ROAD

SITE OF BELBOUCH MANOR HOUSE·

ABBOT OF CROWLANDS MANOR HOUSE

WATER LA.

HIGH STREET

COTTENHAM

SHEEPS GREEN

LONGSTANTON

COLES LA.

THE DRIFT

JUMBLATT WAY

ANGLO-SAXON CEMETERY

OAKINGTON BROOK

HISTON BECK BROOK

BECK BROOK

OAKINGTON CP.

HISTON C

ALEHOUSE GREEN. THE VILLAGE CROSS STILL STOOD HERE IN 1833·

CAMBRIDGE-GODMANCHESTER RD. ELY DRAYTON

CAMBRIDGE ROAD

GIRTON·

to have been surrounded by a wall, and in the 14th century it had a hall, chamber and kitchen. The estate sent much of its grain crop, some-times with pigs and poultry, to Crowland by water, via its manor in Cottenham.

The largest estate in Westwick was Lisles, which was held by Picot in 1086. In the 17th century the lord of the manor was resident in the hamlet and a large house stood here at that time, its site being re-used in the 19th century for Westwick Hall. Another significant manor was Belbouches, which had belonged to Ely before the Conquest. The Belbouche family held it from the late 12th to the 15th century, and their manor house stood between Westwick Hall Farm and Beck Brook, where there are also earth-works that may be part of the medieval village.

Village Development

Oakington's principal early settle-ment was around the church at the north end of the village, lying on a route known in the Middle Ages as Jumblatt Way which ran from the Cambridge-Godmanchester road to the fens. Other medieval centres that may be equally early in origin were located at the south end of the village, where Jumblatt Way was crossed by a major route from Girton to Longstanton, around a village green at the crossroads, later known as Alehouse Green, and at Sheep's Green, where the road to Longstanton left Church Lane.

Pottery of approximately 11th century date found in a ditch during excavation of the Anglo-Saxon cemetery on the south side of the street suggest that a Saxon settle-ment covered a considerable area at this end of Oakington. The Abbot's manor house and the church, where a priest was recorded in Domesday Book, were also in use at this time. The main road through the village was probably Water Lane and there were crofts along both sides of this of which traces can still be discerned as low platforms in pasture, particular-ly at the northern end. At one stage

there was also a track parallel to Water Lane to the south, running past further house-sites. In medieval times the road that looped round to the manor house became more important. There was housing along both sides of this, and traces of more hollow-ways have been noted to the north.

Oakington was quite a large village early in the Middle Ages, with 55 villagers counted in 1086 and nearly 100 tenants in 1279. This figure was maintained up to the mid 14th century, but the Black Death is known to have had a very serious effect on the village, half of the Abbot's tenants dying at this time for example, and in the later 14th century many holdings were empty and only 174 people paid the poll tax. The population stayed modest in the next few centuries, with 43 households in the 16th and 57 in the 17th centuries. By 1801 there were still only 285 inhabitants. This figure grew to 610 in 1851 and then fell before rising again slowly in the early 20th century and more rapidly after 1960. The hamlet of Westwick had only 4 villagers recorded in 1086, but grew to at least 20 households by 1279. After this it fell to 5 households in the late 18th century. In the 19th century the number of residents rose to 80, but there were very few houses in the 20th century. In 1996 the combined population of the two settlements was 1390.

Over

Over is a large parish of 1507 hectares, ideally placed on the immediate fen-edge where the settlement could make full use of fen and upland environments from prehistoric times onwards. The village itself is on a patch of gravel about 15m above sea level. To the south the land, which in this area is mostly clay, rises to about 20m near the Cambridge-Godmanchester Roman road, the southern parish boundary. North of the village there are rich but low-lying alluvial soils up to 1.5m deep, overlying clay and gravels which outcrop on the eastern side, near Willingham. This alluvium was formed by flooding of the River Ouse from Roman times and has therefore covered and protected archaeological traces of earlier land-use. The land is below 5m and much of it was marshy fen that was liable to flood, and so was used as common pasture throughout the Middle Ages. In the north-west of the parish was Willingham Mere, which was not drained until the 19th century. A long stretch of the north-eastern parish boundary is the River Ouse, flanked by a broad band of Ouse Fen that was not ploughed until Enclosure. Much of the boundary with Willingham was not determined until the 17th century as the common land had previously been shared between them. Some areas of fen were enclosed as distinctively regular fields after the first attempts at drainage of the fens in 1628, and the open arable fields to the south of the village were enclosed along with Ouse Fen after an Award was made in 1837. In 1086 Over was Ouere, or 'the bank of the river'.

Prehistoric

On a small ridge of sand and gravel in the north of Ouse Fen a Mesolithic site that probably extends underneath the surrounding alluvium is exposed, with large numbers of flint flakes, fire-cracked stones and bone. This ridge was also used in Neolithic, Bronze Age and Iron Age times. A short distance to the west,

Neolithic pottery and flint flakes were found when ditches were being dug. Important settlement evidence was found during recent investigations of a field near the river where one of the Bronze Age barrows discussed below was located. There were several scatters of Neolithic flint tools and waste flakes, and also groups of pits which contained decorated pottery. Many parts of the site, whose highest parts were only 3m above sea level, seem to have been occupied in short episodes throughout prehistory, from Mesolithic to late Bronze Age times. Worked flints occur in gardens in the village, but otherwise there have been few finds of this date despite an intensive programme of field-walking which has located several other important sites.

During the Bronze Age, about 1500-1000 BC, the fen-edges became significantly wetter and the low-lying area between the present village and the slow and shifting course of the Ouse turned into marshland. The large freshwater lake of Willingham Mere, still visible as an area of pale soil due to the amount of shells it contains, began to form at this time. Interesting sites identified during field-walking were at least eleven Bronze Age round barrows near the river which were blanketed by later alluvium and so remained hidden.

The fields they lie in were first ploughed after Enclosure in the mid 19th century, and by the mid 20th century they were recognised as mounds standing slightly above surrounding soil, though constantly shaved by plough action. One of these barrows and the surrounding fields were examined in 1996. The mound, which was made of turf capped with gravel from its encircling ditch, still stood 80cms high and was 35m in diameter. Around it were ditched fields and droveways from farmsteads that used the site later in the Bronze Age, and at least one round house. This house was set within a ditched enclosure, and was found with pits, ditches and gullies, and the domestic rubbish that accumulated in them.

By the Iron Age there was a great deal of settlement in the parish, using areas of exposed gravel that later became Roman farmsteads. Scatters of Iron Age pottery and occupation debris have been found on these Roman sites, and at least two Iron Age coins are known from the parish.

Roman

On gravel soils in the east of Over, and extending into Willingham, there are crop marks of Roman fields and droveways leading down to the fen. Amongst these, scatters of pottery have been found in localised

Over barrow field from the air.

areas, so there must have been some farmsteads amongst the fields. Further to the south there are other scatters of occupation debris which in two places include remains of kilns and their waste products. Excavations on one of these sites showed that heavy storage jars were being made here in the late 1st and early 2nd centuries. Another of these southern sites had tile and plaster on the field surface, indicating there was at least one substantial building set a comfortable distance back from the fen-edge. Roman material is sometimes found in gardens in the village, especially those close to the church, and two skeletons found in this area may also be Roman.

Medieval

The principal manor was bequeathed in a will in 986, and was held by Ramsey Abbey from 1044 until the dissolution of the monasteries. Its manor house probably stood south of the church on the road to Swavesey. A slight mound at Berry Close may be its site.

Village Development

The village lies on two routes from Cambridge, one of them running around the fens via Histon, Rampton and Willingham, and another via Girton, Oakington and Longstanton. These routes joined with local roads from the fields in the south-west and the fens in the north-east, and used the old river bank, Ouse Fen Bank, to cross the fens north of Over on the way to Earith. The road also ran west to Over Cote where there was a ferry across to the St. Ives road at Needingworth. In the Middle Ages, Over enjoyed a position on a route between the important markets in Cambridge and St. Ives. Other roads went to Swavesey and Longstanton, and there were drove roads to the fens which can still be seen as hollow-ways. Settlements grew up at the junctions of these routes at Church End, Over End and Fen End. However, the village pattern of Over is confused by the efforts of Ramsey Abbey to lay out a regularly-shaped settlement around their church and

Over church, drawn in about 1810.

market and the lode they built to give access to both of these from the fens. This reorganisation probably dates to late Saxon times. There may have been some organic growth around road junctions, although much of the overall pattern we see today presumably dates to later in the medieval period.

Church End included the manor house of the Abbot of Ramsey and a magnificent church standing at the junction of three routes and overlooking the adjacent fens. John Layer described the church in the 17th century as 'very large, beautiful and well built of freestone', and William Cole in the 18th century also called it 'very faire and very beautiful'. The market place was in a rectangle near the Rectory and church, now used for car-parking, where there was also a guildhall. Houses were built along all the three roads in the Middle Ages, and to the east they probably spread all the way to Fen End, more than half a mile away. The separate settlement of Over End is a mile south of the church, and was arranged around a large square green. This green was fiercely defended in 1856 when the lord of the manor tried to enclose it and the villagers burnt his fences overnight.

The medieval economy owed much of its prosperity to use of the fens. There were six fisheries on

Willingham Mere in addition to those on the Ouse, and eels were particularly abundant. Rushes and reeds, cut on a four-year rotation, were a valuable crop. Grazing of cattle and sheep became the most important fenland activity in the Middle Ages, and pasture was valued at twice as much per acre as arable land. Winter flooding only added to its value as it enriched the grass. By the early 17th century there were 1300 cattle and 1000 sheep on one manor, and butter and cheese was supplied to Cambridge in quantity. Much of this grazing was controlled by 134 villagers. Another product of Over was woad, which was grown in the parish from the 10th century and in the Middle Ages was marketed in Swavesey, from where it was sent to the market in St. Ives, the only centre apart from Winchester licensed to export the dye. Teazles, used for dressing wool, were another of Over's unusual crops. In the 16th century orchards played a significant part in the economy and became more important in later years, especially when rail transport opened up markets in the Midlands and the North.

Over's size and natural advantages enabled it to support a large population from the Middle Ages onwards. In 1086 there were 35 villagers counted, quite a modest figure that grew to at least 140 tenants, perhaps 700 people, by 1279. In 1377 there were still 378 poll tax payers, and a slightly increased population was maintained over the next centuries. The size of the population was apparently little affected by the 17th century drainage of its fens, for in the 16th century there were already 124 families that were taxed, the highest figure in South Cambridgeshire. In the 17th century there were 134 families, comparable to Waterbeach and its neighbours Swavesey and Willingham but by now much outstripped by Cottenham. In the 18th century the failures of fenland drainage as the fen soils shrank became apparent and the village was less prosperous, with the population temporarily falling. In 1801 there was a total of

689 people. Introduction of steam power to help drainage was a great benefit to Over, and in 1830, before the changes Enclosure brought, William Cobbett approved of agriculture here and its 'fat sheep and fat oxen'. The population grew fast in the early 19th century, to over 1200 in 1851, when Over was described as 'large and scattered', and its soil was said to be 'rich and produces valuable crops'. It afterwards fell to about 900, and then stayed steady until the 1960s and '70s, when new housing estates were built. By 1996 the population was 2510.

Pampisford

Pampisford is a small parish of 650 hectares, lying mostly on chalk but with strips of gravel near the Cam on the extreme western edge and around Bourn Bridge in the north-east corner. Parish boundaries include short stretches of the Cam in the west, the Granta in the north and the straight line of the A11, a Roman (and earlier) road on the east. A major route of the Icknield Way, now mostly the A505, runs through the parish and was once the central street in the village, which is itself set well away from the river. The only stream in the parish rises in Dickman's Grove and flows to the north of the village and into the Cam. Most of the parish is about 25m above sea level, but near the border with Essex in the south-east there is a steep rise to 50m. Pampisford's open fields were enclosed following an Award made in 1801. Its name in Domesday Book was *Pampesuuorde*, or 'Pampa's enclosure', and it was usually known by variations of Pamsworth until the 17th century, when the ford element was introduced.

Prehistoric

Apart from a few prehistoric flint tools found near the river, little was known about prehistoric settlement in Pampisford until examination of a site at Bourn Bridge, where gravel was due to be quarried for dualling the A11 in 1994, revealed a mass of archaeological features. The oldest artefact found was a Palaeolithic hand-axe, and there was also a Mesolithic axe and a scatter of tiny flint flakes. In the Neolithic period the site was occupied sporadically and pits were dug in which burnt and waste flints, bone, decorated pottery, and charcoal were left. In the Bronze Age there were again short periods of occupation on the site, and also two burials and an interesting funerary monument. The burials were cremations in pits, one of which was surrounded by a small and shallow but broad ring-ditch, just under 10m in diameter, with a partial circle of pits outside the ring and settings for posts within the ditch itself. The central cremation pit had also held a post.

Roman

Small scatters of Roman pottery are found on sites all around the parish, and there are crop marks of ditched enclosures both north and south of the village. To the south-west of the village, on the route of the Icknield Way that runs through the later village centre, there is Roman building material from at least two houses and also a small cremation cemetery, with one fragmentary and two complete pots of 2nd or 3rd century date. During the Bourn Bridge excavations (above) Roman field ditches and a droveway were found, but no other settlement.

Anglo-Saxon

Within the abandoned Roman field system at Bourn Bridge seven sunken-floored huts of early Anglo-Saxon date were excavated and were found to contain large quantities of bone, pottery and daub. The huts each had a post at either end, and one had a clay and stone-lined hearth. Bones found in the huts included roe deer, hare and water fowl as well as the more usual farm animals. The amount of debris suggested that the huts were back-filled with disused rubbish heaps. During construction work on the A11 near to this site more artefacts were collected, including two brooches and a wrist-clasp of the 6th century, which may possibly indicate a small cemetery near the settlement.

One of Cambridgeshire's four defensive dykes, Brent Ditch, crosses the eastern side of Pampisford,

Excavation through Brent Ditch in 1992.

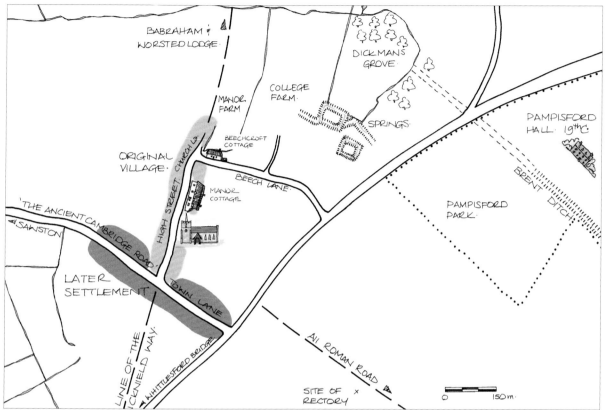

running from the springs in Dickman's Grove across high ground and two routes of the Icknield Way until it reaches the boulder clay plateau in Great Abington. Most of this dyke was levelled at the time of Enclosure, but a shallow ditch and very slight bank can still be seen in the trees of the park around Pampisford Hall. The site of the ditch in an area close to the A11 was excavated before this road was dualled, and was shown to be nearly 3m deep with the flat bottom and steep sides typical of all the Cambridgeshire dykes. Interestingly, at the bottom of the ditch were four Roman coins and a fragment of Iron Age human bone, finds that indicate an earlier ditch on the same alignment.

Medieval

Pampisford has two closely adjoining rectangular moated sites at the north end of the village, fed by the springs in Dickman's Grove. It is not known why two such sites should be needed, or whether they were both used at the same time. They were part of the main estate in the parish, which was given to Ely by Brihtnoth in 991, as were so many manors in Cambridgeshire, just before his death at the Battle of Maldon. However, the Bishop granted the manor to a lay landholder, Walter of Pampisford, and in the 14th century it passed to the Colville family, who held it until it was sold in 1584.

Village Development

The village grew along a single route of the Icknield Way, now Church Lane and High Street, spread between Manor Farm to the north and the Rectory to the south. The church, which is notable for the 12th century figures carved on the tympanum above the south door, was in the middle of the village. The road now effectively ends at Beechcroft Cottage, but once continued north to Babraham and Worsted Lodge until the 19th century. Its southern end had once run on to join the modern A505 and to cross the Cam at Whittlesford Bridge. The present A505 is also a branch of the Icknield Way which divides north-east of the village, both roads eventually meeting as one main Romanised route. By the 16th century it was presumably the main through-route, for people at that time left money in their wills for loads of stones to repair it. As

Beechcroft Cottage, at the end of the old route to Worsted Lodge.

71

12th century carved figures forming a tympanum above the south door of Pampisford church.

the route through the centre of the village became less important, settlement shifted south to the junction of Town Lane and the High Street, leaving Manor Farm, Manor Cottage and a very few houses at the northern end. From the 19th century the road to Sawston became the principal area of settlement. A large area in the north of the village was used as the parkland setting for Pampisford Hall, a large Victorian house described in 1851 as 'a handsome mansion, beautifully situated on an eminence, and surrounded by fine rural scenery'. A conifer arboretum was established in the mid 19th century which has been renewed and is still a renowned feature of Pampisford's landscape. The Parker Hamond family who built the Hall were the first resident lords of the manor since the 15th century and were responsible for supporting new institutions in the village.

Pampisford was fairly small in 1086, with 25 villagers recorded. The population stayed modest, with about 64 tenants, some 320 people, in 1279, and 109 poll tax payers in 1377. There were less than 40 families in the 16th, 17th and 18th centuries, and in 1801 there were still only 202 people in 46 households. In 1859 the population rose to a peak of 359, some of whom were employed in the industries of the neighbouring village of Sawston, though even then the village was described as 'small and rural', and was 'almost entirely composed of poor people'. Afterwards, this figure fell by about a hundred. It was rising by the mid 20th century, but growth has been very restricted, and in 1996 was still only 350.

Manor Cottage.

Rampton

Rampton is a small parish of 550 hectares, including some fields that were added from Willingham in 1981, lying mainly on clay. There are small patches of gravel at the west end of the village, and peat overlies the clay in Hempsals Fen and Iram's Fen in the northern extremity of the parish, providing good grazing until they were ploughed in the 20th century. Most of the parish is just above the area liable to flood, with the village itself on a plateau about 7m above sea level. The parish, which lies on the edge of the fens, is crossed from north to south by the road from Cambridge to Ely via the Aldreth Causeway known as the King's Highway, a major route until the 17th century when a shorter road was opened. The track was finally closed at Enclosure. From east to west the road from Cottenham to Willingham runs through the centre of the village and forms its High Street. Parish boundaries include Westwick Brook, which flows into the Ouse, and also tracks and field boundaries. Longstanton border was moved to follow the railway line in 1985. None of these boundaries appear to be ancient. Those with Willingham may have been fixed when the villages were divided, for it is likely that Rampton was originally part of that much larger parish, and its name in 1086, *Ramtona*, or 'Ram's Farm', indicates a subsidiary settlement. Some land in Rampton's open fields was being fenced in the 17th century, and there were hedged closes in the 18th century. The remainder was enclosed following an Award made in 1852.

Prehistoric, Roman and Anglo-Saxon

Very little early settlement is known in this area of damp low-lying clay soils, despite quite intensive programmes of field-work. Two Neolithic axes were found at the west end of the village, and in Hempsal's Fen in the north there is one enclosure and a few finds of Roman date. An early 20th century description of Rampton by its rector, C H Evelyn

Giants Hill in 1955. The D-shaped ditch was dug by the Home Guard during World War II.

White, claims that 'Large quantities of Roman pottery... had been found in fragmentary form in and around Rampton'. The church itself was probably built in Saxon times, for fragments of at least five decoratively carved grave-covers and part of a cross-shaft were found in it during restoration work, and have been built into the east end of the church.

Medieval

The principal archaeological monument in Rampton is Giants Hill, the site of a castle that was almost certainly built by royal command during the period in the mid 12th century known as the Anarchy, when Stephen and Matilda fought for the crown for eighteen years and barons were free to fight for whichever contestant offered more, or could just engage in their own battles. One of the most powerful of the barons was Geoffrey de Mandeville, an Essex lord who captured the Isle of Ely, from where it was easy to raid the countryside around the fen-edge. Stephen ordered a ring of castles be built to contain him, of which Burwell, Giants Hill and perhaps Swavesey Castle and Caxton Moats are surviving examples. While Burwell was being built, de

Mandeville attacked it and was mortally wounded by an arrow. His rebellion collapsed when he died, and Burwell and Rampton were never finished. The rectangular platform surrounded by a wide not-quite-complete moat, with mounds of earth outside that were intended for the interior, is an excellent example of an unfinished fortification of this period, and has been opened to the public by the County Council. Extending from below the earthen dumps are the low rectangular mounds of houses that were deserted or were deliberately cleared when the castle was built, and the field between the church and castle contains more earthworks of the very early village.

The manor that included most of the parish was held by Ely before the Conquest, but was then effectively taken over by Sheriff Picot. In the 13th century it was granted to the de Lisle family who often lived in the village, probably in a manor house on the castle site, where they were licensed to have a chapel in 1344 and later. Remains of this house were noted by Evelyn-White, and foundations have been found during excavation of trenches by the Home Guard and by local children. The

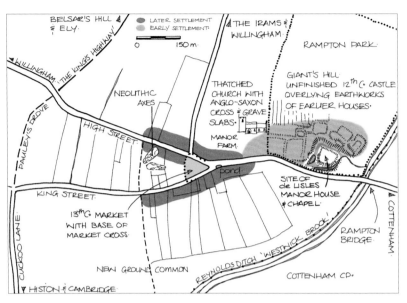

inhabitants, although when the County Council bought land after World War I and let it to small-holders, there were some incomers to the village. Growth was still very slow until the 1960s, after which the population grew to 420 in 1996.

Sawston

Sawston is quite a small parish of 770 hectares, lying on chalk soils to the east of the road that runs through the centre of the village, with gravels and alluvium on the west side, where the parish adjoins an older route of the Cam. The land is fairly level, rising to 25m above sea level in the village and other points in the east, and falling as low as 20m near the Cam, which forms its long western boundary. Most of the northern boundary is the Granta, and a stream, field-boundaries and tracks make up the remaining borders. Though the village is set on higher land away from the Cam, this river has had a dominant effect on developments in the parish. Suitable river crossings at four different locations led to scattered early settlements on significant long-distance routes, and one of the Anglo-Saxon watermills that used this river was developed in the 17th century as a paper mill, leading to the industrial development of the village. There were also many streams and water-filled ditches, especially in the north of the parish, and these had to be regularly cleaned out or there was severe flooding. This was still a problem in the 20th century. In 1918 a whole row of clay-bat cottages in Mill Lane collapsed after being soaked with flood-water, and in 1943 Italian prisoners of war were used to clear ditches on Deal Moor. Closes were being made around the village

land between the castle and the church was made into a park, and village houses were probably moved at this time. In the late 14th century Rampton was sold to Lord Scrope of Bolton, and this noble family held it until the late 16th century, leasing out the manor house. The old manor house was allowed to fall down, and a new one was built on higher ground on the site of the later Manor Farm.

Village Development

The earliest settlement was east of the church, spreading along the High Street to Giants Hill, and low mounds and hollow-ways in a pasture field indicate the houses and a street that ran from the church to the castle mound. Part of the settlement was moved when the castle was built, and the rest may have been deliberately moved to make the village closer to the King's Highway by the lord of the manor, Robert de Lisle. He was granted a market and fair in the late 13th century, and created the triangular green, around which most of the village lies and where the base of the village cross still stands, to accommodate them. This market was not successful. Any remaining houses would probably have been moved when a park was made around the de Lisles' home.

The houses along the two roads, one of which goes to Willingham and the other to Longstanton, were set in long, curving pieces of land that look as if they have been taken from open fields. Later houses were built on the south side of the High Street, on land that was previously part of the village green.

Rampton remained one of the smallest fen-edge parishes, with 19 villagers recorded in 1086 and a maximum of 37 families in the 17th century, until 1801, when there were 162 people in 35 households. The population rose to a peak of only 250 in 1871, the village being described twenty years earlier as consisting of 'the manor house (an ancient building with two wings), and a few cottages', virtually the whole population being labourers. In the early 20th century there were again only 180

The village green at Rampton.

and common land was being illegally enclosed in the Middle Ages, and an Award made in 1811 led to the official Enclosure of the remainder. Sawston was *Salsitone*, or 'Salse's Farm' in Domesday Book.

Prehistoric and Roman

A Neolithic flint axe was found south of the village, and many flint tools, including blades, scrapers and the waste cores left over from tool-production occur near where the old vicarage stood, by one of the ancient routes through the parish. At least ten ring-ditches that were once Bronze Age barrows are grouped around the northernmost of Sawston's route-ways, and a hoard of bronze tools has been found in the parish. This Late Bronze Age hoard, consisting of three axes, two spears and several broken pieces, was typical of the sort of collection likely to be left by travelling smiths on the Icknield Way that were not collected again for some reason. Fragments or complete examples of three other Bronze Age axes have also been noted within the parish.

An Iron Age fort lies on a low promontory of chalk above the gravels of the Cam's floodplain, close to the river. It is about 8 hectares in extent and was once surrounded by a double bank and ditch, although now only slight traces of one bank can be seen. Much of the site has been damaged by industrial developments around Borough Mill and it has also been ploughed since medieval times.

Roman finds are very sparse in this parish. Scatters of pottery have been found at Dernford Farm, which later became one of Sawston's late Saxon settlements, and also near the river-crossing of the Granta to Stapleford. There are also some square enclosures on other ancient routes, near to Babraham.

Anglo-Saxon

One wealthy Anglo-Saxon burial site was found in 1816 when labourers were digging gravel from a local high-point known as Huckeridge Hill, on the road to Cambridge. The finds included a sword, shield-boss, a bronze bowl and snake's headed

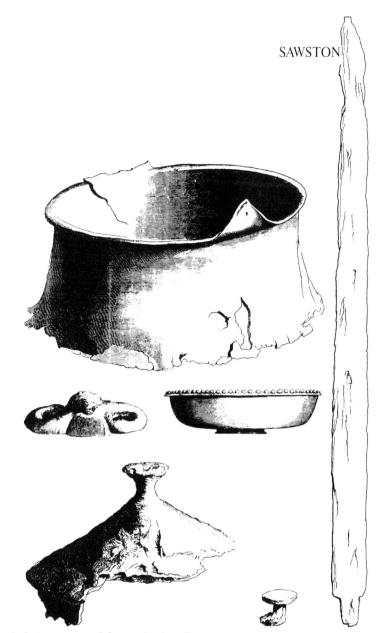

Anglo-Saxon grave goods from Huckeridge Hill.

buckle. Elsewhere in the parish a bronze object which may be a shield-ornament probably also belongs to the 6th century, and there is an iron key from the late Saxon period.

Middle Ages

The main manor in Sawston was Pyratts, a pre-Conquest estate that was held by the Pirot family from the 11th to the late 14th century. Their manor house was on one of the old route-ways, close to the church, and

in the 15th century was a large building that included a hall, 32 other rooms, a gatehouse, dovecote and many other outbuildings. T F Teversham, Sawston's historian, noted traces of this house in the grass during dry weather in the 1940s. This house was still habitable when the Huddlestone family inherited the estate by marriage, by which time it comprised almost all the village. The Huddlestones, who were usually resident in the village until the 20th century, were one of England's leading Catholic families after the change to Protestantism, and they were particularly prominent in the 16th and 17th centuries. They first became famous in 1553, when Queen Mary was protected here on the death of Edward VI, during her flight to Norfolk. When she escaped the next day, according to tradition on the same horse as John Huddlestone, either a Protestant mob or the Duke of Northumberland set light to the manor house. On her accession to the throne, Mary knighted Huddlestone and gave him other honours, and also granted him stone from the castle at Cambridge to help him rebuild Sawston Hall. The new Hall incorporated remains of the older building, and was built on a grander scale. A three-sided ornamental moat was one of the garden features that decorated it, perhaps from the 16th century, though it may be later than this. In the 19th century Sawston Hall was described as 'a large, handsome quadrangular building, surrounded with a park, gardens, and moat, and forms a picturesque and agreeable residence'.

Dale, or Deal, manor was originally part of Pyratt's manor, but was held separately from the 12th until the late 16th century. Its manor house stood within a rectangular moated site with a ditched extension

that lies in Deal Grove, now very overgrown and partly filled with rubbish. The house was recorded in 1279, and again in 1580, when it was leased with an orchard and dovecote, but had disappeared by the end of the 18th century

Huntingdon's manor, another pre-Conquest estate, also had a manor house in a moated site, and was recorded in 1279. This stood near the present Huntington's Farm, on an old route from Whittlesford. In 1580 'The Mannor Place' was described in detail as a tiled timber building with a courtyard, an orchard, a garden that contained a dovecote and fishponds, and a large yard surrounded by stables, a malthouse, granary and two barns. At the entrance to the yard was a timber gatehouse with a slate roof, which was probably replaced in the 19th century by the similar structure that stands there now.

Dernford was an area of early settlement in Sawston to the north of the village, on the northernmost of the ancient routes across the parish. It was recorded in 956 and had a population of 9 families in 1086. William I granted the manor to a French monastery, and it was sold by them in the 14th century, after which it was held with Pyratt's manor. A manor house stood here in 1279, but when a Survey of the Huddlestone's estate was made in 1580 it was stated

Sawston village cross, 1819.

that the house had burned down some years before, though there was still a mill and mill-house.

Village Development

As we have already seen, the early centres of activity in Sawston were on the four routes of the Icknield Way which were able to cross the Cam, running eastwards across Cambridgeshire. Like so many villages in south-west Cambridgeshire, Sawston seems to have started in Saxon times as scattered settlement along these routes, of which Dernford, Pyratt's manor (around the church), and Huntingdon's manor are recognisable throughout the Middle Ages, and the Borough, around Borough Mill, was also recorded on a few occasions. Later in the Middle Ages the north-south route through the village, on the road from Cambridge to Royston and London, became more important than the east-west routes, and the village cross marked the junction of this route and Church Lane. Settlements away from this, even the one around the church, tended to decay, and there was linear development along the present High Street. This layout was consolidated when one of

Sawston Hall in 1840.

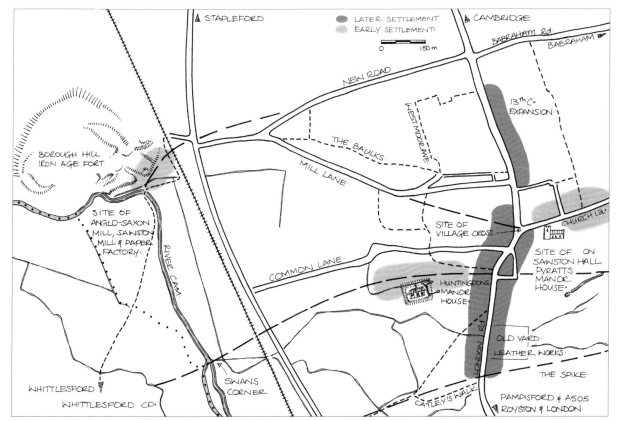

the lords of the manor, probably a Pirot in the 13th century, added a planned extension to the village over open fields at the northern end, on the Cambridge road.

A much later planned development, in the late 19th century, was the Spike, at the southern end of the village, built to house some of the workers of the notoriously harsh industrialist TS Evans. He owned the Old Yard leather works and had managed to quarrel with nearly everyone else in the village. Other industrialists who built houses for their employees were E Towgood, who owned the paper mill and built part of New Road, and J Crampton, owner of a mineral water factory and printing works, who built Crampton Terrace. His printing works was later sold to the Spicer family, and their factory has remained a thriving business. The village in the mid 19th century was already described as 'large and compact', and during that

century all the plots in the main part of the village were infilled.

In 1086 there were 38 villagers recorded in Sawston, and in 1279 this had risen to at least 125 households, perhaps 625 people. By the 16th century this had fallen, but Sawston was still a substantial village of 64 households, and there were 74 families recorded in 1664, several of whom were quite prosperous, as can be seen from some of the houses which survive from this period. Paper making and the leather industry began in Sawston in the 17th century, and with the growth of employment through industry the population rose to 466 in 1801. It continued to rise through the 19th century, to 1882 in 1891, thanks to the success of its leather, parchment and paper works. After that there were years of depression and decline, but in the 20th century there was revival of the old industries and creation of new ones, so the

population grew to 2130 just after World War II. Sawston was chosen as a Rural Growth Area, and both housing and industrial development were encouraged. Its good communications and facilities, including a Village College, made it an attractive area for commercial growth, and in 1996 it had expanded to a population of 7200, making it the largest village in South Cambridgeshire.

Shudy Camps

Shudy Camps is a medium sized parish of 950 hectares, lying mostly on high ground on chalky boulder clay, with its underlying chalk outcropping near the western edge of the parish. Its landscape is more typical of Suffolk, which it abuts, than of Cambridgeshire. Most of the parish is above 100m above sea level, the village itself being about 115m, and on the western edge a plateau rises to over 120m. Considerable woodland is recorded here in 1086 and in the Middle Ages, some of which lasted until the Dayrell family took over much of the parish in the 18th century and felled extensive areas. Part of the boundary with Suffolk follows a stream, but other parish boundaries are mostly field

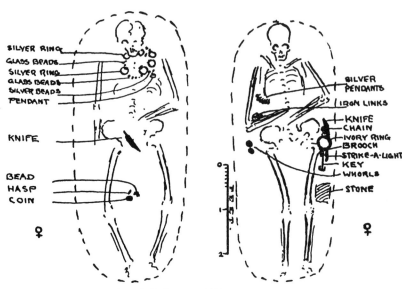

Anglo-Saxon graves excavated at Shudy Camps in 1933.

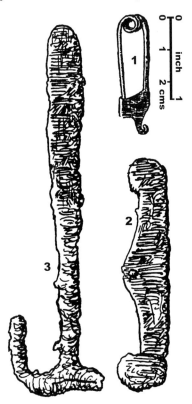

Anglo-Saxon artefacts found in graves at Shudy Camps: 1. Silver brooch, 2. Strike-a-light, 3. Iron key.

edges and seem to have been agreed at a late date, which is reflected in the confusion between the neighbouring parishes in Domesday Book. Parva was added to the village name of Camps by the 14th century, and variations on *Sude* seem to have been used from the 13th. The origin of this is not known, though the suggestion is that it means sheds, a derogatory comparison with its neighbour, *Castle* Camps.

Prehistoric and Roman

Early information about the parish is scarce. Two ring-ditches have been noted on chalk soils near the eastern border, and on the site of one of these there is evidence of Neolithic flint working, and an adjacent sub-rectangular enclosure. A round ditched mound on the western side of Shudy Camps Park has sometimes been described as a Bronze Age or a Roman barrow, and these are both possible suggestions, but it more closely resembles a medieval windmill mound. There are two references to Iron Age coins from the parish, and Roman coins were found near the Horseheath border. At Nosterfield End, in the south-west of the parish, was found a Roman cremation burial in a glass urn, accom-

panied by another small vessel, close to the route of a possible Roman road that joined the Cambridge-Colchester road in Horseheath.

Anglo-Saxon

A major Anglo-Saxon cemetery of 7th century date was excavated in Shudy Camps, near to the Bartlow border, in 1933. It lay on the slope of a chalk hill side, overlooking a stream, and contained at least 145 burials, 78 of whom were accompanied by grave-goods. Children, who made up about a third of the population represented, were often buried with a pot of food, a few beads or a knife. Men had few artefacts other than knives and buckles, and were not generally accompanied by their weapons, as they were in the earlier cemeteries. Of the three spears from Shudy Camps, one was found with a man, another with a woman (as part of a chatelaine set), and the other was with a child, and no shields were discovered. Two men, however, did have daggers in scabbards. The most interesting male skeleton was one who had a set of 56 gaming pieces and a dice. Some of the women had quite lavish jewellery. One necklace contained 27 beads of glass, silver wire and shell, with a

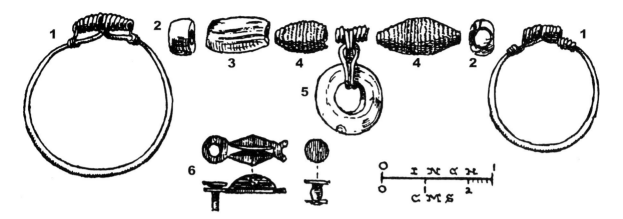

Artefacts from Anglo-Saxon graves at Shudy Camps: 1. Silver ring beads, 2. Glass beads, 3. Shell bead, 4. Silver beads, 5. Silver and glass pendant, 6. Bronze hasp and stud.

green glass bead in a silver sling, and the cemetery include 8 pendants made of gold or silver. Other grave-goods found with women included cowrie shells, amethyst beads, small wooden boxes, iron shears, chains made of iron loops, a silver brooch shaped like a large safety pin, spindle-whorls and one ivory bag-ring. One woman was buried in her iron-bound bed, an extraordinary custom that has also been found at Barrington and Cherry Hinton.

These burials date to a time that was at least notionally Christian, but it is obvious that, although styles of clothing and jewellery had changed from the 6th century, and the symbolism of men carrying weapons was no longer important, the ritual of burial in one's finest clothes and with the personal items normally carried in life was still thought important for a happy after-life.

Medieval

Medieval settlement in Shudy Camps was scattered across the parish in small clusters. These were mostly based around moated sites, of which the sites of at least seven are known. Very fragmentary remains of a moat at Lordship Farm, now lost, existed earlier in the 20th century, and were probably the site of the main manor house of Hanchetts, recorded in 1279. This manor was raided during the Barons War in

1264, when oats, beans, geese and capons were taken from Henry de Hanchet's house, and the vicar was captured and held to ransom. The most notorious holder of this manor was John Hanchach, the leader and 'chief insurgent' of the Peasants Revolt in Cambridgeshire. He was beheaded for his part in the fighting, but his family were not otherwise affected.

Another of the manors was held by Waltham Abbey, and their estate too was raided. This was known as Shardelowes, and was later split into two holdings. One manor house was at Shardelowes Farm, where a 16th century house still stands, although a moat which is shown on a 19th century map finally disappeared in the late 20th century. There are also fragments of two other moats at Mill Green, on the same road as Shardelowes Farm, and these perhaps represent other manor houses on this estate. Nosterfield manor was in the far eastern corner of the parish, close to the possible Roman road, and a small rectangular moat survived here until 1949. Nostresfeld, a name which recorded the Roman straet, was a separate settlement in Domesday Book and in the 12th century. Even closer to the County border is Barsey Farm, where there was an oval moat and a fish pond, both now filled in. This manor was bought by

William de Berardshay, who already held land in Nosterfield, in 1296.

Village Development

The numerous settlements of medieval Shudy Camps include small groups around the moated sites mentioned above, in addition to other hamlets that also occur in early documents. Around the church were a few houses, an area known as Rowhedge in the 16th century. A larger group on the village street, on which were centred the open fields of Shudy Camps, was called Newton in the 16th century, and so was presumably later than other centres despite its position in the parish. Its original form, before modern development, indicates that it had grown up on the verges of an old drove road. One important building on this street is 'Bramleys', a 13th century aisled hall. Northo, north-west of the village, is mentioned throughout the Middle Ages. This early pattern of settlement, which may partly reflect gradual clearance of woodland without any central parochial authority, has, to a large extent, survived into modern times.

Some important changes, how-ever, were made in the 18th century, after Hanchetts manor was acquired by Sir Marmaduke Dayrell. He and his successors built a small mansion in Shudy Camps Park, surrounding it with a 60 hectare park, which involved moving a road and houses. This family bought up much of the other land in the parish amidst considerable litigation and acrimony, but could not touch a large estate that was by that time based at Nosterfield End. That belonged to the Bridge family, who were able to withstand measures that the Dayrells took. William Cole, who was on friendly terms with both sides, describes how:

Mr. Bridge was of a quarrelsome disposition, and meeting with another of the same turn of mind in the same parish there was rarely in my time an assize where there was not a suit between Darell and Bridge, though the two parties were two very different sorts of men, Mr. Darrell being a thorough well bred gentleman and the other as little of it as any man knew.

In 1086 there were a minimum of 22 villagers in Shudy Camps, but this is probably an underestimate because of the exceptionally complicated landownership there. In 1279 a considerable population of 85 tenants can be counted, but the Black Death is known to have left many properties empty, and in 1377 this figure was down to 141 poll tax payers. The population stayed low, with no more than 30 families in the 16th century, and then rose a little in the 17th century and again in the 18th century, with a period of decline in between. In 1801 there were 349 people in total, and this grew only to 418 in 1831, after which it declined. There was a small amount of growth after 1950, but the parish is an area where development is restricted, and in 1996 the population was still only 300.

Stapleford

Stapleford, a medium sized parish of 740 hectares, rises from low-lying gravel and alluvial soils about 20m above sea level near the river, where the village lies, up a chalk slope to Wandlebury and Worsted Street Roman road, which are above 70m. Here a large area of open heathland was used for sheep grazing until the 19th century. Some has been converted back to grass for golf courses and flower-rich fields for amenity purposes. The parish is bounded on the south by the River Granta, on the north by Worsted Street, and by field edges to the east and west. A stream that feeds a moated site runs through the centre of the village, and there are still several ponds. The parish is crossed from north-east to south-west by a route of the Icknield Way which forded the Granta south of the village and then ran past Wandlebury to join Worsted Street. From at least the Middle Ages, and probably much earlier, there was also an east-west route close to the river from Great Shelford to Babraham, and this crossed the Icknield Way route in the village. Open fields in Stapleford were enclosed following an Award made in 1814, and about 300 hectares of sheep walks on the chalk downs were

then ploughed. Stapleford is *Stapleforde* in Domesday Book, meaning 'ford marked by a post'.

Prehistoric
The chalk downs were well used in prehistoric times, and flint artefacts have been regularly found during field-walking. One Mesolithic axe has been found, and Neolithic flints, including arrowheads, axes, blades, scrapers and innumerable waste flakes are especially common. Recent field-work between Wandlebury and Worsted Street identified a Mesolithic flint-working site. On the south side of the modern A1307 opposite to Wandlebury aerial photographs indicate a large circular monument, about 200m in diameter, made up of short lengths of ditch. It is possible that this is a causewayed camp, used for various social and ceremonial functions in the Neolithic period, but there have been no investigations so far to verify this. A few worked flints also occur within the village, close to the river.

A mound called Wormwood Hill, near Wandlebury, has been described as a Bronze Age barrow, but, like Copley Hill in Babraham it is almost certainly a natural chalk knoll. However, two mounds called the Twopenny Loaves, which are near Worsted Street and were mapped in the 19th century, do appear to have

Excavation of the Roman road near Wandlebury, in 1991.

been burial mounds, though the description of skeletons found in them in the 18th century sounds more like Anglo-Saxon re-use than original inhumations.

Stapleford's principal monument is the Iron Age hill fort of Wandlebury, which commands one of the highest points on the chalk ridge, giving control over access to Cambridge, the Icknield Way and the river valley. Excavations in the 1950s showed that the defences were built at two different times. Firstly, in the 3rd century BC, a steep-sided ditch with a bank revetted with timber to give a vertical face topped with a protective palisade was constructed around the perimeter, giving a precisely circular enclosure. Then, when trouble threatened again in the 1st century AD, the fortifications were rebuilt with a double bank and ditch. In 1995-6 there were further excavations, outside and inside the fortifications. These showed that there was abundant evidence for occupation around the fort, suggesting that there was an early undefended settlement here before the banks and ditches were constructed. Numerous pits dated to the early and late Iron Age date, and postholes showed that a variety of buildings stood here. An original entrance on the eastern side was located,

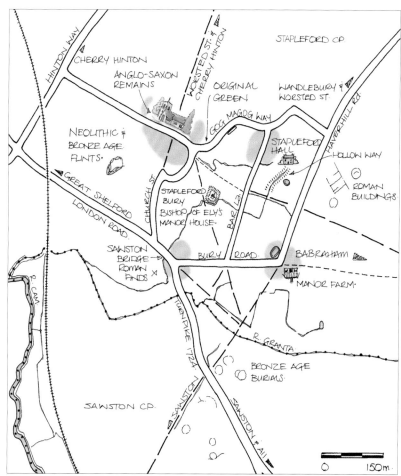

Excavating Iron Age skeletons, probably battle victims, at Wandlebury in 1976.

which, as Cole says, was used until the Godolphins stopped the road through the fort in the 18th century. Also outside the fort, skeletons have been found on several occasions. One particular group, evidently thrown together into a shallow grave, may have been battle victims as they were all adult males and at least one had been wounded in the face by a sword-cut. Wandlebury was extensively landscaped as an ornamental feature in the park that surrounded Lord Godolphin's shooting box and stables in the 18th century. The banks were levelled and one ditch was filled in, the other being altered to suit the new garden's design.

Roman

Wandlebury and its surrounding areas were occupied again in Roman times, particularly in the 2nd century, and the Roman road, which probably uses an older route though its construction phases are entirely Roman, passes very close by it. In the south of the parish there are rectangular enclosures that are probably Roman in date, one of which surrounds the timber posts of an aisled building. It is possible that this is the site referred to in a 19th century account of a hypocaust being turned up during ploughing.

Anglo-Saxon

Six skeletons found in one of the Twopenny Loaves near Worsted Street in the 18th century were described as lying parallel to each other in a north-south direction, with another lying east-west. From the other mound a sword and fragments

Lord Godolphin's house at Wandlebury, 1801.

of human bone were turned up, and it seems likely that these finds represent Anglo-Saxon re-use of earlier burial mounds. Wandlebury itself was used as an official meeting-place in late Saxon times, as it was in the Middle Ages, and was known as Wendlesbiri in the 10th century. At this time land in the parish, previously held by the Crown, was given to Ramsey and Ely abbeys, and by 1066 Ely had acquired the whole parish. Within Stapleford church is a cross base and the carved fragment of its shaft, both late Saxon in date. Ely farmed this estate in hand, with a manor house, Stapleford Bury, in the centre of the village, where there is still a medieval moated site.

Village Development

Stapleford grew up at a crossing-place where several routes met, quite possibly with original centres on all of these routes. After fording the Cam, the Icknield Way from Dernford Farm in Sawston split into tracks which led to Wandlebury and to Cherry Hinton, and these were crossed by the riverside route from Great Shelford to Babraham. At junctions of these routes, particularly near the church, at Manor (or Bury) Farm, Stapleford Hall, and the road-crossing north of Sawston Bridge, settlements may have existed from late Saxon times. In the north-western corner of the village was a large green, of which only a small triangle and a pond survived post-

Enclosure development, with the church and a tithe barn to the west and the principal manor, Stapleford Bury, in a moated site to the south. This belonged to the bishop of Ely from the Saxon period until 1870, although it was leased out from the late 16th century and the Church authorities had lost most of their control by this time. The moat still has a wide wet ditch and is used as a nature reserve within the grounds of the primary school. It is in the centre of the medieval village, but land around it was enclosed in small fields for the home farm, and so remained undeveloped. Later medieval settlement was principally along the roads around the edge of the village and, in later years, along the roads to Great Shelford and Cambridge. The London Road was turnpiked in 1724, by which time it was its southern branch to Sawston that was important, though the Babraham branch was open until Enclosure and was later kept as a footpath.

The population of Stapleford stayed quite low until the 20th century. In 1086 it was given as 20, and in 1377 there were 62 adults. In the 16th and 17th centuries there were generally less than 30 households, and there was only slow growth in the 18th century to a total population of 235 in 1801. This rose to a peak of 594 in 1871, and then fell before rising again in the 20th century. There was particularly rapid growth from the 1950s, largely due

to its proximity to Cambridge, though this expansion was later more controlled. In 1996 the population was 1720.

Wandlebury was used in the early Middle Ages as a place where legal cases could be heard, and it also attracted various magical tales. In 1211, for example, Wandlebiria is where a ghostly knight on horseback could be challenged, and the site, by then known as Gogmagog, was remembered in poetry for its mythical giant in the 16th century. Early in the 17th century John Layer describes 'a fort entrenched', where there was 'a high and mighty portrait-ure of a giant wch the schollars of Cambridge cut upon the Turf'. William Cole was taken through Wandlebury as a boy in the 1720s, when the road to Cambridge from Babraham ran through the fort, and he was shown 'the Figure of the Giant carved on the Turf'. It was these records which led to rather bizarre excavations in the 1950s, resulting in claims that there were Iron Age carvings representing a god and goddess here, although the features exposed have all been shown to be natural hollows.

James II built stables at Wandlebury in the 17th century, and when Celia Fiennes drove past the fort in 1697 she recorded in her diary: 'a great fortification or ruines of a Castle with great trenches one within another, and ...a long string of stables to keep the king's hunting horses'. In the 18th century Lord Godolphin built his mansion there and began the extensive landscaping works that changed the character of the fort. His mansion was demolish-ed in 1955, but the elaborate stable blocks and servants quarters can be seen, and beneath the arch is a monument to the Godolphin Arabian, who made fortunes for the family and was the ancestor of most modern racing horses. Wandlebury remained a family home until the late 19th century. In 1954 the build-ings and land within the fort were given to Cambridge Preservation Society, who now run it as a country park.

Stow cum Quy

Stow and Quy were small parishes which now have a combined area of 764 hectares. Each of the parishes lies above the fenland that surrounded them on three sides. The earliest site of Stow was at the end of a gravel ridge that rises to about 15m above sea level. Quy made use of the same gravel ridge near its church, which was at about 10m, and was also built on the underlying chalky soils which stretch towards Quy Hall, where the land is only about 5m. Much of the land in both parishes is very low lying and was fenland until it was drained in the 17th and 18th centuries. The two villages were combined into one parish by the late 13th century, and their boundaries mainly follow fens and watercourses. Their open fields were enclosed after an Award was made in 1840. Stow is *Stoua*, in 1086, meaning 'place' or, very probably 'holy place', and Quy is *Coeia*, or 'Cow Island'.

Prehistoric and Roman

Peat had not yet begun to form in the earlier prehistoric periods, and areas that later became fen were available for use. Several artefacts have been found from these areas, mostly representing casual losses by people using natural resources or even deliberate deposition of precious items in the marshy landscape for religious reasons, rather than being indications of permanent settlements. Two Mesolithic axes are known from Quy Fen, and another comes from the village of Quy. Four Neolithic axes have also been reported from the fen near Horningsea. In the fen to the north and east of the parish there were found two finely-flaked early Bronze Age flint daggers, and two spear-heads, a rapier and axe, all of bronze. Near to Stow church, on the higher land that was chosen again for settlement in the medieval period, there was a scatter of worked flints, indicating at least temporary habitation in this location. There are also two possible

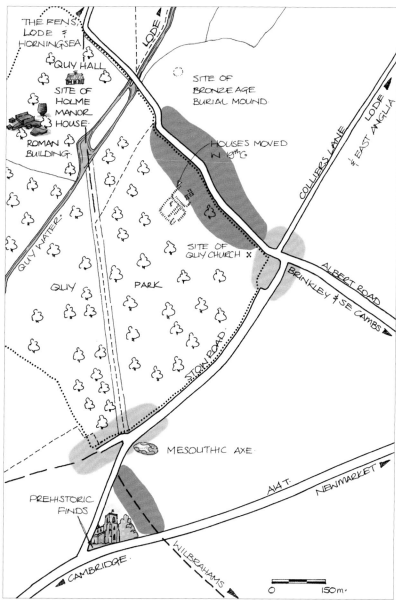

sites of Bronze Age burial mounds. One, immediately on the fen-edge to the north of the Park, was still 30cms high in the 1950s, and another, only recognisable as a large ring-ditch, lies just east of the Hall.

At Quy Hall, very near to the edge of the fen, quantities of Roman pottery and tiles from roofs and heating systems have been found which must have originated from a large building nearby.

Medieval

Quy's parish church stood near the crossroads in an area that is now part of Quy Park. It fell out of use during the Middle Ages, and a few fragments of carved stone in the grounds of Quy Hall are all that remains of it now, although until World War II some of its walling stood about a metre high. Stow's church was remote from its village, set on a high point that it visible for miles in all directions, possibly using the ancient 'holy place' for which the village is named.

Quy Hall was built on the site of the manor of Holme, at the extreme north end of the village. In the mid 15th century, when it was owned by the Ansty family who also held land in Fen Ditton and Teversham, only a hall and parlour were recorded here, but by the 1530s it had been enlarged to include three chambers, a chapel and a gatehouse which blew down in about 1535. In the late 16th century there began a series of rebuildings, but a late 15th century roof was retained, and part of the house is still on a 16th century plan, though it was much altered in later years. From the late 18th century the Martin family was usually resident. The Hall became much grander and the Park was laid out, with a small area to the north of the Hall and an avenue that stretched to the Swaff-hams' road. After Enclosure, leases of the farmsteads south of the Hall were acquired, and the present large area of parkland was created from the open fields, which involved moving two farms and a cottage that appear on maps before that date. A formal garden with a pond and a ha-ha were also constructed at that time.

The main manor of Stow was known as Dengaynes. Before the Norman Conquest it belonged to Ramsey Abbey but was later taken by Picot, sheriff of Cambridge and was held by the Dengaynes from the beginning of the 13th century until its sale in the 16th century. The estate passed to Gonville and Caius College, who sold it to the County Council in 1914. The manor house stood near the church in the 14th century. It was never a significant residence for the owners of the manor, and was sold separately in 1534.

Village Development

Both villages originated on road crossings on a ridge of higher ground that stood above the fen. The road that runs through them was part of a long-distance Cambridge-East Anglia route before the present Cambridge-Newmarket road came into use some time in the Middle Ages, and the village of Stow lay along this route at a point where, later in the Middle Ages, it was crossed by a drove road running south-east to north-west from the Wilbrahams to the fens. The medieval village also had at least one street lined with houses extending to the Cambridge-Newmarket road. Quy lay along the long and ancient track from Brinkley and other south-east Cambridgeshire villages. In the 19th century this route still extended through the fen to Horningsea and the river crossing at Clayhithe, and it was in use as far as Quy Station until this was closed.

Quy Park was created in the 19th century and the old road to the south of it, which had become significant again as the way to Anglesey Abbey, became increasingly important. This led to more houses clustering around its junctions with the old routes.

Before Enclosure the northward route from Stow was effectively replaced by the long straight drive to Quy Hall, and after Enclosure its village street, previously a continuation of the drove road from the Wilbrahams, was moved to its present route east of the church. In Quy, all remains of the village were cleared from the Park in the 19th century.

The population of the two villages was about 20 in 1086, Quy probably being the principal place. In 1377, by which time the parishes were combined, there was a modest population of 148. In the 16th century 31 households paid tax, growing to 45 in the 17th century. In 1801 there was a total population of 235, which grew to a peak of 387 in 1881. In the mid 20th century there was a population of 530, but this fell, and in 1996 had been stable for a decade at 480.

The platform of the disused station at Quy.

Swavesey

Swavesey is a very large parish of 1600 hectares which lies on the edge of the fens, where the resources and communications of this position were used to build a thriving community during the Middle Ages. Most of the parish is on clay soil, but the older parts of the village around the church make use of two gravel islands, and much of the settlement is surrounded on three sides by alluvium that was wet and marshy from Saxon times until Enclosure in the 19th century. Even after the fens were drained some of these areas were often flooded. The highest points in the parish, nearly 20m above sea level, are on the Cambridge to God-manchester Roman road, which forms the southern boundary. From there the land falls gently to the village, which is about 10m at the southern end but rises to 15m on the gravel islands in the north. The surrounding fen is much lower, falling to about 4m. The northern parish boundary follows the River Ouse, and the boundary with Over is the old line of Swavesey drain. Field boundaries and drains separate Swavesey from Fen Drayton and Longstanton. Areas of higher fen near to the village were reclaimed in the Middle Ages, but drainage of most of the fens was not undertaken until the 17th century, and it was only at Enclosure, which followed an Award made in 1840, that enough drains were laid to enable alluvial soils to be ploughed. Swavesey's name in Domesday Book is *Suausheda*, translated as 'the Swabians' landing place', though the 'ey' ending, common in fen names, also means 'island'.

Prehistoric, Roman and Anglo-Saxon

The clay soils of much of the parish were not attractive for early settlement and, if the very low-lying areas were used in prehistoric times, the evidence has not so far come to light despite an extensive field-walking programme in recent years. At Black Horse Lane, on the island where gravel overlies the clay, how-

Earthworks of the Priory, next to Swavesey church.

ever, a late Iron Age settlement and industrial site has been found, with large amounts of pottery in ditches and pits, and kiln debris, suggesting pottery was made here in the early 1st century AD. Roman sites are also scarce in this parish, though small quantities of pottery have been found in the fens to the west of the village, and in Middle Fen, to the north, a small enclosure that survives as an upstanding earthwork may also belong to this period.

Late Anglo-Saxon pottery has been dug up in the churchyard, and the fabric of the unusually long nave of the church itself is also in late Saxon style. This church may have been a minster at this time, with a group of priests serving a wide area, the origin of the late 11th century priory. The Black Horse Lane excavations (above) also produced several large pits and ditches containing pottery of the 11th century, possibly belonging to the original late Saxon settlement. One of the ditches was thought by the excavators to have a defensive function. Later excavations to the west of Black Horse Lane confirm the presence of 10th and 11th century buildings in that area, although by the 13th century settlement had moved elsewhere.

Medieval

The manor of Swavesey was the administrative centre of a large

Cambridgeshire estate of lords who also held extensive estates elsewhere in England from Saxon times and who, after the Norman Conquest, had land in France as well. It was given to Count Alan of Brittany after the Conquest, and the church, probably already served by several priests, was an important part of this estate. It is possible that Count Alan simply converted this church into a priory, which he gave to a French abbey, with a prior appointed from France to rule the existing priests. This small priory, controlled from France until it was given to a priory in Coventry in the 14th century, was in existence in 1086. The monks used the nave of the parish church for their worship, while the villagers used an aisle, and they remained so poor that the priory was reckoned to be a net loss to its mother-house and there were no objections when it was given away. The number of monks is not known, but seems to have been very few, and at times the prior was almost alone. After the 14th century it was treated as a normal manor, paying its rents to Coventry and no longer maintaining monks at Swavesey.

Earthwork traces of banks and ditches in the pasture field north of the church include a semi-circular ditch which may date to its 11th century origins as a minster, and a canal that linked the church and priory to the Ouse. Stone from the priory was used in the 19th century for repairs to the church, and the rectory to the north of the church, of which the last traces disappeared in the early 19th century, contained medieval stonework, including two carved heads, that also originated in the priory.

Swavesey was farmed in hand and was used as a residence by its lords on an occasional basis. Roger de la Zouche was granted oak trees by the

Medieval carved head, photographed at the Rectory in 1934.

king to build himself a house at Swavesey in 1232. In the 14th century a chapel was built here, and repairs are recorded in the 15th century. The site was probably at Manor Farm, opposite the church, part of which is late medieval though it was much altered by Sir John Cutts, also owner of Childerley Hall, whose family held Swavesey manor in the 16th and 17th centuries.

At some stage early in the Middle Ages Swavesey had a castle. It consisted of a mound that has been heavily degraded by quarrying and erosion, and a low bank and ditch that were later incorporated in the town defences and surround a rect-angular area that, judging from traces of ridge and furrow visible until recent years, was laid out over

part of the open fields. The mound itself is sited at the beginning of a causeway that led into the fens, and it must have been intended to prevent access at that point. This location suggests that it may be one of the fortifications King Stephen ordered around the fen-edge during the civil war as protection against Geoffrey de Mandeville, which could explain its unfinished-looking appearance, or it could date to another period of threat such as the 13th century when corn was burnt and the church attacked by de la Zouche's enemies during the Barons War. Optimistic planning of a larger commercial area than was ever needed is another possibility, but lords of the manor seem to have deliberately kept villagers at a distance from this part of the village, so this seems unlikely. The banks may even just be flood-defences or enclosures for animals. However, there were many times in the Middle Ages when wealthy fen-edge manors might be vulnerable. The town-ditch, surrounding the southern gravel island, seems to have been constructed in the 13th century and was kept cleaned out until the late 15th century, on the evidence of excavations in 1984. This ditch would have helped protect the village from flooding, often a worry in this area, but it was also needed to encourage

payment of tolls by making sure traffic used controlled bridges.

Village Development

The original village used two separate patches of gravel at the northern end of the present settle-ment, where the higher ground abutted the fens, probably including the area chosen for use in the Iron Age as well as the extreme northern site where the church and manor house stand. Subsequent settlement by villagers was kept clear of the area occupied by the priory, manor house, church and castle, but it spread to fill the southern gravel island and also stretched for nearly two miles along the road to the south, except for areas kept open as greens and a market place. Apart from the two northern centres there were medieval settlements at Cow Fen Green, Gibralter Green, Thistle Green, Great Green and Boxworth End.

The huge population expansion that occurred in the 12th and 13th centuries as a result of the commercial developments described below may have been accommodated in planned expansions in areas such as Boxworth End, the west side of Great Green, and to the north of the town, and settlement could have

Swavesey manor house.

been almost continuous as far as Boxworth End. The magnificent 13th century farmhouse of Ryder's Farm, well outside the ditched settlement, is an example of wealth in the expanded village. Water transport and a suitable site for building docks was clearly crucial to the early settlers, and the availability of dry gravel soils safely above flood levels was also appreciated. This northern end was linked by road to the Cambridge-Godmanchester road using a ridge of slightly higher ground and a causeway that had to be built up in wetter areas. The causeway stopped to the north of the church, though a track, which was made into a new straight road after Enclosure, continued to Over. Other roads which have continued in use link Swavesey to Longstanton and, again using a causeway, to Fen Drayton. North of the village there was also a canal to the Ouse.

By the late 12th century Swavesey was a port, its profits belonging to the prior. Its economic potential was developed further after 1244 when the lord of Swavesey manor and many other estates, Alan de la Zouche, was given the right to hold a market and fair which flourished for several centuries. He was able to carry out major changes to the town, laying out a precisely straight High Street with a large market place on its eastern side, and he replaced the prior's hythe with a dock at the end of this market place, blocking off the old Back Lane. The dock was the place of trade for neighbouring parishes such as Over and Longstanton, and was still being used, for example for importing coal, until Enclosure, when a new dock was built north of the railway line. This had a short life, as a railway station was opened in 1847. Plots around this market were held by burgesses, free citizens normally engaged in trade rather than being tied to the land like most villagers. The presence of these merchants and the importance of trade, as well as the overall size of the settlement, define Swavesey as a town in the Middle Ages.

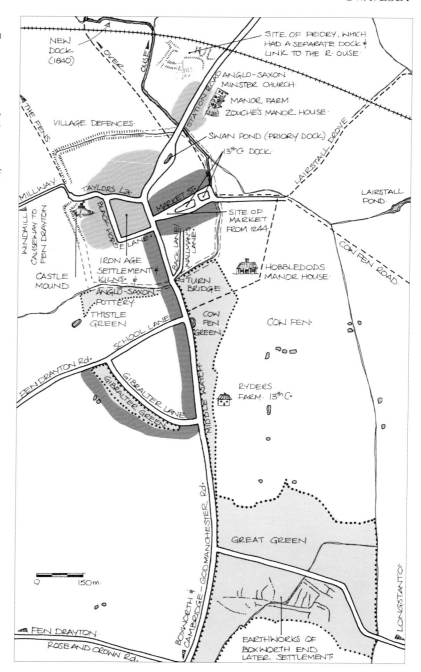

Fenland produce was also important to Swavesey's economy. In 1086 nearly 4000 eels were accounted for annually, the prior had his own fishery and fisherman's house on the Ouse and was given tithes from another. Other fisheries are mentioned during the Middle Ages.

Swavesey's population in 1086 was already very high at 65, and there were at least 200 tenants holding land in 1279. This represents about 1000 people, the highest figure

Swavesey from the air in 1976, showing the line of the medieval town ditch.

in South Cambridgeshire. After-wards it dropped drastically, to 379 poll tax payers, about 493 people, in 1377, and to 78 families in the 16th century. From the 17th century there was growth, to 831 in 1801 and a peak of 1385 in 1851, and it then fell until the 1920s. Growth began in the 1950s, and increased after 1965 when it was accepted that Swavesey was a village where growth should be permitted because of its facilities, which included a Village College. In the late 1980s the village was identified as a Rural Growth Settlement, and the population rose to 2020 in 1996.

Teversham

Teversham is a very small parish of 484 hectares, mostly lying on chalk but overlain by a patch of gravel around the Cambridge-Newmarket road. The land is mainly about 10m above sea level, but it slopes down to an area of fen in the north-east corner of the parish and to Caudle Ditch, its boundary with Fulbourn, in the south-east, and rises to about 18m near Cambridge Airport in the north-west. Other boundaries include Wilbraham River and the

zigzag line of field edges between the parish and Cherry Hinton. There were many closes around the village, and the open fields were enclosed following an Award made in 1815. The parish was *Teuuresham* in 1086, but the meaning of this is not known.

Prehistoric

Bronze Age flint artefacts, including an arrowhead, were found in small quantities in the south of Teversham during investigations of a Roman building, and a bronze axe from Manor Farm was probably dumped with sugar beet brought in from the same field. Two ring-ditches which show on aerial photographs also belong in this period. The gravel area around Newmarket Road attracted settlement in the Iron Age, and a large site of the middle Iron Age that was excavated in Fen

Ditton also extended into the north of Teversham parish.

Roman

A villa near Fulbourn Drift is visible on aerial photographs as small, regular rectangular enclosures and buildings adjacent to a ditched track and larger enclosures. Excavations revealed several periods of occupation from the 2nd to the 4th century, though it was principally used in the 3rd century. Tesserae from a mosaic of three colours were found here, and there was painted plaster from the decorated walls. Foundations of the villa were made of flints with rubble infill, into which were set vertical square-cut timbers. Dressed stones were used at the right angles of the walls, and the roof was tiled. Outside the building was a

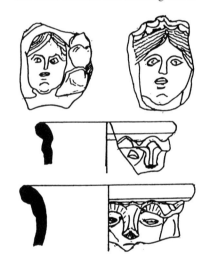

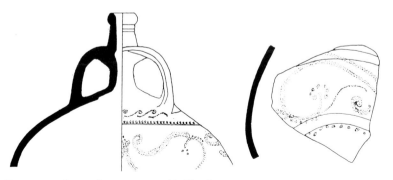

Roman pots and pottery fragments excavated in Teversham.

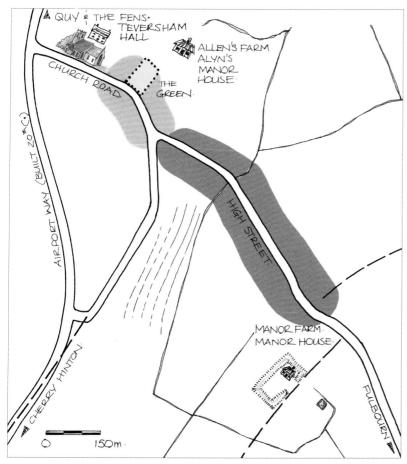

large cobbled yard. Some of the pits contained dumps of clay that would have been suitable for pottery manufacture, and there were stoke-holes that may indicate kilns.

Undated ditches found beneath ridge and furrow close to the village centre may also date to Roman times, and in the north-west of the parish, close to the airfield, a very late Roman settlement, mostly dating later than 350 AD, was discovered when a new road was built in 1997. Walls of its timber-framed buildings were found, and tesserae and tiles on the site suggest another substantial building nearby.

Medieval

Land in Teversham was given to Ely by Brihtnoth in 991, and a church, which is one of only three in South Cambridgeshire to be mention-ed in Domesday Book, seems to have been built on this estate. Ely's manor house may have stood near the church on the site of Teversham Hall, which was rebuilt in the 19th century. This estate, known as the manor of Bassingbourn and Warburton, was given to Gonville and Caius College by Thomas Willows, a Cambridge glove-maker, in 1503. Alyn's manor, whose house stood to the west of the church at Allen's Farm, was also a pre-Conquest estate, and was given to Alan of Brittany before 1086. It later passed to St. Thomas' Hospital. Another manor, known as Dengaines after the family who held it in the 14th century, had a manor house at the far end of the High Street, now called Manor Farm. This is now a much-altered 17th century farmhouse surrounded on three sides by a moat. It probably marks the southward extent of the village in the Middle Ages. The fourth arm of this rectangular moat was infilled in the 19th century. This manor also passed to Gonville and Caius in the 16th century. Boundary ditches and pottery dating from the 11th to the 15th century excavated near the street frontage in the centre of the village suggests that medieval settle-ment stretched for much of the way between the church and Manor Farm.

Village Development

Teversham's church and village green lie near the junction where drove roads from Fulbourn and Cherry Hinton met before they led to the fens, and the original village was presumably located in this area. Later development was along the Fulbourn drove road possibly with well-spaced crofts extending as far as Manor Farm, although at times of contraction some plots would have been empty.

The population was at least 26 in 1086, but by the 16th century had shrunk to only 15 households. In 1664 there were 25 families, but Teversham is only a short distance from Cambridge where there were serious outbreaks of Plague in 1666. This spread to the village, where it caused the deaths of 32 people in the small community that year. In 1801 there was a total of 154 people. The highest population it reached in the 19th century was 276, in 1881. Shortly after this Corney Chalk, a London celebrity and friend of Oscar Wilde, who grew up at Manor Farm, published a description of Teversham at this time:

Picture to yourself, ...some farm build-ings and cottages, the Rose and Crown, ...then more cottages, a farm with orchard containing an excellent mulberry tree, the blacksmiths; then a cottage, then Hancock's the carpenter's house; and then in some meadows or, as we call them, closes, our house! A farmhouse covered with ivy, with pretty lawns and gardens, and a moat running round three-quarters of the grounds'.

In the 20th century Teversham's position near Cambridge led to substantial growth. There were 570 people living here in 1951, and by 1996 it had been allowed to grow to 2620, some of this growth being accommodated on estates near Cherry Hinton.

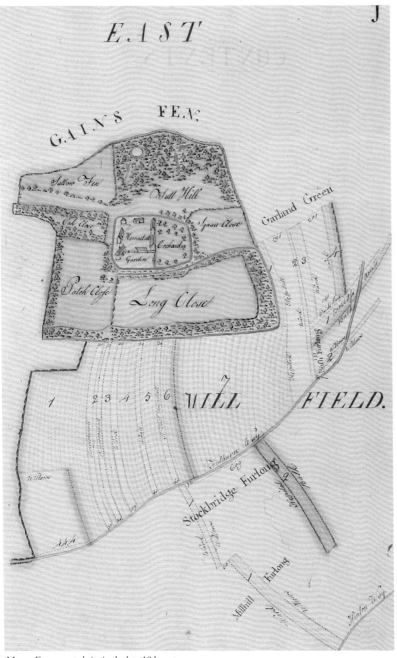

Manor Farm moated site in the late 18th century.

Waterbeach

Waterbeach is an extremely large parish of 2320 hectares, lying very close to the edge of the fens which have determined its development and economy since prehistoric times. The village itself is on an area of slightly higher ground, about 6m above sea level, where clay soils are exposed, and this 'upland' stretches most of the way north from the village towards the monastic settlement at Denny. In the area south of the village there are gravel soils, but to the north of Denny, and on the entire eastern side of the parish, the land falls to less than 1m, and the underlying clay and gravels were covered in peat until at least the 17th century. In some places this peat, which began to form in Neolithic times, is still over 2m deep.

Waterbeach's boundaries include the River Cam, the Car Dyke, Akeman Street Roman road and a 13th century drainage ditch, dug when the common land of Stretham and Waterbeach was divided. The uplands were cultivated as open fields until Enclosure in 1818, and in the 17th century an area of fen in the north of the parish was drained. However, most of the parish was fen pasture until the 19th century and, despite the problems caused by frequent flooding, this was the landscape that allowed the large peasant population of Waterbeach to enjoy the characteristic opportunities of which John Layer so disapproved in his description of the village as: *'a Fenn towne of large extent ...having large and spacious commons and marish grounds as most of the fen towns have, which is the cause that a multitude of poor and meane people do resort and inhabit there, to live an easy and idle life, by Fishing, Fowling and Feeding of Cattle'.*

Waterbeach was known just as *Beche*, or 'Stream' in 1086, with 'Water' added from the 13th century to differentiate it from Landbeach.

Prehistoric

Areas of fen that lay over gravel soils and which were reasonably dry before peat began to form had many uses in prehistory, although they rarely attracted permanent settlements. Gathering of natural resources and felling trees for use elsewhere, for example, were common. This has led to discovery of at least thirteen Neolithic stone axes and other tools scattered in the north and east of the parish, though investigation of their sites has revealed no indications of even short-lived habitation. During the Bronze Age burial sites were constructed at Denny, where a low mound has been identified, and at two sites to the north where there are single ring-ditches. Artefacts of bronze known from Waterbeach are three rapiers and an axe, found in the 19th century. There is also a 19th century account of a bow that was made of a single highly-polished horn, over 1m long, being found in the fens between Waterbeach and Ely. Only two possible occupation sites of Neolithic or Bronze Age date have been discovered so far: one area close to Denny, where a scatter of fire-cracked flints, presumably used while cooking, was identified during recent field-work, and another near Car Dyke where there were single Neolithic and Bronze Age sherds and a sparse scatter of worked flints. In the Iron Age traces of evidence for occupation, mostly pottery, have been found on some of the upland sites that were used intensively in Roman times. This is certainly the case at Stony Hills, a peninsula to the north of Denny, which seems to be an important centre throughout the Iron Age, a time when the fens were becoming much wetter and organisation of its resources was changing.

Roman

In contrast to earlier prehistoric land-use Roman occupation was dense and was entirely concentrated on the upland areas, as by that time most of the peat fens of the parish had developed. Most of it is found in four distinct sites which lie in a row on the west side of the parish, from south of Car Dyke to the earthworks adjacent to Akeman Street at Chittering. Common features on these sites are large numbers of querns and huge quantities of pottery that range from the 2nd to the 4th century in date, but there are few signs of luxury goods or other indications of wealth, with the possible exception of some hypocaust tiles noted on Waterbeach aerodrome. Crop processing on an industrial scale, for exporting via Car Dyke, as well as pottery manufacture, are seen as significant activities on these distinctive sites.

The best-preserved section of Car Dyke in Cambridgeshire runs across the south of Waterbeach, where it is still a flat-bottomed ditch about 20m wide and 2m deep. Banks along both sides were visible until the 1920s, but have now been ploughed away. Excavations show that it was originally nearly 3m deep, and that part of it was recut in the 17th century during the large-scale drainage of the fens, when its function as a catchwater drain was again appreciated. One discovery in the Dyke was a dug-out canoe, found in the 1930s, which from its description would seem to be prehistoric, but, as it was found preserved in the Roman canal, it presumably has to belong to this period. Sites close to it include three small kilns, part of the extensive industrial complex on the opposite side of the river in Horningsea, and finds include dumps of potsherds. In 1997 excavations through the Dyke, close to where it broadened into a hythe on the Cam, uncovered waterlogged remains in the ditch, including a hob-nail boot and a wooden harpoon. A kiln beside it which had most of its kiln-furniture intact. Buildings nearby were raised on sill-beams, and were probably connected with industrial processes here. Crop marks in adjoining fields include trackways with small paddocks ranged along them.

About a mile north of Car Dyke, on the airfield, is a Roman site

Excavations to the base of Car Dyke in 1994 and (above) of a Roman pottery kiln and Car Dyke in 1997.

Denny Abbey in 1730.

where late Roman pottery and coins were found with hypocaust tiles and nails, suggesting more elaborate buildings than those normally noted in the fens. Further north again, around the site later used for Denny Abbey, extensive Roman remains have been found in field-walking and excavations. Earthworks that were first ploughed in the 1950s and now survive as crop marks reveal ditch systems, with droves and paddocks that would be well suited for stock-rearing. Just to the north of these is a large occupation site at Stony Hills, and here the evidence is more domestic in character, with quantities of animal bone, oyster shells, tile, burnt stone and other refuse on the field surface. Around Chittering, which is close to Akeman Street and to the edge of the fens, upstanding earthworks of the northernmost of these groups of ditched fields survive.

Anglo-Saxon

Immediately south of Car Dyke, on sites that were still in use late in the Roman period, there appears to be an unusually extensive area of early Anglo-Saxon settlement. Three huts were located on the lip of the Dyke, at the Lodge, in the 1920s, and proved to be the customary sunken-floored type. Parts of the wattle walls were found, and there were piles of rubbish which included decorated pottery, five beads of red,

yellow and green glass, bone and bronze needles, a brooch fragment, three spindle-whorls, a perforated boar's tusk and fragments of ivory bag-rings, in addition to some Roman items which may have been deliberately collected. In the middle of one of the floors was buried a large dog.

Less than half a mile to the south, also close to Car Dyke although not adjoining it, more areas of early Anglo-Saxon have been located by field-work. Investigations with small trenches have shown that these areas contain buildings both of the sunken-floored type, like those at the Lodge, and also long halls, possibly similar to the ones excavated at Hinxton.

Further finds of similar date found near this site, at the point where the Car Dyke entered the Cam, are probably the remains of a disturbed cemetery. Parts of two swords were dredged up, together with a shield-boss, spear and human skulls. Some years later a fragment of gilded bronze, part of either a pendant or brooch, was found in the same area.

Medieval

Denny Abbey is the principal medieval monument in Waterbeach, and is opened to the public by English Heritage. The site, which made use of the promontory of upland with fen on three sides where

the Romans had also settled, has a complicated history of religious use. The first church here, built in the 12th century, was given to the monks of Ely so that they could have some respite from their life in the main monastery. After a few years, perhaps to repay a debt, it was given to the Knights Templar, the religious and military order that was created in the early 12th century to defend the Holy Sepulchre in Jerusalem and to protect pilgrims travelling to Palestine. They also became known for academic learning that was eventually seen as witchcraft, as well as for immense wealth. They used

A priest's door at Denny, in 1780.

Denny from 1170 until the early 13th century, principally as a hospital for their elderly and sick monks. As the Order became rich, and was seen as over powerful by the king because it was subject only to the pope, suspicions of magic were used as an excuse to suppress it, imprison its members and seize its assets. The buildings at Denny then stood empty for some years before being taken over by the Countess of Pembroke. She converted them into a convent suitable for nuns, the Franciscan Poor Clares, who had been living at Waterbeach abbey, where they suffered frequent flooding and were perhaps thought to be too close to the village. The Countess also spent much time here, and special quarters were built for her.

The nuns stayed at Denny until the dissolution of the monasteries. After this, some of the religious buildings were demolished, and others were either converted to agricultural uses (the refectory, for example, became a barn), or were encased in brick so that they appeared to be a farmhouse. These buildings have now been restored sufficiently for their different architectural periods to be understood. Other parts of the site have been excavated, revealing the ground plan of the 12th century church, monastic gardens, and some of the Templar and Franciscan buildings. Features discovered during this work included a lead-working pit, water cistern and several wells. Finds from the site include many decorative tiles and fragments of window glass.

The site where the nuns originally lived is now a pasture field to the south of the church containing the earthwork remains of the religious house and its outbuildings. Small-scale excavations have traced the wall-footings of buildings whose stone-work was later dug out for road repairs and other uses. Some of the decorative tiles and wall-plaster that were used in the nunnery were found for, although it was short lived, it had been built to quite a luxurious standard for nuns, many of whom were of noble birth and had previously lived in France. Despite

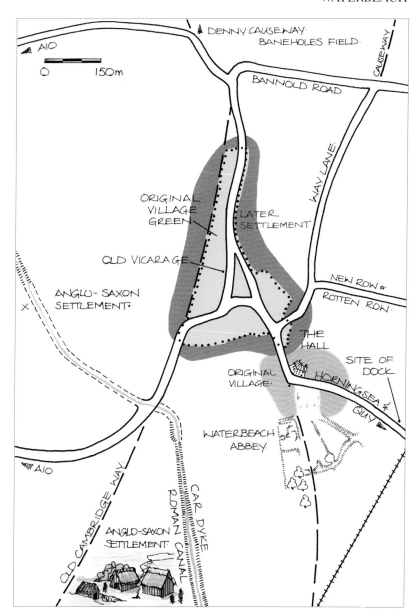

the drawbacks of this site, the nuns were very reluctant to move to Denny, and force was eventually used to get them there.

Village Development

The original village was probably at the southern end of the present settlement, on an area of relatively high land near to the church and accessible to the old docks which gave access to the Cam. The manor

house was presumably on the site of the later abbey, for the whole manor was given to found the religious site by their owner, Denise de Munchensy. From the church, the road ran south through the abbey site to the river, and north through the present airfield, using causeways to cross wet areas before reaching Denny. This route probably became more important when the Templars developed Denny in the 12th century. The road

18th century gravestone in Waterbeach church-yard.

from Cambridge entered the village in a direct north-easterly direction, between the present road and Car Dyke, meeting the north-south route in the north of the village. The two roads thus formed two long sides of a large triangle, which became Waterbeach's well-used village green. In the 17th century there was considerable encroachment on this green. The cottages built upon it had long curving plots behind them which had been taken from the open fields. One of the buildings here was the vicarage where William Cole lived miserably as a curate. He complained about how he had 'a long, dirty walk of a quarter of a mile or more' to the church, and was driven out of his damp, smoky parlour in wet and windy weather. Eventually, 'not being a water rat', he moved to a drier house at Milton, though he continued as Water-beach's curate. His diaries include graphic descriptions of the effect of wet weather in this parish in the 18th century, when villagers would be called out in the night to raise the banks at Denny and Chittering. Later roads were built towards the fens as the number of poor villagers increased. One of these was New

Road, where single room 'chambers' were built on very small plots in the 14th century and were maintained so badly the road was renamed Rotten Row in the 16th century. There was also a settlement at Clayhithe, where the ferry crossed the Cam. The site of an old dock near Clayhithe is now a caravan park.

The population in 1086 was already substantial, with 47 villagers. In 1279 it was very large, with at least 180 tenants, about 900 people. By 1377 this had fallen to 205 tax-payers, and in the 16th and 17th centuries there were 70 and 106 families respectively. This figure fell in the 18th century, but by 1801 there were 553 inhabitants. The population rose quickly through the 19th century, despite considerable emigration to Australia and America, and reached a peak of 1619 in 1871. It then fell a little, but recovered in the 20th century. Creation of an airfield and barracks in World War II increased the population to 2630 after the War, and since then there have been several new areas of development, resulting in a population of 4680 in 1996.

Weston Colville

Weston Colville is a large parish of 1300 hectares, lying mainly in rolling chalky boulder clay country-side, with underlying chalk emerging to the west of the village. Like several parishes in this area, Weston Colville is long and narrow, stretching from high ground on the Suffolk border, over 120m above sea level, for about 6 miles across a plateau which reaches 130m, then dropping to 30m at its western end. A stream that flows across the parish, through the

hamlet of Weston Green, is one of the headwaters of the Stour, and elsewhere in the parish water is retained in ponds and moats on the heavy clay soil. Settlement in Weston Colville, again like other parishes near the Suffolk border, is made up of scattered farmsteads and hamlets, of which the principal ones are Church End and Weston Green. This reflects a Saxon pattern of settlement which did not change significantly in medieval or modern times. Weston Colville still had considerable wooded areas in 1086, and some of these survive to the east of the village, despite much felling that was record-ed in the 17th century. The parish contained several small fields that had been created from forests during the Middle Ages, and the open fields were enclosed at an early date follow-ing an Award made in 1778, a time when virtually all the parish was in one ownership. Weston Colville was *Westone*, or 'West Farm', in Domes-day Book, 'Coleville' being added in the 13th century, after the family of that name.

Prehistoric, Roman and Anglo-Saxon

Two Neolithic axes and one Bronze Age example have been found in the parish, and there is one possible Bronze Age ring-ditch near the western boundary. Elsewhere, Mesolithic and later worked flints have occurred during excavations between the village and the West Wratting boundary, and along the road to Weston Green, and small quantities of Neolithic or early Bronze Age pottery were found in ditches during excavations immediate-ly east of the church. Similarly, small quantities of Roman pottery were noted in disturbed areas of soil in Weston Green and during excava-tions within Weston Colville moat. A dense scatter of early Anglo-Saxon pottery on a local high point mid-way between the villages of Weston Colville and West Wratting may mean there was a settlement here before either of the villages were created. In the late 10th century a manor at Weston was given to Ely abbey, and it was probably at about this time that numerous other sites

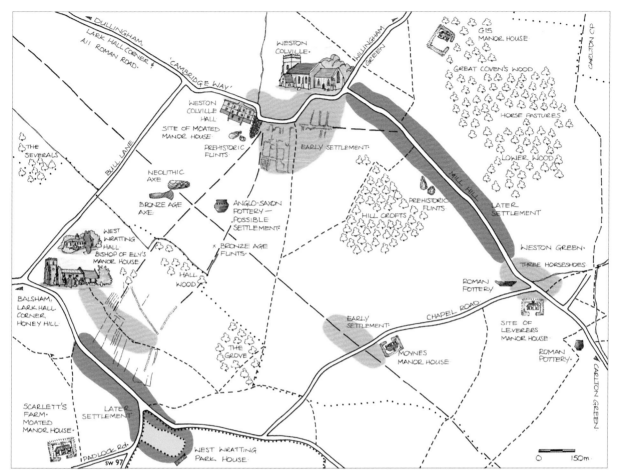

that we can recognise later in the Middle Ages were founded.

Medieval

The principal manor was Colvilles, which probably had a manor house west of the church where there are fragmentary traces of a moat near the present Weston Colville Hall. Though it had been given to Ely, this estate was in the hands of the powerful de Warenne family soon after the Norman Conquest, and it continued to be owned by wealthy absentee land-owners, including the Colvilles. In the 15th century the estate was united by marriage with the other Weston Colville manors of Moynes and Leverers, and it is possible that at this time a new house was built in the substantial square moat, now

covered in trees, to the north-east of the village, where pottery of the 14th and 15th centuries, in addition to Roman remains, has been excavated. If so, it was a short-lived move, for by the 16th century, this site stood empty, and Weston Colville Hall, described in the mid 19th century as 'an ancient looking mansion with a good north front', was built on the old manor site, which had come to be used as a farmhouse. William Cole dined here with Col. Hall, whose wife shared his antiquarian interests. He complained of 'the shortest and poorest dinner I ever sat down to for company. Cards. I lost'.

Another Anglo-Saxon manor that stood well away from the village was known as Moynes, after the Great Shelford family who held it in the

late 13th and early 14th centuries. The manor house was in a moat, of which fragments remain, that is still known as Mincs Farm, on the road leading south-west from Weston Green. This estate was impoverished by problems caused when its owner, John Bunting, was imprisoned for robbery in the 14th century. The site of its manor house, like that of Leverers manor, which probably stood at Pound Farm in the centre of Weston Green, continued to be used for later farmhouses.

Village Development

Weston Colville is notable for the scattered nature of its settlement and for its density of population, which was unusually high for this part of Cambridgeshire until the problems of the 14th century, after which there

Weston Colville church, 1997.

West Wickham

was a steep decline. There was no real recovery until the 19th century, and by then there was no impetus to develop a nucleated village, and the scattered distribution of settlement was maintained. One centre was around the church, which lies on a north-west to south-east road known in the Middle Ages as the Cambridge Way, at the point where it crossed one of the many winding north-east to south-west routes linking the hamlets and farmsteads that are typical of this landscape. Weston Green is in a similar location, and Carlton Green and Mines Farm are also on minor crossroads. Both archaeological and historical evidence show that there were early medieval settlements, probably Saxon in origin, at each of these locations.

The archaeological evidence of pottery scatters, earthworks and excavated remains show that the settlement around the church was once much larger than the few houses that stand there now, but by 1612, when a map was made of the parish there were only six houses here. At this time there were about eighteen houses at Weston Green, which has remained the larger hamlet, and there were several more houses than there are at present along the road from Weston Colville to Weston Green. Scatters of pottery also confirm that the medieval village filled most of the gap between what appears now to be two hamlets.

In 1086 there was already a substantial population of 40 villagers, about 200 people, recorded in Weston Colville, and this would have increased considerably in the next two centuries. The effects of famine and the Black Death, however, were severe in this part of Cambridge-shire, and in 1377 the population was recorded as 119, or about 155 people. In the 16th century a maximum of 28 households were taxed, rising to 45 families in 1664 and a total popula-tion of 318 in 1801. In the 19th century this figure rose to 574 in 1851, at which time it was described as 'small and irregularly built', and it then fell again. It has risen since the 1960s, but in 1996 there were only 430 people living here, the majority of whom were in Weston Green, with others still spread throughout the extensive parish.

In the mid 19th century a villager from Weston Colville, J R Withers, became a poet, and one of his poems celebrates his boyhood in the parish, recalling the annual fair that was held at Weston Green:

Just down the road , beside the bowl-
ing green,
The weather-beaten sign-post still is
seen;
Here once a year at what was called a
fair -
Though horse was never bought nor
cow sold there -
Here met the village youth on pleasure
bent,
And the long-hoarded halfpence freely
spent....'

West Wickham, a large parish of 1184 hectares, lies mostly on chalky boulder clay, with a small area of the underlying chalk exposed near the western edge of the parish. It is on high ground, rising from about 80m above sea level in the west to 100m in the village and the hamlet of Streetly End, and then up to 130m on the Suffolk border. The parish is bounded by Worsted Street Roman road on the south and by field edges and former woodlands on the other sides. There was still much woodland here in medieval times, and woods mentioned in the Middle Ages, such as Leys Wood, Cadges Wood, Over Wood and Hare Wood, survive today. Medieval woodland around Yen Hall was cleared after Enclosure. Small streams which rise in this parish flow to the north, south, east and west, and there were previously many ponds and moats with standing water on the retentive clay soil. The medieval population was scattered around the parish, and some early settlements are still ham-lets or farmsteads. There were many closes around medieval settlements, especially on the eastern side where land was taken into cultivation dur-ing the medieval period. The rest of the open fields were enclosed follow-ing an Award made in 1822. West Wickham was *Wicheham* in 1086, possibly from the Latin *vicus*, indicating that the area was still recognisable as a Roman administrat-ive unit, which is supported by the archaeological evidence from the sites around Yen Hall. 'West' was added in the 13th century. The hamlet of Streetly End, close to Worsted Street, is *Stretlaie*, 'wood or clearing by the Roman road', in 1086.

Prehistoric and Roman
Prehistoric finds from West Wickham are scarce, with just one ring-ditch and occasional pieces of worked flint discovered at Yen Hall, but in the Roman period the parish was extensively settled, despite its

heavy clay soils. The main site was found in an area that was woodland in the Middle Ages. This was a villa or similar tiled building, dating from the 2nd to the 4th century, and near it were found areas of metal-working and artefacts such as brooches, buckles, plumb-bobs, a spoon, bracelet and coins. Many Roman coins were reported from West Wickham in the 19th century, and small scatters of finds such as pottery and coins are known throughout the parish. Some of these have been found near the church, some in Streetly End, close to a Roman site excavated in the parish of Horseheath, and others occur as single finds in remote locations.

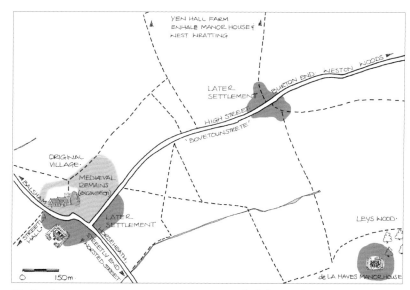

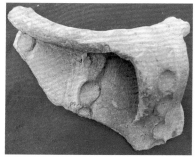

Late Saxon Thetford ware, excavated near West Wickham church.

Anglo-Saxon

Early Anglo-Saxon burials are known from objects found in the ploughsoil around the site of the ring-ditch mentioned above and close to the area of intensive Roman occupation. These include brooches, of which some fragments had been cremated, a 'girdle-hanger', shield-boss and decorated pieces of a cremation urn, showing that there was a cemetery here where both cremation and inhumation were practised. An adjacent site was Yen Hall, which is referred to in documents dating back to 974 as a manorial site and settlement, where large quantities of late Saxon pottery have been found. More pottery of this date has also been found near the church, so there must have been at least two established settlements well before the Norman Conquest.

Medieval

Enhale, or Yen Hall, the pre-Conquest estate, was given to the de Warennes after the Norman Conquest, and under them it was held by the de Rosey and then the Manners families. A manor house within the moat is recorded in 1315, and it was probably a residence for the lord of the manor at this time, for hunting rights were granted and his widow tried to keep it as a dower house after his death. In the 16th century it was sold to the Alingtons of Horseheath, who were acquiring most of West Wickham. The unusual

rounded shape of the moat suggests a possibility it could have originated at the time of the pre-Conquest manor.

A rectangular moat at Manor Farm, opposite the church, may have been the site of the manor house for Bernhams manor, which was created from part of another pre-Conquest estate and which was originally held by Aubrey de Vere. The other part of this estate was given to the de la Hayes and may have been based on a manor house at Hill Farm, where there is a disturbed moated site near Leys Wood. Both these estates later

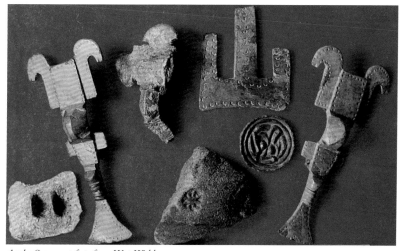

Anglo-Saxon artefacts from West Wickham.

passed to the Alingtons. A manor at Streetly was also in existence before 1066, when it was owned by the abbey of Ely. Its manor house, known as Streetly Hall, was recorded in the 13th century, and its park was noted in the late 14th century.

Village Development

As we have seen above, three manors were in existence before the Norman Conquest, in the north, south and centre of the parish. The population in 1086 was made up of ten families each at Yen Hall and Streetly, and thirteen in Wickham itself. The church was built on the central site of Wickham, and that effectively became the focus of the village. It was situated on the road from Balsham to Worsted Street and also where roads from Streetly End, Streetly Hall and Horseheath met. The village lay principally to the north of the church, where there was a back lane that is now a footpath and where there are earthworks and pottery that indicate Saxon and medieval settlement. Burton End, to the east of the main village, was known as Bovetownstreet in the 14th century and, although this hamlet now appears to be a continuation of settlement along the village street, it was previously separated from Wickham by a long gap, and it had its own north-south routeways. As usual in parishes in the south-eastern corner of Cambridgeshire, the separate settlements continued to be populated throughout the Middle Ages and some are still distinctive hamlets. Yen Hall declined in importance by the 13th century, but the settlement at Streetly End continued to develop on a site to the east of Streetly Hall, where it had a village green in the 15th century.

The scattered population amounted to 33 villagers in 1086, and at least 50 tenants in 1279. In the 16th and 17th centuries there were a maximum of 33 households. In the 17th and 18th century much of the village was owned by the Alington's Horseheath estate, and some substantial houses which still survive were constructed. When Horseheath Hall was demolished in the late 18th

century materials were taken from it for use in West Wickham. The total population grew at this time to 332 in 1801, and then to a peak of 572 in 1841. It then fell, and, despite local authority housing built on the road between West Wickham and Burton End, and other areas of infilling, the population in 1996 had only risen again to 370.

West Wratting

West Wratting is a large parish of 1430 hectares, lying mostly on chalky boulder clay at about 125m above sea level, with underlying chalk exposed in the west, where land reaches 110m. Parish boundaries, which were recorded in the 10th century, include Fleam Dyke, track-ways and what were then woodland edges. There are two small streams in the parish, one in the south which flows towards Weston Green, and the other running across the western side of the parish, from Oxcroft Farm, where a medieval manor house had a fishery in the 14th century, to Wadloes Farm. Much of the parish was woodland or heath in the Middle Ages, and there were still extensive sheepwalks when the open fields of West Wratting were enclosed in 1813. Heathland in the west of the parish, around Dungate Farm, was used for horse racing from the 17th century, and there were racing stables at Valley Farm and Oxcroft. Large areas of common land at the east end of the parish were known as Great and Little Shrub. This became an airfield during World War II, and is now Wratting Common. In 1086 West Wratting was *Waratinge*, or 'place where cross-wort grows', and 'West' was added in the 13th century.

Prehistoric, Roman and Anglo-Saxon

There are few early sites known on the heavy soils of West Wratting,

although on the west side of the parish there are soil marks of ring-ditches and also pits and fragmentary enclosures that probably belong to Iron Age or Roman times. Two Neolithic axes were found near Fleam Dyke, and an Iron Age coin comes from this parish. The only Roman site where there is clear evidence for settlement is between the church and the boundary with Weston Colville, where scatters of pottery dating from the 1st to the 3rd century found with areas of dark soil and burnt stones indicate a small farmstead. Despite documentary references to West Wratting in the 10th and early 11th centuries, there is not yet archaeological evidence for the village at this time.

Medieval

In the late 10th century the main manor, West Wratting Hall, was given to Ely abbey. During the Peasants Revolt local villagers broke into Ely's manor house and burnt the Court Rolls, and the rectory was also burgled, even though the stolen items included a sword and a bow which were presumably intended to help defend the property. The estate passed to the dean and chapter in the 16th century, and they held it until the 19th century, then selling it to the Frost family who were already resident at West Wratting Hall, which they had leased for many years. They bought up most of the parish during the 19th century. The 18th century manor house for this estate, West Wratting Hall, known as the Old Hall, still stands on a site that may well date to Saxon times, immediately to the north of the church and close to the Roman site mentioned above. The Hall is surrounded by the Frosts' park, which contains a hollow-way and other remains of the medieval village.

Another large estate was held by free men before the Norman Conquest but was afterwards given to Hardwin de Scalers, holder of extensive Cambridgeshire estates. In the 16th century it was acquired by Andrew Perne, who gave it to his college, Peterhouse. In the 18th century they leased it to Sir John

A green and cottages at the east end of West Wratting.

Jacob, who built the red-brick mansion known as West Wratting Park House, set in a large park at the south-eastern end of the village. This park absorbed part of a village green and the sites of houses that had previously stood around it. The house was owned by various titled families before it was sold to the Frosts in the late 19th century. William Cole was friendly with Sir Robert Smyth, who bought the house from the Jacobs and 'greatly added to it and furnished it in a most polite and gentile taste.' The following owner also 'made improvements at a vast expense, both in house and garden', before shooting himself following losses in horse racing. When the house was sold in 1780 it was described as having 'a most beautiful park or lawn in front, containing 84 acres of rich meadow'.

Other West Wratting manors were scattered around the parish, well away from the village. Parys manor, first mentioned in 1312, had a manor house that was still standing when the Enclosure map was drawn, sited at Brook Farm, where a stream crosses the road to Haverhill. Oxcroft manor was a Saxon estate whose manor house stood next to a stream close to Balsham on West Wratting's southern boundary. Scarletts manor was subdivided from Oxcrofts in the 13th century, and its

manor house presumably occupied the large square moat that still surrounds Scarletts Farm, to the south of the village. Another manor, Hammonds, not recorded until the 16th century, had a manor house on the north side of West Wratting green when the Enclosure map was drawn.

Village Development

As in other parishes near Suffolk there are several settlements scattered around the parish, which is more than six miles in length. The village itself had two distinct centres in medieval and later times, based on the estates held by Ely and by de Scalers. One was close to the church, where there are earthwork remains of medieval date, and where the rectory and West Wratting Hall are situated. Roads from Weston Colville, Balsham and Six Mile Bottom meet here. The de Scaler settlement was around the green at the east end of the High Street, part of which now has cottages built upon it. These settlements are joined by a street which, according to a map made in the early 18th century, was once lined with houses. Both of these centres were cleared of earlier dwellings in order to create parks around the new style of mansion, probably at times when few dwellings remained. There are also some

indications in the soil marks near Brook Farm that there was medieval settlement linked to Parys manor, on the edge of West Wratting Common.

West Wratting was a fair sized village with 33 villagers in 1086, and then grew before, like most clayland parishes, being badly affected by bad weather and the Black Death in the 14th century. In 1377 it contained 180 tax-payers, and in the 16th century only 47 families. In the 17th century there were 76 households, but this figure fell to about 250 people in the early 18th century, before rising to 541 in 1801. In the 19th century the population rose to a peak of 912 in 1841, but then fell rapidly as the villagers found employment elsewhere, or emigrated. It continued to fall in the early 20th century, and, despite new housing which has virtually joined the two main parts of the village together, there were still only 460 people living here in 1996.

The Wilbrahams

Great and Little Wilbraham are separate parishes of 1180 and 800 hectares respectively, both containing low-lying areas of fen and alluvial soils though most of their land is chalk. Around the village of Little Wilbraham and at Wilbraham Temple this chalk is overlain by glacial gravels. In the late 18th century the agricultural writer Vancouver complained that the 500 acres of fen in Little Wilbraham 'produces little else than sedge, and rushes, which are mown for litter'. In contrast, the higher chalkland in the south of both parishes was a dry area of downland that was used for sheepwalks.

Springs that rise at Shardelowes Well at the end of the upstanding section of Fleam Dyke flow into Wilbraham River, part of the boundary

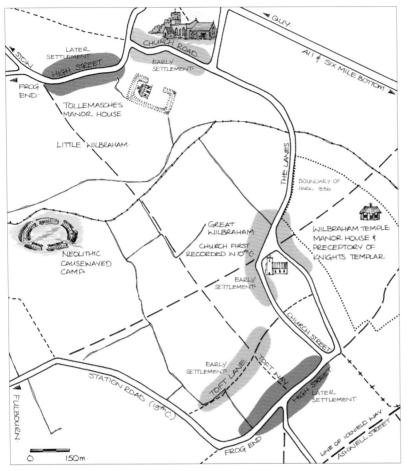

between Fulbourn and Great Wilbraham, and are joined by a tributary which rises near Wilbraham Temple and then forms the parish boundary between Great and Little Wilbraham. The remainder of the boundary with Fulbourn is Fleam Dyke, on which lies Mutlow Hill, the meeting place of four parishes and three hundreds in Saxon and medieval times, and also a prehistoric burial mound. The land falls from uplands which reach 50m above sea level near Mutlow Hill, to about 15m in the villages and about 8m in fen areas to the north. The Wilbrahams are crossed by Ashwell Street, and by the A11 from Cambridge to Newmarket, a Romanised route of the Icknield Way that was made a turnpike road in the 18th century. Several tracks led from the Icknield Way to the fens, of which a few survive. The open fields of both parishes were enclosed following Awards made in 1801, although extensive areas of commonland still survive near the streams. In Domesday Book the Wilbrahams are *Wiborgha*, or 'the village of Wilburgha', just possibly a reference to the sister and successor of St. Etheldreda, founder of Ely and daughter of King Anna of East Anglia.

Prehistoric

Neolithic axes are commonly discovered in and near the areas of fen in these parishes. Nine of them are so far recorded, all found singly and without other artefacts, apart from a hoard of four axes, all unfinished and unused, that were packed together in a pit near to the springs at Wilbraham Temple. Sites close to springs certainly attracted deposits of ritual offerings at many periods, of which this may be an example, or it could have been a convenient place for a craftsman to store some of his stock.

In another wet area, adjoining the stream that flows from Wilbraham Temple, is a site which would definitely have been used for ritual as well as social events. This is a causewayed camp, a type of monument that was constructed in many areas of Britain in Neolithic times for communal activities such as organisation of land, exchange of goods and livestock, and religious and social ceremonies. It consisted of a double sub-circular arrangement of short, straight segments of ditches, with a maximum diameter of about 200m. Small-scale excavations on this site discovered large quantities of pottery, animal bone and worked flints, showing that it was used for more than occasional or ritual use, and ditches that were still waterlogged contained organic material such as wood, seeds and pollen. Aerial photographs also show two other monuments close to Wilbraham River, one in Great and one in Little Wilbraham, that could possibly be of a similar type and date. They are both large circles, about 100m in diameter, one of which has part of a concentric palisade within it and curving segments of ditch nearby, and the other has indications of a concentric ring on the outside.

On the high areas of chalk downland in the south of Great Wilbraham aerial photographs reveal the ring-ditches of at least nine Bronze Age burial mounds, and just to the north of Little Wilbraham, close to the hoard of Neolithic axes, a similar mound was still visible in ploughsoil in the 1960s. At Shardelowes Well, near the termination of Fleam Dyke, more ring-ditches have been observed, and cremated remains have been ploughed from one of them. A Late Bronze Age axe has also been found in this area.

To the south of Shardelowes Well, where Fleam Dyke meets an area of fenland and ceases to exist as an upstanding monument, maps that were made in the 18th and 19th centuries and aerial photographs indicate that the earthwork continues as a slighter structure across low-lying land to the junction where two streams meet, near the Neolithic causewayed camp described above. Where it was cut by a pipeline, the ditch of this extension was recorded, and was about 10m wide. This seems to be different structure to the Anglo-Saxon dyke that runs from Fulbourn to Balsham, and it is more likely to belong to its predecessor, perhaps constructed in the Iron Age.

Roman

There are two important sites in Great Wilbraham where domestic buildings are mingled with religious remains. One is close to Wilbraham Temple and was investigated when a water pipeline was cut through it. This site is also close to Ashwell Street, known here as Street Way. Two rooms of a Roman villa were exposed, each with a floor of rammed chalk. One room had wall-foundations of mortared flints and other stones, and the other had walls supported by large timbers that were set in pits and in beam-slots. Outside the building, which probably extended well beyond the width of the pipe-trench, was a courtyard, beyond which were rubbish pits and enclosure ditches. At the edge of the courtyard was a low chalk plinth, and in the centre of this was a pit in which had been hidden a stone altar, fragments of a pillar, a cornice stone, and an object of twisted iron, possibly for holding candles. Elsewhere on the site a Roman pewter plate had also been deliberately buried in the 4th century, shortly before the villa was abandoned, and not far away part of a lead christening vat was found above a cobbled surface.

On the western side of Great Wilbraham aerial photographs show an area of enclosures and trackways, and small-scale investigations have started to reveal features that include cobbled yards and ditches. Much pottery, great numbers of coins, mainly of 4th century date, a

Excavating two rooms of a Roman building in 1990 and (below) a stone altar and carved pillar, found in a pit just outside the villa.

bronze disc on which the Christian fish symbol may be detected, and a knife handle in the form of a lion's head have been found on this site. Other items of a religious nature found at Great Wilbraham are a miniature enamelled altar found near the village, and material found at Mutlow Hill, which lies partly in this parish. (See Fulbourn)

Anglo-Saxon

A very rich Anglo-Saxon cemetery of the 5th and 6th century was excavated at Little Wilbraham, only a short distance from the villa described above. The great majority of the site was excavated in 1851, and there was some further work in 1926/7. A total of 200 inhumations and well over 100 cremations were found, even though many had already been destroyed or were considered too damaged to invest-igate. Cremations and inhumations were found mixed together, some-times one above the other, and the artefacts with them showed that they were culturally the same and were buried in the same years.

The unusual wealth of this cemetery is illustrated by four male graves that contained swords, normally only found in highest-status graves. These swords had scabbards with bronze fittings, and three of them were decorated with large coloured

Cremation urn from Little Wilbraham.

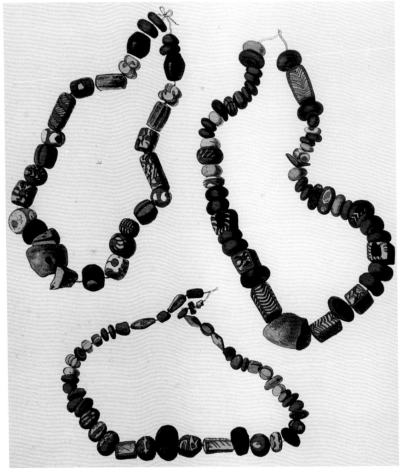

Anglo-Saxon necklaces from Little Wilbraham cemetery.

glass beads. One man with a sword was also accompanied with a complete horse skeleton, with its bronze bridle-bit and silvered harness fittings, and another had a bronze-mounted drinking horn and a cauldron as well as his spear and shield. Women, too, had many grave-goods, including 125 brooches, many of which were described as 'thickly gilt', and more than a thousand beads were collected. Though the cremated objects were very similar to those buried with inhumations, there were some differences, such as more common occurrence of iron tools. An adze, axe, pincers, hooks, a pair of shears and five pairs of iron tweezers, for example, were cremated, and nearly all the burials had

fragments of bone combs. All the excavated cremations were in urns, some of which were decorated. Being so close to the villa, it is not surprising that some Roman objects were collected and kept. Amongst these were 35 Roman coins and the bowl of a spoon, this last item being fixed to the chatelaine of a woman who also carried a strange amulet of wood bound in a sling of bronze, presumably for magical purposes.

Other early Anglo-Saxon items have occasionally been found in Great Wilbraham, particularly near to Fleam Dyke, but only in one area is there clear evidence of a settlement. This is in the grounds of Wilbraham Temple, where piles of clay loom-weights, typical of those

found in the sunken-floored huts of the time, were found.

By the 10th century it is known that a church stood in Great Wilbraham, for a landowner here became a monk at Ramsey Abbey and gave part of his estate and the church of that parish to the abbey, who later exchanged it with Ely. Other estates are known from charters of the same period.

Medieval

The larger of the two Saxon manor in Great Wilbraham was held by the king before and after the Norman Conquest. Part of this estate was later given to Nigel the Chamberlain, and later passed to the Loveday family. The remaining half was retained by the Crown until the 13th century, when it was passed to the Knights Templar. An inventory of the Templars estate in the 13th century suggests only a small establishment, with a Preceptor, or head of the holding, one brother, one chaplain and some servants, including a porter, baker and bailiff. At this time two watermills and one windmill stood on this manor. After the Templars' assets were confiscated in the early 14th century Wilbraham Temple was given to the rival organisation, the Knights Hospitaller, who held it until the dissolution of the monasteries. In both the 14th and 15th centuries a temple garden is specifically mentioned, and there was a dovecote. A late 15th century timber building with an original doorway survives from this period. Mary I later gave the estate to the Huddlestones of Sawston, in gratitude for the support they had given to her before her accession, and they also acquired other estates in the two villages. The oldest parts of Wilbraham Temple itself are early 17th century, built for Robert Huddlestone when he married and moved here. Later, a park was created around the house.

Another Saxon manor in Great Wilbraham was given to Alan of Brittany and was subsequently subdivided. Part was later held by the Lovetots who, in the late 13th century were first given hunting rights in

Great and Little Wilbraham and then, in 1281, were granted a weekly market and annual fair, neither of which survived. In the 17th century Lovetots manor passed to the Alingtons of Horseheath, and 'Lufters', a 16th century house on Church Street was probably used as the farmhouse for their estate here.

Little Wilbraham, previously a Saxon estate, was given to the de Veres of Castle Hedingham after the Norman Conquest, and it was later sub-let it to families within the village, principally the Tollemasches and the Chamberlains. When the priory of Anglesey took over part of the Tollemasches estate in the 13th century they were required to keep in repair the houses of that manor, which included a chapel, grange, ox-stall and a small house with its close. In 1279 a Hall with a chapel and a dovecote are noted. This manor house presumably stood in a moated site near the church, which partially survived when the Enclosure map was made. The estate that the priory acquired was later given to the city of Coventry, for charitable purposes.

Village Development
Both villages grew up along drove roads running from the Icknield Way routes down towards the fen. These ways linked the grazing land on the chalk downs with summer fenland pastures to the north, and also served many parishes on the heavier soils of south-east Cambridgeshire. In Great Wilbraham they were crossed by three routes running east from Fulbourn. The southernmost of these, following the ancient route of Ashwell Street, was a well-used east-west drove road that was particularly popular when tolls were charged on the Cambridge-Newmarket road. The church lay on the northernmost route, where it crossed the main north-south road. This route was diverted after Enclosure by an expansion to the park around Wilbraham Temple. The village pound stood on the triangle adjacent to the Poor House, later a Reading Room, which contained a lock-up known as the 'cage'.

In 1086 there were 33 villagers on the manors that are already recognisable as Great Wilbraham, and 20 in Little Wilbraham, although the villages do not acquire these separate names until the 13th century. In 1377 Little Wilbraham still had 108 tax-payers, and in the 16th century Great Wilbraham had 50 households, and Little Wilbraham only 21. By the 17th century there were 61 families in Great Wilbraham, but Little Wilbraham had shrunk further, to 11. There was some recovery by 1801, when the villages had 354 and 183 people respectively. In the mid 19th century Little Wilbraham was described as 'small and irregularly built'. The villages grew to 19th century peaks of 644 in Great Wilbraham in 1851, and 412 in Little Wilbraham in 1871, though a number of these lived in the hamlet of Six Mile Bottom, where cottages were built around after the railway was opened in 1848.

Willingham

Willingham is an extremely large parish of 1880 hectares lying on the edge of the fen and benefiting from the natural advantages of that environment. It is flat and very low lying, some of it less than 2m above sea level though it rises to 5-7m in the village and 9m in the south. Clay underlies most of the parish, and is covered by glacial gravels within the village and land to the west. There are patches of gravel on slightly higher areas (about 2-3m) in the fens, and these were widely used in Roman times. The lowest lying areas are covered in peat which was forming in Neolithic, Bronze Age and Iron Age times. Virtually all the northern half of the parish was fenland in medieval times and its alluvial soils covered the many

Roman sites. There were also two meres which began to form in the Iron Age and were open water until the 17th century. The northern parish boundary is the River Ouse, that on the south mostly follows tracks and pre-dates arable cultivation, and those on the east and west were not fixed until the 17th century, when a 4m wide ditch was dug to divide commons that had previously been shared by Willingham and Over. About half the parish was fen and was used as common pasture until Enclosure in 1853, though small areas had been made into closes in the early 17th century, when such actions were met with violent and litigious objections by the villagers. In 1086 Willingham was *Wivelingeham*, 'the home of the people of Wifel'.

Prehistoric
Even the gravel areas in Willingham seem to have been surprisingly little used in prehistoric times, and flint artefacts, including waste flakes, have rarely been found. One possibly Palaeolithic flake and a few other prehistoric fragments were excavated on a Roman site just within the fen to the north of the village, and two Neolithic axes come from a similar location. A Palaeolithic scraper was also found in material dredged from the Ouse. Three ring-ditches that may once have surrounded Bronze Age burial mounds or Iron Age huts are recognisable on aerial photographs, two to the north of the village on Roman sites, and one to the south. The only Bronze Age find reported so far is a bronze axe found in the 19th century.

During the late Bronze Age and the Iron Age the fens were becoming wetter, and evidence of deposits found in Willingham Mere show that this area, which had already been deforested by rising water levels, became fen carr and sedge fen, and then open water. Single sherds of Iron Age pottery have been noted on many areas of Roman occupation, suggesting there was a low level but widespread usage of land use around the fens before the dense settlement pattern that was to follow, and one

Bust of Antoninus Pius.

places and a ditch with a maximum depth of 1m and width of 8m. It lay within the open fields of Willingham and so was ploughed throughout the Middle Ages, and in the late 19th century ploughing right over the banks was occurring on the eastern side. The situation on a promontory that was surrounded by marsh on three sides gave it a strong defensive position, and its position at the head of the Aldreth Causeway, an artificially raised track that gave access to the Isle of Ely on the south-western side from prehistoric times, gave it considerable military value and also significance in controlling trade.

Roman

The Roman period saw very intense use of the fen edge, particularly on a broad band of sites running right across the parish to the north of the village, on land that was just above 2m above sea level and which, it was observed during the 1947 floods, was also above flood levels at that time. The sites represented almost all seem to be peasant farmsteads with few signs of wealth beyond occasional tiling on house roofs. Great quantities of pottery have been collected from these sites (described as being 'by

the bucketful'), and this appears to confirm that there was extensive Roman settlement in the 1st, 2nd, and 4th centuries, with some sort of withdrawal in the 3rd century, due to flooding. Crop marks reveal numerous small rectangular enclosures and many ditched droveways, both of which were presumably used for the control of stock. Although the buildings were humble, there are also signs of hoarded wealth, some of it related to religious depositions, and there are indications of at least four small square timber temples, probably similar to one excavated on the opposite bank of the Ouse at Haddenham, and to examples nearby in Cottenham.

The most spectacular of the Willingham hoards was ploughed up in Hempsals Fen, probably in one of the small temples, in 1857, shortly after Enclosure brought this area under cultivation. It consisted of a wooden box which contained pieces of a tubular bronze baton or sceptre ornamented in high relief with figures of a naked god trampling on an enemy, an eagle, wheel, bull and dolphin, together with a small bust of the 2nd century emperor Antoninus Pius, which may have been part of the sceptre. There were

of the principal Roman occupation and religious sites, at Milking Hills, includes ditches that the excavators thought were Iron Age. Close to the village another site has been discovered through field work which revealed a thin scatter of early or middle Iron Age sherds.

The principal site of this date, however, is the circular fortification of Belsars Hill, which commands access to the Isle of Ely along the Aldreth Causeway. Dating for this monument is still not conclusive, and its re-use and refurbishment in medieval times is highly likely, but close examination of its structure and comparison with other Iron Age forts in this region, particularly those at Borough Fen and Arbury, show that its origins are most probably in this period. The earthwork consists of an almost circular bank and ditch, 250 by 225m in diameter, with a bank still surviving up to 2m high in

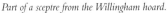
Part of a sceptre from the Willingham hoard.

Three Roman pewter plates, one inscribed with the Christian symbol of Chi-Rho and (above) two bronze figurines, from the Willingham hoard.

also remains of two more knobbed batons and other pieces of bronze, including a part of a bridle. Other items were found with these, but it is difficult to tell from the description published in 1883 whether they were all together or scattered in the field, though the former is perhaps more likely as they are small and not easy for a ploughman to find if they were much dispersed. These include 'several curious little bronze figures of horsemen', of which two survive, an eagle, owl, bull's head, ram's head, 'several diminutive human masks', of which one was a three-headed goddess, and two large opaque blue glass beads. Some of these items are priestly regalia, but as this mixture includes symbols that range from emperor-worship to a Celtic wheel-god, with classical, Celtic and eastern religions apparently intermingled, it is impossible to tell who was actually being worshipped.

Other hoards from Willingham include about 500 3rd century coins dug up on the edge of the fens later in the 19th century, apparently on an occupation site, and a recent discovery of three 4th century pewter plates, one inscribed with the Christian chi-rho symbol, in a small pit that also contained two cattle skulls, two sheep jaws, a horn core and other cattle bones. The plates were neatly stacked, as if for safe-keeping.

Anglo-Saxon

Evidence for Anglo-Saxon land-use in Willingham is still very fragmentary, but it is now becoming clear that, despite worsening climatic conditions, the late Roman farmsteads were not totally abandoned, although the sites where people lived were moving to higher ground in the parish. There are unconfirmed reports of cemetery remains, and, within the village at Berry Croft, excavations in 1995 and 1997 have uncovered a large early and middle Anglo-Saxon village. There were two halls here, at least six other smaller rectangular buildings, and one wattle-lined well. Most of the dating evidence from the site is early Anglo-Saxon, with some middle Saxon pottery. Later Saxon pottery was found in the boundary ditch which separates the Berry from the back of the properties fronting Church Street.

By the late Saxon period Willingham had become an important centre that was almost entirely in the ownership of Ely, and its church had probably been developed by the abbey into a minster that served a group of nearby parishes. Within the present church are fragments of a cross and also parts of two stone grave covers carved with plaitwork decoration, presumably used on the graves of monks who served here. Elsewhere in the parish a large hoard of 11th century coins was discovered, and two lead vats, thought to belong to a similar period were found near the Ouse, on the boundary with Cottenham.

Medieval

The manor of Willingham was given to Ely in about 1000 AD, later passing to the bishop, who held it until 1600. Its manor house stood in an enclosure to the north of the church, and was large enough to entertain the king's household in 1244, a few years after the king had given the bishop fifty oak trees to repair it. In the 14th century its treasury and chapel were dilapidated but otherwise it was a sound and substantial building. In the 15th century the bishops leased out all their land in Willingham and the manor house fell out of use. In the

Excavation of the Anglo-Saxon settlement at Berry Croft in 1997.

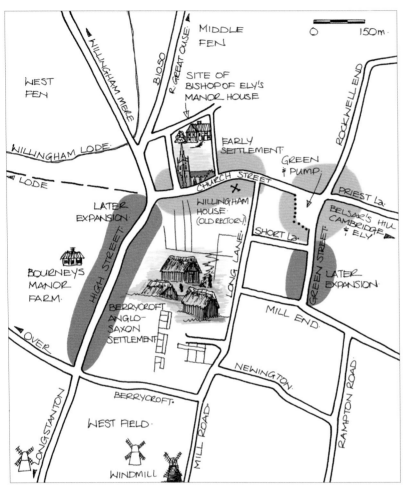

the north of the Anglo-Saxon settlement, near to the unloading point for Willingham Lode, which was constructed to import their building materials. There may also have been another early settlement around the green at the east end of the village street, now Church Street, which wound between the church and its rectory and continued to Belsars Hill and the junction of routes to Cambridge, Ely and Rampton. After the Saxon period it was the sites close to the fen-edge, with excellent communications by road and water in addition to easy access to the fen-land resources, which were the most attractive areas for settlement, and the Berry Croft was no longer occupied. Subsequently the other two fen-edge centres grew and joined together.

Later in the Middle Ages the pressures of an expanding population in a village severely constrained within the small area that was available for house building led to the development of a compact settlement arranged around three sides of a rectangle. By the late 16th century, when a survey of the village was made, the north-south road that is now High Street, running to Long-stanton, was built up with close and regularly spaced houses set within long thin curving plots. Less organised groups of dwellings at the north end of the village had no land attached to them, and there was another short row with small strips of land built along a fen drove road north-east of the church. Green Street and Rockmill End were also built up. A map made in 1603, which survives as a copy made in 1793, shows the village as compact and densely built-up, with larger plots for the rectory and Bourneys manor house. All the available land along the street frontages is filled with cottages in narrow plots, with no signs of shrinkage or desertion.

By the 18th century some plots had been divided for yet more houses, and additional areas were built up to the south, at Mill End and the end of the High Street. Most of the houses in the village were poorly made and have not survived. Only a few

late 16th century three houses and a barn stood in the close. The estate was sold to Miles Sandys, and he and his son attempted to reverse Ely's custom of leasing out their rights and lands to villagers, but were blocked at every turn by the independent-minded inhabitants. Some changes were made, with the Berry Croft, for example being enclosed, but the villagers exacted full compensation for anything they had to give up. Much of the land was sold in small lots, and the Sandys eventually went bankrupt, partly as a result of litigation expenses. After further sales, what remained of the manor was owned by the Hattons of Long-stanton from the mid 18th century.

Bourneys was a small manor that was created out of land leased from

the bishop from the 13th century. Its manor house stood on the west side of High Street, where its site is now occupied by a 17th century building, Bourneys Manor Farm. The rectory was another substantial building which in the 17th century had at least eight hearths and where there were farm buildings that included two stables, a malt kiln and a dove-cote. It was rebuilt in the late 19th century and is now used by the County Council as an old peoples' home. Like other buildings on Church Street its holding stretched back to a ditch that was constructed in late Saxon times.

Village Development

The church, rectory and manor house were built a short distance to

The village green at Willingham, still regularly flooded in the early 20th century.

farmhouses were not burnt down in arson attacks and other fires of the 19th century, but some 17th century houses, such as Church Farm, can still be seen in Church Street and the High Street. In the 19th century the increasing population was packed into even more houses on the three original streets and on new roads such as those built at the south end of the village, Over Road and Berrycroft.

The east-west road through the village and past the church ran to Over and the river crossing to St. Ives and so was a significant through-route. It was said that before the Ely-Cambridge turnpike was built in 1768 the only route suitable for a carriage on the journey from Cambridge to Ely went through Willingham. Droveways led from the village through the fens to the meres and river-crossings. On the east side of the parish the King's Highway from Cambridge met the Aldreth Causeway and other minor routes at Belsars Hill, which they had to run around, not through. The Causeway itself was the main, and sometimes the only, route onto the Isle of Ely. It was maintained by the villagers as part of their labour-service to Ely, a duty recorded in Domesday Book.

The economy of Willingham was, of all the fen-edge villages, the one that was most affected by the

peculiarities of its location. Only about a quarter of its land was used for arable farming, and villagers were able to earn a good living even when they owned virtually no land. In the 17th century, and probably also in the Middle Ages, it was normal for peasants to own about a dozen cattle in addition to sheep, pigs and, in some cases, horses. There was free grazing for all these animals, and even those who held no common rights might inherit part of a pond, for example, which evidently was enough to live upon. With these resources the village became famous for its export of cheese, often sold under Cottenham's name, and it was possible to subdivide holdings to support an expanding population. Wills that were written at the time might provide for the next generation with an inheritance as humble as 'two cows, all my lodge with the fodder... my boat in the fen, my boots and a pair of high shoes'. Fisheries on the two meres and fish-ponds in many areas of fen are mentioned in documents from Domesday Book to the 17th century, and fishing, fowling and cutting reeds and willows were always lucrative.

In 1086 the monks' estate included a vineyard, and orchards later became an important part of the economy. They were recorded in the 16th century, but many were probably

planted long before this. In later centuries fruit and cheese were sent to Cambridge and St. Ives, and when rail transport arrived there was large-scale export to London and the Midlands. In the late 19th century glass-houses were extensively used for soft fruit, salad crops and flowers.

Willingham became one of Cambridgeshire's largest villages but in 1086 it was still small, with 23 villagers, about 115 people in all. This population grew to 79 holders of land in the mid 13th century, and in 1377 there were 287 tax payers. Like its neighbours, Cottenham and Over, the village expanded considerably in the 16th and 17th centuries, a time when villagers with very small plots of land, or even none at all, could make a living from grazing cattle on the commons and fishing in the fens and meres. Even when drainage works began in the 17th century the population continued to rise, and there were 183 families, 795 inhabitants, in 1801. Enclosure was not allowed to affect common rights until 1853, and the population was able to rise rapidly in the early 19th century, to a peak of 1600 in 1851. After this there were short term gains and losses, and in 1951 the population was about the same as it had been a century earlier. In 1965 it was decided that development should be allowed in Willingham to relieve pressure in the south of the county and in Cambridge, and in 1989 it was identified as a Rural Growth Settlement. There has therefore been considerable expansion since the 1970s, and it in 1996 it had a population of 3510.

Population figures for South East Cambridgeshire and the Fen Edge

Notes:

C19 - The maximum population of each village in the 19th century .
ha - hectares, approximately 2.4 acres. This relates to the size of the parish in 1996, which may not be the same as its medieval extent.

Figures in bold italics are derived from numbers of tenants and slaves given in Domesday Book (1086), numbers of tenants recorded in the Hundred Rolls (1279), numbers of adults over 14 and therefore eligible to pay the Poll Tax, and households assessed for the Subsidy Rolls (1563) and Hearth Tax (1664). They have been multiplied to give a rough estimate of the total population of the time, but none of these figures are very accurate, and probably err on the low side. Subsequent figures are derived from census returns and the County Council forecasts for 1996, based on 1994 figures.

Parish	1086	1279	1377	1563	1664	1801	C19	1996	ha
Abington, Great	*14 / 70*	*48 / 240*	*96 / 125*	*32 / 144*	*44 / 189*	272	382	840	661
Abington, Little	*20 / 100*	*35 / 175*	*45 / 58*	*25 / 112*	*21 / 90*	185	339	500	545
Babraham	*38 / 190*	*60 / 300*	-	*36 / 162*	*29 / 130*	196	304	250	970
Balsham	*26 / 130*	-	*255 / 331*	*80 / 360*	*104 / 447*	542	1352	1400	1830
Bartlow	-	-	*32 / 42*	*20 / 90*	*8 / 34*	83	123	90	218
Carlton	*24 / 120*	-	*71 / 92*	*22 / 99*	*36 / 155*	229	469	190	974
Castle Camps	*27 / 135*	*87 / 435*	*113 / 147*	*37 / 166*	*43 / 185*	546	949	620	1256
Cottenham	*60 / 300*	*134 / 670*	-	*121 / 544*	*230 / 989*	1088	2300	4840	2914
Fen Ditton	-	-	*330 / 429*	*55 / 247*	*58 / 249*	337	680	730	600
Fen Drayton	*23 / 115*	*55 / 275*	*111 / 144*	*40 / 180*	*58 / 249*	265	450	810	600
Fulbourn	*91 / 455*	-	*426 / 554*	*52 / 234*	*91 / 391*	702	1807	4920	2124
Hildersham	*20 / 100*	-	*47 / 61*	*17 / 76*	*24 / 103*	170	248	210	616
Hinxton	*38 / 190*	-	*115 / 150*	*43 / 193*	*46 / 198*	270	465	270	632
Histon	*75 / 375*	*189 / 945*	-	*54 / 243*	*89 / 383*	523	1000	4310	710
Horningsea	*51 / 255*	*86 / 430*	-	*32 / 144*	*57 / 245*	293	435	320	663
Horseheath	*29 / 145*	*80 / 400*	*121 / 157*	*34 / 153*	*32 / 138*	342	578	440	777
Impington	*24 / 120*	*45 / 225*	*57 / 74*	*14 / 63*	*35 / 150*	92	600	3230	736
Landbeach	*32 / 160*	*55 / 275*	*114 / 148*	*36 / 162*	*68 / 292*	235	526	790	932
Linton	*61 / 305*	*172 / 860*	*155 / 201*	*92 /414*	*166 / 714*	1157	1858	4070	1600
Longstanton	*67 / 335*	-	*267 / 347*	*42 / 189*	*52 / 224*	400	600	2370	1120
Milton	*36 / 180*	*75 / 375*	*146 / 190*	*36 / 162*	*38 / 163*	273	576	4320	800
Oakington and Westwick	*59 / 295*	*120 / 600*	*174 / 226*	*43 / 193*	*57 / 245*	285	690	1390	833
Over	*35 / 175*	*140 / 700*	*378 / 491*	*124 / 558*	*134 / 576*	689	1200	2510	1507
Pampisford	*25 / 125*	*64 / 320*	*109 / 142*	*31 / 139*	*37 / 159*	202	359	350	650
Rampton	*19 / 95*	-	*82 / 107*	*31 / 139*	*37 / 159*	162	250	420	550
Sawston	*38 / 190*	*125 / 625*	-	*64 / 288*	*74 / 318*	466	1882	7200	769
Shudy Camps	*22 / 110*	*85 / 425*	*141 / 183*	*30 / 135*	*41 / 176*	349	418	300	950
Stapleford	*20 / 100*	-	*62 / 81*	*28 / 126*	*23 / 99*	235	594	1720	740
Stow cum Quy	-	-	*148 / 192*	*31 / 139*	*45 / 193*	235	455	480	764
Swavesey	*65 / 325*	*200 / 1000*	*379 / 493*	*78 / 351*	*128 / 550*	831	1385	2020	1600
Teversham	*26 / 130*	-	-	*15 / 67*	*25 / 107*	154	286	2620	484
Waterbeach	*47 / 235*	*180 / 900*	*205 / 266*	*70 / 315*	*106 / 456*	553	1619	4680	2315
Weston Colville	*40 / 200*	-	*119 / 155*	*26 / 117*	*45 / 193*	318	574	430	1300
West Wickham	*33 / 165*	*50 / 250*	-	*33 / 148*	*30 / 129*	332	572	370	1184
West Wratting	*33 / 165*	-	*180 / 234*	*47 / 211*	*76 / 327*	541	912	460	1430
Wilbraham, Great	*33 / 165*	-	-	*50 / 225*	*61 / 262*	354	644	640	1180
Wilbraham, Little	*20 / 100*	-	*108 / 140*	*21 / 94*	*11 / 47*	183	412	370	800
Willingham	*20 / 115*	-	*287 / 373*	*105 / 472*	*135 / 580*	795	1600	3510	1880

Bibliography

Abbreviations:-
Antiq. J. The Antiquaries Journal; Archaeol. J. The Archaeological Journal; CCC Cambridgeshire County Council; CAU Cambridge Archaeological Unit; CLHS Cambridge Local History Society; CUP Cambridge University Press; HDAG Haverhill and District Archaeology Group; OAU Oxford Archaeological Unit; PCAS Proceedings of the Cambridge Antiquarian Society; TCHAS Transactions of the Cambridgeshire and Huntingdonshire Archaeological Society; VCH The Victoria County History of the County of Cambridgeshire and the Isle of Ely.

Many works on the archaeology and history of Cambridgeshire have been used repeatedly, and so have not been listed separately. These are:

Fox, C. *The Archaeology of the Cambridge region*, CUP, 1923.

Gardner, R. *History, gazeteer and directory of Cambridgeshire*, R. Gardner, 1851.

Haigh, D. *The religious houses of Cambridgeshire*, CCC, 1988.

Hall, D. *Cambridgeshire survey, Isle of Ely and Wisbech, Fenland Project 10*, East Anglian Archaeology, 1996.

Hall, D.N. *Fenland survey: an essay in landscape and persistence*, English Heritage, 1994.

Hart, C. *The early charters of England*, Leicester University Press, 1966.

Ravensdale, J.R. *Liable to flood*, CUP, 1974.

Malim, T. *Archaeology on the Cambridgeshire County Farms Estate*, CCC, 1990.

Malim, T. et al. 'Recent work on the Cambridgeshire Dykes', *PCAS*, forthcoming.

Meaney, A. 'A Gazetteer of the Hundred and Wapentake meeting places of the Cambridge region', *PCAS 82*, 1993.

Munby, L. *Fen and upland*, Swavesey Village College, 1961.

Oosthuizen, S. *Cambridgeshire from the air*, Alan Sutton, 1966.

Palmer, W.M. *John Layer of Shepreth*, Cambridge Antiquarian Society, 1935.

Palmer, W.M. *The Peasants Revolt in 1381*, Cambridge Antiquarian Society, 1935.

Palmer, W.M. *William Cole of Milton*, Galloway and Porter, 1935.

Reaney, P.H. *The place names of Cambridgeshire and the Isle of Ely*, CUP, 1943.

Taylor, C.C. *The Cambridgeshire landscape*, Hodder and Stoughton, 1973.

Essential reference books that have been widely used are:

Royal Commission on theHistorical Monuments of England, *North-East Cambridgeshire*, HMSO, 1972.
  For Fen Ditton, Horningsea, Stow cum Quy and Teversham.
VCH II, 1948.
  For descriptions of earthworks.
VCH VI, 1978.
  For the Abingtons, Babraham, Balsham, Bartlow, Carlton, Castle Camps, Shudy Camps, Hildersham, Hinxton, Horseheath, Linton, Pampisford, Weston Colville, West Wickham and West Wratting.
VCH VII, 1978.
  For Roman sites.
VCH IX, 1989.
  For Cottenham, Fen Drayton, Histon, Impington, Landbeach, Milton, Oakington, Over, Rampton, Longstanton, Swavesey, Waterbeach and Willingham.

In addition, the Cambridgeshire Sites and Monunents Record, (SMR), maintained by Cambridgeshire County Council, has been used throughout this work.

The Abingtons
Oxford Archaeological Unit, *Four Wentways (A11/A604), Little Abington , Cambridgeshire*, 1994.

Palmer, W.M. *The neighbourhood of Hildersham and Abington*, Cambridge Chronicle, 1924.

Seaman-Turner, G.W. *The Abington story*, private, 1968.

Taylor, H.M. and Taylor, J. *Anglo-Saxon architecture* Vol I, 1965, 17-18.

ARCHAEOLOGY OF SOUTH EAST CAMBRIDGESHIRE

Babraham
Hatton, A. *Human remains and medieval pits at Babraham Hall* (Rpt 109), CCC, 1997.

Balsham
Fox, C. 'Saxon grave-slab, Balsham, Cambs', *PCAS 32*, 1921, 51.
Tweddle, D. 'A Fragment of pre-conquest sculpture from Balsham, Cambs', *PCAS 68*, 1978, 17-20.

Bartlow
Gage, J. '.... an account of Roman Sepulchral relics....', *Archaeologia 25*, 1833, 1-23.
Gage, J. '....an Account of the final Excavations made at the Bartlow Hills', *Archaeologia 29*, 1842.
Gage, J. '....further discoveries of Roman Sepulchral relics at the Bartlow Hills', *Archaeologia 28*, 1850, 1-6.
McIntosh, J. and Wait, G. *The Romans in Cambridgeshire*, CCC, 1992, 39-41.
Neville, R.C. 'Investigations of Roman remains in the County of Essex', *Archaeol. J. 10*, 1852, 14-21.
Seaman-Turner, G.W. *Story of a village*, private, 1988.

Castle Camps
Charge, B.B. 'A Romano-British Camp at Castle Camps, Cambridgeshire', *HDAG 6*, 1996, 98-109.
Charge, B.B. 'Castle Camps Survey', *HDAG 7*, 1997 forthcoming.
Neville, R.C. *Sepulchra exposita*, (1848), 50-58.
Palmer,W.M. and Fox, C. *Shudy Camps, Castle Camps and Walton's Park, Ashdon*, Cambridge Chronicle, 1924.
Taylor, C.C. 'Motte and Bailey Castle and Deserted Village, Castle Camps', *PCAS 64*, 1973, 38-43.

Cottenham
Clark, J.G.D. 'Report on Excavations on the Cambridgeshire Car Dyke, 1947', *Antiq. J. 21*, 1949, 145-163.
Cottenham Village Society *Cottenham: a glimpse into the past*, 1977.
Evans, C. 'Sampling Settlements: Investigations at Lingwood Farm, Cottenham and Eye Hill Farm, Soham', *Fenland Research 8*, CAU, 1994, 26-30.
Evans, C. and Mortimer, R. 'Excavations at Lordship Lane, Cottenham, Cambridgeshire', CAU, 1996.
Royal Commission on Historical Monuments of England *Bullock's Haste, Cottenham, Cambridgeshire*, 1996.
Taylor, A. 'Prehistoric, Roman, Saxon and Medieval artefacts from the Southern Fen Edge, Cambridgeshire', *PCAS 74*, 1-52, 1987.
Taylor, C.C. *Village and farmstead*, George Philip, 1983, 157-8.

Fen Ditton
Chadwick, D.V.M. 'Some notes on the Biggin, Fen Ditton', *PCAS 48*, 1954, 1-5.
Lethbridge, T.C. 'The riddle of the dykes', *PCAS 51*, 1958, 1-5.
Briscoe, G. et al. 'Finds from the Fleam Dyke', *PCAS 57*, 1964, 125-6.
Hinman, M. *A Middle Iron Age settlement at Greenhouse Farm, Newmarket Road, Fen Ditton*, CCC, 1997.

Fen Drayton
Mortimer, R. *Archaeological excavations at Low Fen, Fen Drayton, Cambridgeshire*, CAU, 1996.
Wait, G. *Excavations at Fen Drayton reservoir, Fen Drayton* (Rpt 73), CAU, 1992.

Fulbourn
Clarke, E.D. 'An Account of some Antiquities found at Fulbourn in Cambridgeshire', *Archaeologia 19*, 1821, 56-60.
Crane, D. *Fulbourn highways and byways*, private, 1991.
Fox, C. 'Excavations in the Cambridgeshire dykes I', *PCAS 24*, 1922, 45-51.
Gdaniec, K. *Archaeological investigations at Fulbourn Hospital, Fulbourn, Cambridge* (Rpt 83), CAU, 1993.
Lysons, D. and S. *Magna Britannia*, EP Publishing Ltd., 1978 (1808), 196-9.
Neville, R.C. 'Account of Excavations near the Fleam Dyke, Cambridgeshire, April 1852', *Archaeol. J. 9*, 1852, 226-30.
Oxford Archaeological Unit *Excavations at Fulbourn Hospital*, 1996.

Hildersham
Lethbridge, T.C. 'Bronze bowl of the Dark Ages from Hildersham, Cambs', *PCAS 45*, 1952, 44-47.
Palmer, W.M. *The neighbourhood of Hildersham and Abington*, Cambridge Chronicle, 1924.

Hinxton
Alexander, M. and Hill, J.D. *The excavation of a Late Iron Age cemetery at Hinxton, Cambridgeshire* (Rpt 159), CAU, 1996.

Evans, C. *Archaeological investigations at Hinxton Quarry, Cambridgeshire* (Rpt 88), CAU, 1993.

Roberts, J. *Hinxton Hall to Great Chesterford* (Rpt A81), CCC, 1995.

Wait, G. *Archaeological assessment of a Roman settlement at Hinxton, Cambridgeshire* (Rpt 38), CCC, 1991.

Histon
May, S. 'Three earthwork surveys', *PCAS 81*, 1993, 39-49.

Walker, R. *A church in the landscape*, 1993.

Horningsea
Evans, J. *An examination of some pottery from Cherry Hinton and Horningsea, Cambridgeshire*, unpub. thesis, 1978.

McKenny Hughes, T. 'On a potter's field at Horningsea...', *PCAS 10*, 1902, 174-94

Walker, F.G. 'Roman pottery kilns at Horningsea, Cambridgeshire', *PCAS 17*, 1912, 14-69.

Horseheath
Parsons, C.E. 'A Romano-British site in Horseheath', *PCAS 31*, 1929, 99-104.

Parsons, C.E. 'Horseheath Hall and its owners', *PCAS 41*, 1948, 1-51.

Parsons, C.E. Some recollections of Horseheath, typescript, 1952.

Impington
Evans, C.E. *Archaeological investigations at Arbury Camp, Cambridgeshire* (Rpt 3), CAU, 1990.

Landbeach
Macaulay, S. *An archaeological investigation of Akeman Street Roman Road and a Romano-British settlement at Car Dyke, Landbeach*, CCC, 1997.

Ravensdale, J.R. 'Landbeach in 1549: Ket's rebellion in miniature', *East Anglian Studies*, ed. L.M. Munby, Heffer, 1968.94-114.

Ravensdale, J.R. *Landbeach: the old village*, Landbeach Village Society, 1972.

Ravensdale, J.R. *The Domesday inheritance*, Souvenir Press, 1986.

Linton
Brown, A.E. and Taylor, C.C. 'A relict garden at Linton, Cambridgeshire', *PCAS 80*, 1992, 62-7.

Brown, A.E. and Taylor, C.C. 'Little Linton and the Linton landscape', *PCAS 84*, 1996, 91-104.

Ette, J. and Hinds, S. Excavations at Linton Roman villa (Rpt 88), CCC, 1993.

Fell, C.I. 'An Early Iron Age settlement at Linton, Cambridgeshire', *PCAS 46*, 1953, 31-42.

Lethbridge, T.C. 'Romano-British burials from Linton, Cambridgeshire', *PCAS 37*, 1944, 67-71.

Neville, R.C. *Antiqua explorata*, 1847, 1-9.

Neville, R.C. 'Anglo-Saxon cemetery excavated January 1853', *Archaeol. J. 11*, 1854, 95-115.

Stevens, R.C. *Linton, the story of a market town*, 1992.

Palmer, W.M. *The antiquities of Linton*, private, 1915.

Potter, L. 'A perambulation of the manor of Barham, Linton, Cambridgeshire, in 1721', *PCAS 84*, 1996, 105-12.

Longstanton
Evans, C.E. *Archaeological investigations at Hatton's Farm, Longstanton, Cambridgeshire* (Rpt 57), CAU, 1991.

Milton
Clay, W.K. *History of Milton*, Cambridge Antiquarian Society, 1869.

Denham, T. et al., 'Field-Work in Cambridgeshire', *PCAS 84*, 1996, 173-4.

Humphries, K.P. *New Romano-British pottery sites in the Cambridge region at Milton*, private, nd.

Humphries, K.P. 'The ancient face of changing Milton', *CLHS 20*, 1964, 10-21.

Robinson, B. and Guttman, E.B. *An archaeological evaluation of the proposed site of the Cambridge Rowing Trust rowing lake at Milton and Waterbeach, Cambridgeshire* (Rpt 120), CCC, 1996.

ARCHAEOLOGY OF SOUTH EAST CAMBRIDGESHIRE

Oakington
Hines, J. and Taylor, A. 'An Anglo-Saxon cemetery at Oakington, Cambs.' *PCAS*, forthcoming 1998.

Over
Lee, C. 'A history of Over', *CLHS 33,* 1978, 6-17.

Phillips, C.W. *The fenland in Roman times*, Royal Geographical Society, 1970, 189.

Evans, C.E. *The archaeology of Willingham/Over* (Rpt.), CAU, 1992.

Evans, C. and Knight, M. *The Over lowland investigations, Cambridgeshire, Part I*, CAU, 1997.

Pampisford
Browne, G.F. 'Notes on the tympanum of the south door of Pampisford church, and on the rectory of Pampisford', *PCAS 6*, 1888, 284-94.

Pollard, J. *Excavations at Bourn Bridge, Pampisford, Cambridgeshire* (Rpt 140), CAU, 1995.

Rampton
Taylor, C.C. 'Cambridgeshire earthwork surveys II', *PCAS 67*, 1977, 97-9.

Sawston
Clarke, E.C. 'Observations on some Celtic remains... near... Sawston...', *Archaeologia 18*, 1817, 340-3.

Taylor, C.C. et al. 'A prehistoric enclosure at Sawston, Cambridgeshire. A Survey by the Royal Commission on Historical Monuments of England', *PCAS 82*, 1994, 5-9.

Taylor, C.C. 'Dispersed settlement in nucleated areas', *Landscape History 17*, 1995, 31-3.

Teversham, T.F. *A history of Sawston*, 1943, 1947.

Shudy Camps
Palmer, W.M. and Fox, C. *Shudy Camps, Castle Camps and Walton Park, Ashdon*, 1924.

Lethbridge, T.C. *A cemetery at Shudy Camps, Cambridgeshire*, 1936.

Stapleford
Clark, W. *Once around Wandlebury*, Cambridge Preservation Society, (1985).

Hartley, B.R. 'The Wandlebury Iron Age hill-fort, excavations of 1955-6', *PCAS 50*, (1957), 1-27.

Pattison, P. and Oswald, A. *Wandlebury hillfort, Cambridgeshire*, Royal Commission on the Historical Monuments of England, 1996.

Taylor, A. et al. 'Field-Work in Cambridgeshire', *PCAS 83*, 1995, 176.

Taylor, A. and Denston, B. 'Skeletons on Wandlebury hill-fort', *PCAS 67*, 1977, 1.

Swavesey
Cooper, S. and Spoerry, P. *Late Saxon and medieval activity at Barwells Engineering site, Black Horse Lane, Swavesey* (Rpt 136), CCC, 1997.

Davis, E.M. 'Ryder's Farm, Swavesey: a late 13th century timber-framed aisled hall', *PCAS 72*, 1984, 59-61.

Haigh, D. 'Excavation of Swavesey town ditch', *PCAS 73*, 1984, 45-53.

Ravensdale, J.R. 'Swavesey, Cambridgeshire: a fortified medieval planned market town', *PCAS 72,* 1984, 55-58.

Sutherland, T. and Hatton, A. *Medieval features outside the town defences at Swavesey*, CCC, 1996, 124.

Evans, C. Archaeological investigations at Swavesey, CAU, 1990.

Palmer, W.M. and Parsons, C. 'Swavesey Priory', *TCHAS 1*, 1904, 29-48.

Teversham
Kemp, S.N. *Pembroke Farm, Teversham, an archaeological evaluation*, CCC, 1996.

Pullinger, E.J. and White, P.J. *Romano-British sites at Hinton Fields, Teversham, 1978-86*, private, 1991.

White, P. et al. *Teversham Chronicle and notes on the history of Teversham*, Fieldfare Publications, 1993.

Waterbeach
Cra'ster, M.D. 'Waterbeach Abbey', *PCAS 59*, 1966, 75-95.

Christie, P.M .and Coad, J.G. 'Excavations at Denny Abbey', *Archaeol. J. 137*, 1980, 138-279.

Lethbridge, T.C. 'An Anglo-Saxon hut on the Car Dyke at Waterbeach', *Antiq. J. 7*, 1927, 141-6.

Macaulay, S. and Reynolds, T. *Car Dyke, a Roman canal at Waterbeach* (Rpt 98), CCC, 1994.

Ravensdale, J.R. *Liable to flood*, CUP, 1974.

Robinson, B. and Guttman, E.B. *An archaeological evaluation of the proposed site of the Cambridge Rowing Trust Lake at Milton and Waterbeach, Cambridgeshire* (Rpt 120), CCC, 1996.

Weston Colville
Boast, R. *The archaeology of West Wratting* (Rpt 23), CAU, 1991.

Palmer, W.M. *A history of Weston Colville*, typescript, 1937.

West Wickham
Charge, B.B. 'Fieldwork and excavation at West Wickham, Cambridgeshire, 1987-8', *HDAG 5*, 1990, 1-38.

Charge, B.B. 'Field survey of sites at Yen Hall, West Wickham, Cambridgeshire', *HDAG 6*, 1995.

The Wilbrahams
Ette, J. and Hinds, S. *Great Wilbraham Roman villa and Fleam Dyke* (Rpt 87), CCC, 1993.

Frend, W.H.C. and Cameron, A. 'Survey excavation on the Long Field at Rookery Farm, Great Wilbraham', *PCAS 81*, 1993, 13.

Lethbridge, T.C. 'Anglo-Saxon cemetery at Little Wilbraham', *PCAS Quarto series 3*, 1931, 71-4.

Neville, R.C. *Saxon obsequies*, J. Murray, 1852.

Stokes, H.P. *History of the Wilbraham parishes*, Cambridge Antiquarian Society, 1926.

Willingham
Connor, A. and Robinson, B. *Excavations of Anglo-Saxon settlement at High Street, Willingham, Cambridgeshire*, CCC, 1997.

Dickens, A. *An archaeological assessment at High Street, Willingham, Cambridgeshire* (Rpt 139), CAU, 1995.

Kenney, J. and Oswald, O. 'Belsar's Hill, Willingham, Cambridgeshire: a survey by the Royal Commission on Historical Monuments of England', *PCAS 84*, 1996, 5-14.

Norris, H.E. *The village of Willingham*, 1889.

South aspect of West Wratting church in 1746

Sources of Illustrations

Key
AT   **Alison Taylor**
CAS   **Cambridge Antiquarian Society**
CUMAA **Cambridge University Museum of Archaeology**
            and Anthropology
GR   **Geoffrey Robinson**
RR   **Richard Relhan**

Cover
  Anglo-Saxon button brooch from Great Wilbraham. AT

Half-Title Page and throughout book
  Motif - Roman bronze lamp from Bartlow Hills.
  McIntosh and Wait 1992, p41

Frontispiece
  Wandlebury Iron Age hill fort. © GR

Title page
  Stained glass representing an Old Testament prophet,
  excavated at Denny Abbey © Archaeological
  Journal, Christie and Coad, 1980

Contents page
  Roman lamp holder from Bartlow Hills. Gage 1842,
  Archaeologia 29

Page

1. *How the fens were formed.* © Sarah Wroot

2. *The Cam at Horningsea.* AT

2. *Palaeolithic tools found at Fen Drayton in 1997.* AT

3. *Jadeite axe from Histon.* © CUMAA

3. *Belsars Hill in Willingham, 1988.* © GR

4. *Iron Age cremation pits at Hinxton and two of the pots found in them.* © Cambridge Archaeological Unit

4. *Plan of a Roman villa excavated at Linton in 1849.* Neville 1847, pl.I

5. *Roman pewter plate from Willingham.* © Joanna Richards

5. *The Car Dyke at Waterbeach in 1988.* © GR

6. *Ancient route ways.* © Sarah Wroot

7. *An Anglo-Saxon necklace from Linton.* © CUMAA

7. *Visitors to an excavation of a Saxon village at Hinxton in 1993.* AT

9. *The Biggin at Fen Ditton in the early 19th century.* RR, © CAS

10. *Even with a fire-engine stationed in the village...* Cambridgeshire Collection

10. *Time-line.* © Sarah Wroot

12. *The church at Little Abington, with its blocked Anglo-Saxon door.* AT

12. *A hollow-way in Little Abington churchyard marks an old route between the two churches.* AT

15. *Statue of Jonas Webb and the wall separating Babraham Park from the High Street.* AT

16. *Anglo-Saxon grave-slab in Balsham church.* © CAS

16. *The present tower of Balsham church dates to the 13th century, with buttresses added in the 16th century.* AT

16. *The graves of medieval priests in Balsham churchyard.* AT

17. *Nine Chimneys in 1997.* AT

17. *Nine Chimneys before 1930.* Cambridgeshire Collection

18. *Bartlow Hills in 1821.* RR, © CAS

19. *Copy of an enamelled cauldron found in Bartlow Hills.* AT

19. *Bronze wine flagon and iron folding chair from Bartlow Hills.* McIntosh and Wait 1992, p 40-1

20. *Bartlow church.* AT

20. *Wall-painting in Bartlow church, recorded in 1928.* Cambridgeshire Collection

21. *Carlton and Willingham Green, in 1767.* CRO, R54/21/1

22. *Camps Castle from the air, 1993.* © Essex County Council

23. *Roman figurines of a frog and a goddess.* AT

23. *Camps Castle, about 1810.* RR © CAS

24. *Excavating a Bronze Age wheel in Lingwood Fen.* AT

25. *Bronze Age wheel.* © Cambridge Archaeological Unit

25. *Bullocks Haste Roman settlement and canal from the air, 1988.* © GR

27. *The Emperor Commodus.* © CUMAA

27. *Roman coin hoard from Cottenham.* AT

28. *Figurines of Sol and Luna.* © CAS

30. *Roman snake's head ring.* © CUMAA

30. *The Biggin, drawn by William Cole in 1780.* © British Library. BM Add. Ms. 5809.9

30. *The Biggin in 1997.* AT

31. *Giant-deer skull and mammoth bone found at Fen Drayton.* AT

33. *Fen Drayton Green and lock-up.* AT

33. *Remains of the wharves near the Three Tuns.* AT

80. *Excavation of the Roman Road near Wandlebury, in 1991.* AT

81. *Excavating Iron Age skeletons at Wandlebury in 1976.* AT

82. *Lord Godolphin's house at Wandlebury, 1801.* RR © CAS

84. *The platform of the disused station at Quy,* AT

85. *Earthworks of the priory next to Swavesey church.* © Ben Robinson

86. *Medieval carved head, photographed at the Rectory in 1934.* Cambridgeshire Collection

86. *Swavesey manor house,* AT

88. *Swavesey from the air in 1976, showing the line of the medieval town ditch.* Bill Vaughan, from the collection of John Shepperson

88. *Roman pottery excavated in Teversham.* © J Pullinger and P White

90. *Manor Farm moated site in the late 18th century.* © Master and Fellows of Gonville and Caius College

91. *Excavations to the base of Car Dyke in 1994.* AT

91. *Excavation of a Roman pottery kiln and Car Dyke in 1997.* AT

92. *Denny Abbey in 1730.* Engraving by S. and N. Buck

92. *A Priest's door at Denny, drawn in 1780.* Cambridgeshire Collection.

94. *18th century gravestone in Waterbeach churchyard.* AT

96. *Weston Colville church 1997.* AT

97. *Late Saxon Thetford ware, excavated near West Wickham church.* AT

97. *Anglo-Saxon artefacts from West Wickham.* AT

99. *A green and cottages at the east end of West Wratting.* AT

101. *Excavating two rooms of a Roman building in 1990.* AT

101. *A stone altar and carved pillar, found in a pit just outside the villa.* AT

101. *Cremation urn from Little Wilbraham cemetery.* Neville 1852

102. *Anglo-Saxon necklaces from Little Wilbraham cemetery.* Neville 1852

104. *Bust of Antoninus Pius.* © CUMAA

104. *Part of a sceptre from the Willingham hoard.* McIntosh and Wait 1992, p36

105. *Figurines from the Willingham hoard,* © CUMAA

105. *Three Roman pewter plates, one inscribed with the Christian symbol of the chi-rho.* AT

105. *Excavation of the Anglo-Saxon settlement at Berry Croft in 1997.* © Cambridgeshire Archaeological Field Unit

107. *The village green at Willingham, still regularly flooded in the early 20th century.* Cambridgeshire Collection

113. *South aspect of West Wratting church, drawn by William Cole in 1746.* © British Library BM Add MS 5810.101

Maps © Sarah Wroot, 1998

Index